The **Northwest Review** is deeply grateful to the following individuals and institutions. Without them we would not be in print.

Patrons
($100 or more per year)
Robert D. Clark
Mrs. Virginia Haseltine
Ken & Faye Kesey
Albert R. Kitzhaber
Glen Love
Mr. & Mrs. Carlisle Moore
Mrs. H. H. Strelow
George Wickes
The Autzen Foundation
Coordinating Council of
 Literary Magazines
Oregon Arts Commission
Weyerhaeuser Company

Donors
($25 per year)
Mr. and Mrs. Roland Bartel
Mr. and Mrs. Edwin Bingham
Mr. and Mrs. Robert A. Eisen
Alice Henson Ernst
Mr. & Mrs. Thomas Fagan
Mr. and Mrs. Otto J. Frohnmayer
Walter Havighurst
Stanley Maveety
Waldo F. McNeir
Carolyn and Ernest Moll
Clarence W. Schminke
John C. Sherwood

Contributions may be sent to the University of Oregon Development Fund designated for the **Northwest Review** and are tax deductible.

This project is jointly sponsored by a grant from the Oregon Arts Commission and the National Endowment for the Arts.

an ANTHOLOGY *of*

NORTHWEST WRITING:

1900-1950

Edited by Michael Strelow
and the NORTHWEST REVIEW staff.

NORTHWEST REVIEW BOOKS

English Department, University of Oregon

This book constitutes Volume XVII, Numbers
Two and Three of the **Northwest Review.**
ISSN 0029-3423

Northwest Review Books edition, 1979
FIRST EDITION

Copyright © 1979 by Northwest Review Books

All rights reserved under International and Pan-American Copyright Conventions. Published in the United States by Northwest Review Books. Library of Congress Catalog Card Number: 79-11606
Printed and bound in the United States of America

Library of Congress Cataloging in Publication Data

Main entry under title:

An Anthology of Northwest Writing: 1900-1950

    (Northwest Review; v.17, no. 2-3 ISSN 0029-3423)
      1. American literature—Northwestern States.
2. American literature—20th century I. Strelow, Michael, 1943-   II. Series.
AP2.N855 vol. 17, no. 2-3 [PS570]   [810'.8'09795]
ISBN 0-918402-04-2   081s 79-11606
ISBN 0-918402-03-4 pbk.

Acknowledgments

"A Note on Poetry," "Logging Trestle," "Cool Country," "Storm," "Wine Ship," "Lai," "The Orchard Spring," "Provincial II," from **Cool Country in Five Young American Poets**, © 1940 by New Directions and Mary Barnard. "The Fitting," "The Whisperer," "Anadyomene," "Inheritance," "Midnight," from **A Few Poems**, © 1952 by Mary Barnard.

"Consider the Unspeakable Pardons," from **The Illiterati**, © 1945 by Glen Coffield.

"Kettle of Fire," by H. L. Davis © 1959 by Elizabeth Hobson; "The River People," © 1925 by Elizabeth Hobson; both used by permission from Shirley Collier Agency; "Status Rerum," © 1927 by H. L. Davis and James Stevens used by permission.

Of Men and Mountains by William O. Douglas. Copyright 1950 by William O. Douglas. Reprinted by permission of Harper and Row, Publishers, Inc.

William Everson, **The Residual Years**. Copyright © 1948 by New Directions Publishing Corporation. Reprinted by permission of New Directions.

April: A Fable of Love (1937), **The Antelope Sonnets** (1927), **Toilers of the Hills** (1928) by Vardis Fisher. Copyright © by Opal Fisher. Used by permission of Opal Fisher. **Toilers of the Hills** also by permission of Houghton Mifflin Company.

"Wind is a Cat," "Slippers," "Winter Orchard," "A Song for Churning," from **White Peaks and Green** by Ethel Romig Fuller © 1928 by Binford and Mort Publishing Company. Used by permission.

Woody Guthrie songs, introductions, story and poem © Copyright 1979. Woody Guthrie Publications, Inc. 250 West 57 Street, New York, N.Y. 10019. Used by Permission.

"Nakedness," "The Way She Walks," "Three Girls," "The Singing," from **Walkers** by Hazel Hall Copyright © 1923 by Dodd Mead and Company. Used by permission. "Inheritance," "Submergence," "Any Woman," "Flight," "Slow Death," "Here Comes A Thief," from **Cry of Time** by Hazel Hall. Copyright 1928 by E. P. Dutton Co. "Night Silence," "Two Sewing," from **Curtains** by Hazel Hall. Copyright 1921 by John Lane Company.

The Adventurers by Ernest Haycox. Copyright © 1954 by Mrs. Ernest Haycox. Used by permission.

None More Courageous (1942) and **The Columbia** (1956) by Stewart Holbrook, copyright © by Sibyl Holbrook Strahl. Used by permission.

Evergreen Land by Nard Jones. Copyright, 1947 by Nard Jones. Reprinted by Permission of Brandt & Brandt Literary Agents, Inc. **The Great Command** by Nard Jones. Copyright © 1959 by Binford and Mort Publishing Company. Used by permission.

At the End of the Carline (1942) and **How Could I be Forgetting** (1933) by Ben Hur Lampman. Copyright © by Binford and Mort Publishing Company. Used by permission.

Fifty Years of Free Thought by George McDonald. Copyright 1945 © by Gordon Press Publishers. Used by permission.

Campus Sonnetts by Ernest G. Moll, copyright © 1934 by Ernest G. Moll. Used by permission.

Our Promised Land by Richard L. Neuberger. Copyright © 1938 by Maurine Neuberger. Used by permission.

"War in Patterson," from **An Anthology by John Reed.** Copyright by Progress Publishers, Moscow, USSR. 1966.

Nisei Daughter by Monica Sone, copyright 1953 by Monica Sone. By permission of Little Brown and Co. in association with The Atlantic Monthly Press.

"Search," "CO's Work on a Mountain Road," by William Stafford, originally printed in **The Illiterati**, Summer 1943, Wyeth, Oregon. Copyright © 1943 by William Stafford.

"Oratorical Medicine," from **Paul Bunyan** by James Stevens. Copyright © 1926 by Alfred A. Knoph, Inc. Used by permission. **Status Rerum** by James Stevens and H. L. Davis, copyright © 1927 by James Stevens and H. L. Davis, used by permission. "Three Bartenders," from **Homer in the Sagebrush** by James Stevens. Copyright © 1928 by Mrs. James Stevens.

Fiddler's Green by Albert Richard Wetjen. Copyright 1931 by Albert Richard Wetjen. Reprinted by permission of Brandt & Brandt Literary Agents, Inc.

Beyond the Garden Gate by Sophus Winther. Copyright © 1946 by Sophus Winther. **Mortgage Your Heart** by Sophus Winther. Copyright © 1937 by Sophus Winther.

Special thanks to the University of Oregon Library Special Collections for photos throughout this book and for support throughout the entire project.

NORTHWEST REVIEW

Editor
Michael Strelow

Fiction Editor
Deb Casey

Poetry Editor
Jay Williams

Assistant Editors

in Fiction
Deb Lavine
Dolores Stockton
Robert Ward

in Poetry
Tom DuVal
Cecelia Hagen
Lucille Handy
R. A. Larson
Karen Locke
Rodger Moody
Jonathan Monroe
Mark Thalman

Advisory Editors
Kenneth O. Hanson
William Stafford
George Wickes

Cover design and layout: Deb Casey

Circulation: Claudia Kraehe

The **Northwest Review** is published three times a year at the University of Oregon. All correspondence should be addressed to Northwest Review, University of Oregon Eugene, Oregon 97403. Submissions of poetry and fiction are welcomed. Unsolicited manuscripts will not be returned unless accompanied by a stamped, self-addressed envelope. Each contributor will receive three copies of the issue in which his work appears. Copyright © **1979** by the **Northwest Review.**
Subscriptions: One year $6.00   Two years $11.00   Three years $16.00
Students: one year $5.00,   two years $10.00   Single copies $2.50
ISSN 0029 3423. Member CCLM and COSMEP.

TABLE OF CONTENTS

Eva Emery Dye	The Brigade to California	2
	Christmas at Fort Vancouver	5
	both from *McLoughlin and Old Oregon*	
Nard Jones	Government Man	13
	from *The Great Command*	
H. L. Davis	The Kettle of Fire	24
Richard Albert Wetjen	Ben the Bosun	44
	from *Fiddler's Green*	
George MacDonald	An Editor in Snohomish	52
	from *Fifty Years of Free Thought*	
Nard Jones	Pioneer Picnic	63
	Reminds Me of a Story	75
	both from *Evergeen Land*	
Sophus Keith Winther	from *Mortgage Your Heart*	85
John Reed	War in Paterson	89
Hazel Hall	An Essay by Eleanor H. Matthews	98
	from *Curtains* two poems	104
	from *Walkers* five poems	105
	from *Cry of Time* six poems	108
Ernest Haycox	from *The Adventurers*	112
H. L. Davis	one poem	121
James Stevens	Oratorical Medicine	125
	from *Paul Bunyan*	
James Stevens and H. L. Davis		
	Status Rerum	140
James Stevens	Three Bartenders	147
	from *Homer in the Sagebrush*	
Ethel Romig Fuller	four poems	161
	from *White Peaks and Green*	

viii

Vardis Fisher	Susan Hemp from *The Antelope Sonnets, Toilers of the Hills,* and *April, A Fable of Love*	164
Ben Hur Lampman	He Was a Country Doctor from *How Could I Be Forgetting*	173
Woody Guthrie	Introduction to Ten of his Songs Faces and Places and People Seven Songs State Line to Skid Row	175 181 184 196
Richard L. Neuberger	The Promised Land from *Our Promised Land*	210
Ernest G. Moll	four poems from *Campus Sonnets*	222
Ben Hur Lampman	One poem from *At the End of the Carline*	225
Mary Barnard	An Essay by Anita Helle A note on poetry and seven poems from *Cool Country in Five Young American Poets* Five poems from *A Few Poems*	227 233 239
Monica Sone	Pearl Harbor Echoes in Seattle from *Nisei Daughter*	243
Stewart Holbrook	Bulkeley the P.T. Boat Man from *None More Courageous*	259
William Everson	Note on poetry and five poems from *The Residual Years*	271
William Stafford	Two poems	277
Glen Coffield	One poem	278
Sophus Keith Winther	Nobody Tells the Truth from *Beyond the Garden Gate*	280
William O. Douglas	from *Of Men and Mountains*	286
Stewart Holbrook	from *The Columbia*	292

INTRODUCTION

The Pacific Northwest was full of stories and poems before the white man got here. Shoshone, Tchinouk, Chehalis, Tillamook, Chilkat, Cayuse, Clatsop, Tlinglit, Umatilla, Kwakiotl—the names are almost poems; the stories of how these Indian tribes came to be, who they fought with, what lived on their mountains, where their dead rested forever, are beginning to surface again from some of the last people to know. Henry David Thoreau insisted that somehow the histories, the stories, the poems and songs reverberated in the woods as long as some of the wild lands were left. In the Northwest, if he was right, the air is packed with literature and we need only breathe it in.

But as for the kind of record you can mark in the margins, there have been only one or two attempts to bring Northwest literature together in representative cross-section. The most notable of these is Alfred Powers' *History of Oregon Literature* (1935). Though Powers titles his collection around Oregon, there are writers included from Idaho, Washington, and Montana. Powers recognized what is still true today, that the fine dark lines on maps have never prevented the restless movement of people back and forth, up and down the Northwest. In the East a family belonged to a town, and certain names were as familiar as the pump handle. But the names in the nineteenth century Northwest —Gray, Allen, Whitman, Eells, Spaulding, Hargreaves, Applegate, Hedges—didn't belong to towns. Like fruit tree scions certain names began appearing all over the Northwest, and each branch traced its vigor to some legendary vitality in a forbear. Names came to be associated with deeds. And the geography in the Northwest often appeared in writing as the challenge that called forth the deed.

The doing in the Northwest was as varied as the land itself. The Applegates wrote territorial legislation, cowboy stories, diaries, memoires, letters, diatribes, bills of lading and travelogues. H. L. Davis set type on several newspapers, wrote poems, then short stories, herded sheep, wrote book reviews, punched cows, wrote pamphlets, worked the woods. Nard Jones wrote every conceivable kind of thing from radio spots to lumber company brochures. James Stevens retold the stories of Paul Bunyan that had made their way from Scandinavia, through the upper Midwest and then to Washington and Oregon—stories that followed first-growth timber. Hazel Hall worked at stitchery in her rooms in Portland and wrote poems that are infused with the same strong sense of life that her hardier Northwest contemporaries discovered in the calloused hands of ranchers or the telling lines around the eyes of coastal fishermen. During the Russian revolution, another Portlander, John Reed, the son of a wealthy family, took his writing skills and political sympathies to Russia and the result was *Ten Days that Shook the World*, a biography of V. I. Lenin, and many short pieces—almost all published in Russia by Progress Publishers. Reed is buried in the Kremlin.

This volume doesn't attempt to catalog or represent all the authors in the Northwest between the years of 1900 and 1950. What it does try to do is provide selections from authors who may best represent a *kind* of writing. For example, Eva Emery Dye wrote good fictitious histories about Oregon and Washington and serves to represent at least four other female writers who also wrote either fictionalized history or historical fictions. Ella Hig-Higginson, Allis McKay, Sheba Hargreaves, and Abigail Scott Duniway all wrote either historical romances or romanticized versions of history. Abigail Scott Duniway is especially interesting because she was a farmer's wife who rose to regional, then national prominence in the women's suffrage movement and still found time to write her romances, run the dairy part of the farm, raise children, make speeches, and, like H. L. Davis, appear to be everywhere at once. But finally, it is the work of Eva Emery Dye that was chosen for this anthology, because her writing is the most polished, her subject matter most representative, and her place in the history of literature of the Northwest unassailable.

And so the principles behind selection for this anthology are several: 1) an author wrote fine quality prose or poetry that remains engaging to this time, 2) an author represents a kind of writing that took place at a certain time or in a certain place in the Northwest and the writing stands as a kind of historical artifact, 3) an author has made the Northwest geography a strong part of prose or poetry (and done it well) or, 4) for all or any combination of the above reasons, the author has become an integral part of the history of literature of the Northwest.

This anthology is arranged historically rather than according to the chronology of composition. That is, a writer publishing in the 30's or 40's, but writing about the time just after the turn of the century, or even writing about the pioneers, appears early in the collection. The literature about the wars, the dust bowl immigrations, the internment camps, etc. appears in an historical context surrounded by works whose time-subject is the same. We have kept the work of poets all together, but, as in the case of H. L. Davis—poet, short story writer, novelist, reporter—we have sometimes separated works by a single author and placed the characters where they belong in history.

The advantage of this order is that each historical period is rendered from several points of view and from various time-frames. And so, Eva Emery Dye writes historical fiction about John McLoughlin and the settling of the Oregon country from the viewpoint of the turn-of-the-century. Nard Jones' book, *The Great Command* (1959) treats the same era through different characters. H. L. Davis' short story, "Kettle of Fire" is still another view of pioneer life. And each author brings to the material not only historical research but particular sensibilities and contemporary values. Davis' story asks questions about survival and individual worth; Dye engages the social customs and manners of pre-territorial high life; Jones finds daily acts of bravery made up the larger historical movements. But all three find the setting both imposing and subtley responsible for how people acted. There are always two references, then, to these selections— the publishing date following the author's work, and the order in which the work is placed in the context of the growth of the Northwest.

Looking at the dates attached to each entry, you will find a few that go beyond 1950. A chapter of Monica Sone's book, *Nisei Daughter* (1953) is included becaues it is a foil to the wartime view of the Japanese in Stewart Holbrook's selection from *None More Courageous*. Perhaps an even better foil might have been John Okada's, *No, No Boy* (1959). But by 1959 a large part of the sensitivity of the 40's, before, during and after the war, had slipped away into a kind of anger and internalized anguish that, though it starkly and convincingly confronts the reader with the Asian-American dilemma during this period, rings false to the whole tone of Northwest Literature in the 40's. *The Adventurers* (1954) by Ernest Haycox, though it is past the cut-off date, represents not only other writers' western and historical novels like Robert O. Case, Edison Marshall and Archie Binns, but the selection from Haycox's novel also treats a recurring Northwest myth—the Sasquatch or Big Foot.

This myth is as old as the world—Easau of the hairy hands, Gilgamesh, wild-man tales of every continent and age—but takes on a special significance in the Northwest where there are still large tracts of land where no one goes, and consequently, absolutely anything could be there. The myth thrives best in places where the "wilds" still has a grip on the imaginations of the people who live on the edge of the woods. A friend has suggested that Big Foot is not a breeding population of ape-like creatures, but, instead, is generated one at a time: there in the misty river valleys west of the mountains, in the high, dry fringe areas east of the mountains, people live in isolation for a time and then, like specimens out of Lamarckian theory, grow longer and longer hair, sharper, thicker nails, stomachs with new acids to digest the rough foliage, and day by day prepare to leave the world of man for the world of beast until they pop back through the veil of thousands of years of genetics to scrabble among the rocks and trees with nothing but a (by this time emblematic) fear of man and a constant hunger. This theory of the Sasquatch is not original with my friend and in varying forms has accompanied the hairy-man myth throughout history. But the important thing about this theory is that it captures something identifiable about Northwest literature: from the most genteel poem written in Seattle, Boise, or Portland, to the coarsest rendering of experiences in the woods or the high country, there is an over-riding sense of *possibility* to Northwest Literature. Natural barriers like the Columbia River or the Cascades or the huge, dry plateaus east of the mountains become gradually transformed in the literature into what they might *potentially* be—irrigation and hydroelectric power from the Columbia, dry land bursting with grasses and crops, vast mountain playgrounds. The land's potential becomes human possibility. It is possible for the natural waterways to become the roads of a new empire, possible to take life in manageable chunks instead of the reckless choking gulps of a California with gold fever, or Chicago with the din of commerce in its ears.

In the character of Susan Hemp, Vardis Fisher gives us some one who is full of the possibilities of the Northwest. She is a woman living alone in defiance of men—white and red—and what these men believe to be woman's limited role in the settlement of the new country. But Susan Hemp also becomes a product of her own isolation and the magic the land works on her. She tirelessly works merely to survive. She shoos man, woman and child away from her door with a wave of her shotgun. She scorns even the notion of love to the one person she lets into her protected life, because her own survival in this rugged land in Idaho has required that she place love in the same category as coyotes, bad Indians, and drunken whitemen. In order to survive she has had to deal with love as so much romantic claptrap—a weakness of character—that would have threatened her very existence had she let it in the door of her rugged cabin hermitage. Her shotgun, her bitterness, and her lonely life bring to mind D. H. Lawrence's phrase describing the typical American (male) hero of Cooper's Leatherstocking Tales: like Natty Bumppo, Susan Hemp is "hard, isolate, stoic, and a killer" (*Studies in Classic American Literature*, p. 62); she has had to be because of the lack of rain and the threat of men and animals. She has become what the land required her to become.

In the two selections by Sophus Winther, two fathers struggle with the life the land has given. On a farm in Nebraska Peter Grimsen is bothered every time one of his able-bodied sons sits down in the house during a rainstorm. There's so much to do. Weeds to pull. Weeds that choke out the corn with every day they are left in the ground, weeds that grow in idle boys who long to go into town for "fun." The fence needs attention, the cows need attention, the land needs attention, and staying alive on the land demands full attention.

Another father, this one in Eugene, Oregon, finds himself occupied by other sorts of things. He lives in the hills overlooking the town. His sons do as they please. His worries: the bad taste Tennyson leaves in his mouth; when's a good time to begin reading Proust aloud with his wife? real pancakes—how can people eat that prepared stuff? And still something is unsettled in his mind, as unsettled as the new people coming to the valley. The land is asking something of him, a gentler asking perhaps, but just as insistently as it asks Peter Grimsen.

The physical Northwest appears in literature as an answer as often as it does a question. For the Arkies and the Okies that Woody Guthrie followed out in the biggest movement of people into the region since the wagon trains of 1843, the valleys that ran the length of Oregon and Washington were a promised land. Everywhere the travelers stopped they asked the natives about rainfall. Too much rain? Impossible! And so they settled again when they could go no farther west. From California to Puget Sound, from the grapes and oranges to the hops and wheat, the farmers dug in again. Guthrie saw the long, wet valley on the west of the mountains as the biblical end to a seeker's journey—the land of milk and honey where rivers ran everywhere and everything was green enough to overgrow the bad memories of the dustbowl. Even on the dry side of the mountains a farmer could get water for irrigation. And not incidentally, since there was no more westering when you got to the Northwest, things *had* to be better because there was no place else to go. If there was a hope left, it was in the Northwest. Most of the songs Woody Guthrie wrote about the Northwest (some of which appear for the first time here) have this double edge to them: the land is rich and waiting for the people, but so is greed, big business, and bad bosses who use men up then discard them like ragged shirts. The possibilities are there in the timber, fish, and farmland. But working people will lose it all as they lost it before if they don't stand together. The music to most of these Guthrie songs can be found elsewhere. The stories the songs tell surrounded by the stories and poems of other writers like those of the conscientious objector camp at Waldport, Oregon, stand together to tell how the injustices of the forties followed on the heels of the great hopes of the thirties.

The poetry of Mary Barnard had sadly been out of print for years when we went looking for representative selections. Her work in the book, *Cool Country*, could only be found in special collections in a few libraries. *A Few Poems* (1952) was printed in a limited edition of 300 and these are being hoarded by private collectors. This year, however, Breitenbush Publications in Portland, Oregon, is bringing out a collection of her work, which will include more of her crafted excellence for readers who get their first taste of Mary Barnard here. In some important ways her poetry captures more completely than any other selection in this anthology the complexities and resonances of the Northwest.

A Northwest poet whose best poems and largest body of work fall outside our time restrictions is William Stafford. The two poems here are meant to fill out the section by writers interned in the C.O. camps and certainly not to represent his later work. In a previous issue of the *Northwest Review*, Stafford made this statement about the importance of a region to an artist. He called it, "On Being Local," and it reads in part:

> All events and experiences are local, somewhere. And all human enhancements of events and experiences— all the arts—are regional in the sense that they derive from immediate relation to felt life.
>
> It is this immediacy that distinguishes art. And paradoxically the more local the feeling in art, the more all people can share it; for that vivid encounter with the stuff of the world is our common ground.

And though "regionalism"—really the basis for this collection —will continue to be discussed, whether in bars or academic conferences, this statement engages the center of the matter. A region with the kinds of contrasts the Northwest has, seems to generate strong feelings of place out of the sheer variety of possibilities for feeling "local." If there is anything common to all the artists represented here, besides the time frame and the geography, it is this feeling expressed many different ways of having written out of contrasts—maybe paradox is better—a context of naturally occurring contradictions.

One of the earliest novels written in the Northwest, *The Prairie Flower*, by Sidney Walter Moss (1843, begun on the wagon trip out during the first big immigration and then finished at Oregon City) represents what for a long time was the relationship between literature of the Northwest and the big publishing houses of the East. Moss's book had just been published when an edition of it appeared in the East under the name of Emerson Bennett. Bennett stole the work, signed his name to it, and began assiduously collecting royalties. Moss eventually gave up trying to fight the injustice of it all and settled back to run his hotel in Oregon. The East had picked its first plum from the Northwest. While the plagiarism stopped with new copyright laws late in the nineteenth century the flow of literature west to east was really just beginning.

Looking at the *Union Catalogue* or the records of the Library of Congress we find Northwest writers (poets, novelists, story writers, essayists alike) often began publishing in Seattle, or Boise, or Portland, and as their work grew in stature and popularity, suddenly they were published and distributed exclusively from the East. There are certain exceptions. Caxton Printers in Boise, and Binford and Mort of Portland, (and a few others) have been publishing the literature of the Northwest since just before the turn of the century. In the last thirty years small press publishers have joined Caxton and Binford and Mort in finding the new writers of the Northwest. But only recently have the small presses learned enough about production and distribution to adequately represent their authors—both new and established—in a national market place. Now, more and more often—especially in poetry—the best editions come out of small, regional publishers. Northwest publishing is catching up to Northwest literature.

There is an excellent bibliography of Northwest literature by Richard Etulain, in the summer, 1973, number of *Idaho Yesterdays*. In his introduction, Etulain documents both sides of the literary/historical arguments about whether claims to a true Northwest literature are exaggerated, or, indeed, understated. Those critics who see the literature of the region as especially vital and telling with respect to culture have interpreted "literature" broadly to include work by historians, journalists, and political writers. This anthology takes the same view. Richard L. Neuberger was primarily a journalist writing for magazines and newspapers, but his works collected in book form not only give a strong historical perspective, but ask hard questions about what it is in the Northwest that brought people here, what broken promises the "Promised Land" visited upon its pioneers and new folks alike, and generally, how the lavish open lands and valleys of the Northwest demanded as much of their inhabitants as they promised to them.

Missing from this book are considerations of the other arts and how they followed the movements of people into the Northwest. For example, a partial list of painters to document twentieth century Northwest art might include the following: Mark Tobey,

Morris Graves, Guy Anderson, Kenneth Callahan, James Fitzgerald, Carl Morris, Louis Bunce and others. It would be interesting to have well-chosen examples from these to show the reader the development of painting. But the work of these artists is reproduced well, often in color, elsewhere and is available from any good Northwest library as are sculpture, histories of dance and theater, politics, economics and social movements. What has not been collected up to this point—and what we are trying to provide with this anthology— is a cross section of literature showing the growth of a conscious culture in the Northwest.

*   *   *

Is "region" a useful concept in assessing literature (or any of the arts), or does it force diverse works into a mold, a mold false to the value of any single piece? Does a regional collection of literature such as this help you understand growth and change in other regional arts? What do you know about the Northwest—after reading this collection—that you didn't know before? The answers to these questions will depend on how you view the growth of art and culture and, ultimately, I suppose, how much you care about the complex interweaving of those attitudes, events, and things that make up culture. What has become clearer while collecting Northwest literature for this anthology is that a tradition of rich variety already exists—in the land, the people, and in the art of the Northwest.

Michael Strelow

John McLoughlin

Eva Emery Dye

From *McLOUGHLIN AND OLD OREGON* (1900)

XII

The Brigade To California

1839

Dr. McLoughlin had much to do in gathering up the threads of routine. "Where is our Spanish Brigade?" he asked.

"Ready equipped at Scappoose Point," answered Michel La Framboise. "We start tomorrow."

There was always bustle when a brigade set out. At daylight two hundred horses were pawing at Scappoose Point just across the western end of Wapato. Tom McKay had a ranch there, rich in sleek horses and cattle, and oceans of grass. A string of boats came down from the fort with a jolly picnic party to give the trappers a send-off. The cottonwoods were yellow on Wapato, sprinkling with gold the old council ground of the Multnomahs. October russet dotted the Scappoose hills. The Cascade Mountains lay in banks of crimson against the sunrise. The ladies from the fort leaped to their saddles tinkling with tiny bells. The gentlemen rode at their sides, gay as Charles's cavaliers, with lovelocks round their faces.

As usual, Dr. McLoughlin took the lead on his Bucephalus. Madame rode Le Bleu, a dappled white and sky blue, that in her day had galloped seventy-two miles in eight hours, to carry the tobacco, the *sine qua non* of an Indian trade. David mounted Le Gris de Galeaux like a Cassock. Rae and Eloise followed on Guenillon and the snowy Blond, all favorite horses at Fort Vancouver. Ermatinger with his Bardolphian nose cut a laughable figure on Le petit Route by the side of his fair bride Catherine on Gardepie.

After the gentry came La Framboise at the head of his long array of French trappers in scarlet belts and Canadian caps, with their picturesque Indian families, the plumes of men and women dancing and waving in the wind, brilliant as a hawking party in the days of medieval song.

Michel La Framboise had a famous voyageur, one of the picked few sent out by John Jacob Astor. He could flip his canoe over the choppy waves where no one else would dare to go. Now, every autumn after the harvest was over, he led the horse brigade to the Spanish country.

The trappers always travelled with their families; the mother bestrode the family horse, with its high-pommelled Mexican saddle; the children jogged along on their Cayuse ponies and slept until night, when down they slid, full of glee, gathered flowers, shooting their little arrows, and listening to tales of grizzly bears and Blackfeet.

La Framboise was proud of his half-breed wife, Angelique, his Grande Dame, in her bloomers of beaded blue broadcloth; Angelique was proud of the pretty white pappoose that dangled from her pommel, asleep in its little *miau* of beads and ribbon. Close behind came the children, with elfin locks and flashing eyes, with one hand whipping their horses to make the bells go "zing-zing-zing," with the other hugging tight the buckskin dollies with blue bead eyes and complexions chalked to the whiteness of the charming missionary women.

The Indian boys brought up the rear, lashing their unruly pack-horses heavily laden with camp equipage and Indian goods. All were in fine feather; the capering steeds, the crisp air, the scintillant sun, the tuneful meadow lark, harmonized completely with the bursts of song and gay and lively laughter.

The Willamette was carpeted with green from the early autumn rain. Scarlet-flaming thickets of vine maple glowed along the watercourses. Every hill-slope was a bank of burning ash. The cavaliers were armed to the teeth; from every belt depended a leathern firebag with pipe, tobacco, knife, and flint and steel. There were hunters in that brigade, rough as the grizzlies they hunted; hunters keen as the deer, suspicious as the elk; hunters that read like a book the language of tracks. Leaning over their horses' necks, they could discern the delicate tread of the silver fox, the pointed print of the mink, and the otter's heavy trail. With whip-stock in hand La Framboise points—"A bear passed last week," "An elk yesterday," "A deer this morning." In a moment a deer tosses its antlers, sniffs the wind, then bounds with slender, nervous limbs into the thickest shade.

A brisk morning ride over the Scappoose hills and down into the Tualatin plains was followed by a picnic dinner around a gypsy fire, then McLoughlin dismissed the trappers into the Indian country.

The parting cavalcades looked at each other from their curveting steeds. "Beware on the Umpqua," called the doctor. "If the new men get the fever give them plenty of broth and quinine." Again he turned with a parting word and gesture: "Look out for the Rogue-Rivers; they'll steal the very beaver out of your traps."

With gay farewells the fort people galloped back to the crossing at Wapato. The California brigade followed along the winding trail to the south. La Framboise always touched at La Bonté's, a solitary garden spot in miles and miles of prairie. "How much land *do* you own, monfrère La Bonté?"

"Begin in the morning," the old trapper was wont to say,—"begin in the morning on a Cayuse horse. Go west till the sun is very high, then go south till it is around toward the west, and then back to the river; that is my manor."

And, too, there was always a stop at Champoeg,—every man at Champoeg was "mon frère" or "mon cousin" to La Framboise. Beside his wide hearth for many and many a year La Chapelle loved to sit and tell of the days when he, too, was *bourgeois*, and Madame his wife was the grandest dame that ever bestrode a pony. And for the thousandth time the good dame brought out the dresses stiff with beads that were worn in that gay time when the Monsieur led the hunt to the head waters of the Willamette.

The head waters of the Willamette was a royal beaver republic. There the little colonies cut down whole forests, built up wonderful dams and bridges, scooped out lakes, and piled up islands. With their long sharp teeth they cut up the timber and shaped their houses, plastering them neatly with their broad, flat tails. They had room in their houses and dininghalls and neat doorways, these deft little builders, more cunning than the fox, more industrious than the bee, more patient than the spider, more skilful than the Indian. "The beaver can talk," says the Indian. "We have heard them talk. We have seen them sit in council on the lazy ones. We have seen the old chief beat them and drive them off."

Two hundred miles south of the Columbia, La Framboise descended from a high ridge of mountains down to a little plantation on the banks of the Umpqua, the fortalice of old Fort Umpqua. Carronades peeped from the donjon tower. Tom McKay built it after that disaster to the American trappers—sometimes they called it Fort McKay. Here a solitary white man ruled the Umpqua. Jules Gagnier was a Frenchman, the son of an honorable and wealthy family in Montreal. In vain they made efforts to reclaim him from his wanderings and his Indian wife. Hither, twice every year, La Framboise came, twenty miles off his trail, to bring Gagnier Indian goods and to carry away his beaver. Here, summer and winter, year in and year out, the jolly, genial Frenchman traded with his red friends and cultivated his little patch of garden. Such were the first white men who broke the way for pioneers on the northwest coast.

La Framboise's brigade wound along gorges and canyons, through the Rogue River valley with its orchards of sunlit manzanita and hillsides of gnarled madrona and chinquapin, into the Switzerland of America, where Mt. McLoughlin on the summit of the Cascades was the most conspicuous landmark on the southern trail. One more pull—over the Siskiyous—and they have crossed the Spanish border. As a rule the brigades started early, to avoid the snows of Shasta, where once they lost the whole of their furs and three hundred horses. All day long, for days and days, the triple peaks of Shasta watched them winding down the Sacramento. La Framboise set his traps. Sutter's men began to look with unfriendly eye upon the intruders from the Columbia, but the Hudson's Bay Company had a permit from the Spanish Governor Alvarado.

Christmas At Fort Vancouver

1839

December arrived. Basil's Christmas fires kept up incessant roaring. The rafters of the provision house creaked under the weight of birds picked smooth and white. The high-backed settees took on a knowing air as Dr. McLoughlin walked through the kitchen. The tin and copperware winked on the wall. Even the kitchen had Christmas greens.

Burris set all his Kanakas in a whirl. Some turned the plovers on the spit. Some set the quails on the gridiron. Burris kept an eye on the sun-dial, and every now and then took a sly nip of ale behind the buttery door. With a thump of the rolling-pin he announced the Christmas dinner. Fat goose, cranes, swans, so fat they swam in grease, plum-duff crowned with holly, ducks, showing the rich red after the knife, and baked quails, white to the bone,—these the Oregon epicures ate for Christmas dinner in 1839.

The tables were removed, and the governor in flowing peruke and ruffled waistcoat led the dance with Madame. The hall blazed in greenery. The tall central posts were wound with the holly-leaved Oregon grape, the Christmas candles were wreathed in ivy. A Yule-log of fir beaded with globules of resin snapped and sparkled. Scotch clerks and English kissed the pretty girls beneath the mistletoe, plucking each time a pale gray berry from the bough.

And who were the pretty girls? Eloise, of course, and Catharine —the Canadian Lily. Six weeks Ermatinger duly courted her; and then they were married. From the mouth of the Columbia there came the handsome Birnie girls, whose father, James Birnie, a genial, jolly Aberdeen Scotchman, kept the only hostelry from Vancouver to the sea and from Sitka to San Francisco. Old Astoria, renamed Fort George, had been abandoned; but after the Clatsop trouble Dr. McLoughlin had sent Birnie there to keep a lookout for passing ships. Here he cultivated a little garden, did a little Indian trading in salted salmon and sea-otter skins, kept a weather eye out on the bar over which at long intervals a ship came into the river. Astor's old post was burned; only the scarified and blackened chimney stood among the ruins that were overrun with briar and honeysuckle. The latchstring of Birnie's log house on the hillside was out to the trapper, the trader, the Indian, and the sailor. More than one old missionary has paid tribute to the housekeeping virtues of his pretty wife, the daughter of a Hudson's Bay trader in the north country. Her blazing hearth, clean-scrubbed fir floor, and neat pine table of snowy whiteness, offered cheer and comfort to all the early wanderers who came "the plains across or the Horn around." Sole Saxon of the forest, Birnie's flag was first to welcome the incoming ship, and last to wave a farewell from the shore.

Chief Factor Pambrun, the *tinas tyee* (little chief) that held in check the upper tribes, sent down his fair Maria, the pride of Walla Walla. Pambrun himself was a blond with thin light curls. This in his child developed into peach-bloom red and white, blue eyes, and the midnight hair of her mother rolling in her father's curls. Very well Miss Maria remembered the urbanity of that accomplished Captain Bonneville who came riding so gayly over the mountains, and then—rode back again. With his feet under Astor's table in New York City, he told Irving a pretty tale of "Pambrun's attractive wife and her singularly beautiful children."

The chief factor's daughter had seldom passed beyond the stockade of Walla Walla except to the neighboring mission, where she became the favorite pupil of Mrs. Whitman. The good Chief Factor Pambrun himself was a great friend to Dr. Whitman,—more than once he called the Indians to task for some act of discourtesy to the devoted missionary. There was a young American at Whitman's, Cornelius Rogers, an enthusiastic missionary, and the finest Indian linguist in the upper country, who madly lost his heart to the curly-haired daughter of the chief factor. Maria was a beautiful singer. Rogers taught her music. Her visits to the mission became events in his life—she seemed a child of joy and beauty. The pensive, studious young missionary watched her from afar as she rode with her father after the fox-hounds, like Christine of Colvile, like Eloise of Fort Vancouver.

This feudal life of the Hudson's Bay Company reproduced in the western wilds the feudal age of Europe. The chief of nearly every post had a beautiful daughter who sat behind her casement window, harp in hand, and sang songs of France. Many of the chief factors took pride in the education and companionship of their children, the nearest links to the Saxon world from which they came. The sons were sent abroad to be educated; some of them are influential chief factors in the North today. The girls were sent to Red River or Montreal. Even Maria had once started for Montreal. It was during one of her father's long absences that the fur-traders were sometimes obliged to make. An uncle sent for the little girl to come to Montreal for her education. For her child's good Mrs. Pambrun consigned her weeping little daughter to the care of the east-bound brigade. Somewhere in the north country, on Rainy Lake, Lake of the Woods, or contiguous waters, the little girl lay sleeping in the bottom of the canoe. Suddenly she heard a well-known voice, her father's voice, crying his orders. Up popped the curly head. The west-bound brigade was flying past them toward the sunset. "Papa," she screamed.

"Why, Maria, is that you?" exclaimed the astonished chief factor. "Where in the world are you going?"

"They are sending me to school at Montreal."

"I guess not. Come," said the chief factor, holding out his arms. With one leap the lovely child cleared the intervening space and nestled her head on her father's bosom with a little cry of joy. From that hour they had never been separated.

Poesy and song found its way into those old forts; it was no rare thing to find a chief factor's daughter far better instructed than many an Enid or Elaine of Tennysonian song. The clerks went wild over these beautiful girls, so fair in contrast with their dusky surroundings. Cornelius Rogers, the missionary, went to the chief factor.

"Marry her? Marry my daughter?" ejaculated the chief factor. "With all my heart, young man, with all my heart. I shall be proud to call you my son-in-law."

But Maria's blue eyes flashed, "Father, I do not care to marry, and when I do I prefer a Hudson's Bay man."

"Do not urge your suit now—time will do wonders," said the chief factor to the impatient American. But that Rogers should marry his daughter became the chief wish of the factor's life. He discussed it with Dr. Whitman, he consulted Dr. McLoughlin; he made a will bequeathing a thousand pounds sterling to Cornelius Rogers.

Every autumn of her life Maria Pambrun had walked the ramparts of Fort Walla Walla, watching for the Montreal express. Somehow, in her romantic little heart, she believed that a knight would come out of that north from some castle beside a distant sea, and then—then— Day after day she sat there and dreamed, beading the moccasins in her lap. Along the northern wall rolled the wild Columbia, sucking in the lesser Walla Walla in its mighty sweep to the sea. Eastward, the Blue Mountains purpled in the sun. The bunchgrass prairies were covered with horses. Close around the fort lay the ever drifting, shifting, changing sands of the peninsula, darkening the sky in summer and sweeping in gales at night. And now, with such dreams in her head, she had come down to Christmas at Fort Vancouver.

At this Christmas festivity, Douglas and his wife Nelia, Rae and Eloise, Maria and the clerks, and the Birnie girls and Victoire, the daughter of La Bonté from the valley, all whirled in the dance together. Dr. Barclay lifted his eyes to the unexpected beauty of Maria Pambrun "in her girtle green and a rosebud in her hair." She danced with David McLoughlin. David's long black locks had a careless grace; he had his father's fine, straight nose, and his mother's squareset mouth; there was a ring on his finger and a sword at his belt. Dr. Barclay's eyes followed the pair with a strange surprise, and David—cared for no one yet.

"Ah, I beg your pardon." It was unusual for David to do an awkward thing, but he trod on Bruce's toes, and Bruce had corns. Snuff-box in hand, the old Scotch warder reposed from the care of the flags, the guns, the garden, and the gate, sleepily watching the weaving dancers and thinking—of Waterloo, perhaps. Burris, portly and rubicund, resplendent in a huge roll of colored neckerchief and horn spectacles astride his nose, slipped out again—to take a nip of ale behind the buttery door.

To be the governor's guest at Christmas was no light honor. Monique and Charlefoux were there in their gayest dress, fine cloth coats and silver buttons, crimson caps and golden tassels, cutting pirouettes and pigeon wings, stamping in the noisy rigadoon, and heeling it and toeing it on air. Tom McKay alone made no change in dress. With the free, frank manners of the Scot and the grace and affability of the Frenchman, he came in his hunting outfit. Scorning the effeminate foppery of the Canadians, he wore as usual his leathern belt, from which depended the powder-flask, the bullet-pouch, and the long scabbard that concealed the swordlike hunting-knife. Tall, dark, powerful, Tom McKay acknowledged no master save McLoughlin. No other man could do what McKay did at Fort Vancouver or on the trail. His name was a terror in the mountains. The Indians believed this Hudson's Bay cousin of theirs bore a charmed life; the whites knew him to be an unerring shot. But with all his fierceness Tom McKay had the gentle heart of a woman.

Past midnight the dance, half Highland with a dash of Indian, ceased, and the dancers disappeared. Old Burris returned in his peaked nightcap and carefully bore away the last brand of the

Yule-log to light the next year's Christmas fire. And he took a nip of ale behind the buttery door.

From Christmas to New Year's, feudal hospitality reigned at Fort Vancouver. The servants' rations were doubled, and they danced more madly. On New Year's every employé put on his best and mounted the flight of steps to the governor's door. Madame and her daughter stood at the heaped and laden tables, and with gracious air dispensed English candies, cakes, and coffee to the governor's guests.

Far away in the dim recesses of the Oregon woods an altar was reared that Christmas night. Before a green bower lit with candles and hung with garlands stood the Jesuit Father, De Smet, among the Flatheads. A hundred lodge-fires burned, a thousand red men slept. At a signal gun the Indians rose. The midnight mass, the mystery, the swinging censers, the decorated altar, the solemn ceremonial awed the savage heart. Indian voices chanted the Kyrie Eleison and the Te Deum, Indian fingers signed the cross and took the beads. The baptismal rite was read with the rising sun. The neophytes knelt with fluttering hearts. "Receive this white garment," said the smooth-shaven priest. "Receive this burning taper." The red hand received it from the white, robed in a flowing sleeve. One by one the untutored red men retired, proud of the white vestment and deeply impressed with the Black Gown's method of making medicine.

So ended the Oregon Christmas of 1838.

Eva Emery Dye

Elijah Bristow built this house, the first in Lane County, in 1847

Nard Jones

From *THE GREAT COMMAND* (1959)
(On Marcus Whitman, pioneer doctor)
Chapter 21: "Government Man"

During the height of the discord among the American Board missioners Elkanah Walker ventured the suggestion that perhaps they should sell a station or two to the Methodists.

In his more discouraged moments Whitman had thoughts along a similar line. Eells had no first conviction on the subject one way or another, but Henry Spalding was shocked at the very idea. He avowed that never would he desert Lapwai and the Nez Percé, and rather favored the notion of keeping the Methodists out of interior Oregon altogether.

Marcus Whitman and Jason Lee apparently never seriously discussed such a deal. Lee was having troubles of his own. Too many of the erstwhile passengers of the *Lausanne* had become disenchanted with their leader. Not a few were beginning to feel that his interests were too commercial and political.

One of his severest critics was as political as any man in Oregon. "A sleek-looking gentleman" and "a quick talker" was Doctor Elijah White, a native of New York State, who had arrived as a physician among Lee's first reinforcements. By the time the second band arrived in the *Lausanne* the windbag doctor had become so obnoxious that Lee dismissed him. The Methodist leader confided to Whitman that probably Oregon had not heard the last of White.

Lee was right. After serving as physician to the Methodist Mission for three years White returned to the States in the *Lausanne*. He was thoroughly convinced that the missionaries—Methodist, American Board, and Catholics—were not handling the Indians right, and that there should be an official representative of the United States government in Oregon. Nor was there any question in his mind as to who that federal agent should be.

On the long voyage home he and Captain Josiah Spaulding of the *Lausanne* had plenty of time to talk it over. Certainly there was collusion of a patriotic sort, as evidenced by the captain's report to Congress. Nearly everybody who had been anywhere near Oregon made a report to Congress if they returned safely, and Captain Spaulding was not exceptional. But his scurrilous view of the machinations of the Hudson's Bay Company must have come from White. In any case, that view gave Senator Linn of Missouri an excuse to recommend the appointment of an Indian agent to Oregon—and there was Elijah White, ready, willing, and, in his opinion anyhow, able.

The office itself meant little; much of the authority that White later assumed was the product of his own imagination. He was in reality a sub-agent, and his powers ambiguous. But in the very ambiguity of White's role lay considerable strength, making the move a bold one for the United States.

So it was in the shape of a thirty-five-year-old, fast-moving doctor that we began to make concrete pretensions to the wilderness north of California, and between the Rockies and the Pacific. In effect, he was to be the nondenominational shepherd of our orphans in Oregon, looking after relations between the natives and the citizens of the United States. It was something that would make Jason Lee sit up and take notice, and White intended that it should.

On his way back to the Far West, White stumped lustily for the cause of Oregon, ignoring as best he could those who remembered hearing Jason Lee on the same theme. He drew drafts on the government to advertise in newspapers, and lectured wherever he could find an audience.

"Last night," he reported en route to St. Louis, "all the other appointments were taken up to hear me lecture on Oregon, as the weather was fine and the traveling good, the noble church was filled, the pulpit lined with ministers of all denominations, and I talked an hour and a half with all my might." He advised his superiors in Washington that interest in Oregon was running high, as most certainly it was.

By May 14, 1842, at a rendezvous twenty-five miles southwest of Independence, there were assembled eighteen covered wagons and a hundred and twelve persons. Although White's lectures and advertisements had warmed imaginations that would take fire the following spring, not many of this first train to Oregon had been induced to go by him. There would not have been time.

This assemblage at Elm Grove was moved by many people and events, some of them remote in time. They had been moved by the feats of Lewis and Clark, or the dreams of Nathaniel Wyeth, or the verbal pyrotechnics of Hall Kelley, or Jason Lee and his Indian lads. They had been moved by stories in the religious magazines of the bravery of Eliza Spalding and Narcissa Whitman, and the knowledge that these mortal women were keeping house out beyond the Rockies.

The poet that lies within the heart of every mystic pioneer was moved by the very name "Oregon" repeated over and over again in the news from East and West. Some were excited by the implied struggle with an old enemy, Great Britain, and had heard of the arrival of Lord Ashburton to negotiate a treaty that might include Oregon.

And of course some had been driven to Elm Grove by discontent, or simple avarice, or the law. Whatever the causes, the sunset was in their eyes and they were bound for Land's End. They were the product of the *Zeitgeist*, the marriage of time and spirit. They were the first of the tide race to Oregon, and the tideway would be deepening.

Fifty-two of them were men over eighteen; the rest women and youths and children. They were not all of a kind, and several were remarkable. Most prominent at the moment was of course Elijah White, who had expected to be elected captain of the train, and was. But only for a month, because Americans are cautious when it comes to the tenure of their elected leaders.

As he remembered, not long after, the eighteen Pennsylvania wagons "with their snow white coverings, winding down the long hill" were followed by an immense train of animals whose drivers walked by their side "merrily singing or whistling to beguile their way."

Among the other more outstanding members of the party were Lansford Hastings, a strong-minded character who would receive the captaincy the moment White's month had expired; and Medorem Crawford, who in Oregon would teach, run a ferryboat, go to the legislature, and catch the eye of President Lincoln.

A young quick-tempered bachelor from Massachusetts was

along, hoping for adventures more exciting than could be found in New England lawyering. A. L. Lovejoy did not dream the adventures would include being a trail companion to Marcus Whitman, fighting Cayuse with the rank of adjutant-general, serving a spell as mayor of Oregon City, and co-founding a town which—by the flip of a coin—would be named after Portland, Maine.

There were three Smiths, one of whom is down in the record as father of such comely daughters that the Sioux braves were forever pestering to buy them. And riding home in the train were the two McKay boys, grandsons of Mrs. McLoughlin, who were doubtless closely watched by a friend of their father, Stephen Hall Meek, the brother of Joe. By profession Steve Meek was a guide who would become almost as famous as his brother, but by the dubious feat of discovering a short-cut so disastrous that it would be known forever after as "Meek's Horrible Cut-Off." Fortunately he was not hired by the White party. But perhaps the most uncommon individual in the train was a Kentucky stonecutter called Sidney Walter Moss, a man of many parts and talents. He would become Oregon's pioneer hotel keeper, a most wealthy merchant, and would survey Oregon City's townsite with an old pocket compass and a piece of rope which, on dry days, was exactly a rod in length.

And in one of the Pennsylvania wagons—possibly that of the Smith with comely daughters—was a girl who would inspire Moss to begin writing, en route, the first novel of Oregon. It would be called *The Prairie Flower*, sell ninety-one thousand copies, and inspire many another young fellow to go west. But it would bring Moss neither fame nor fortune. An enterprising "author" named Bennett would in the east appropriate most of the chapters, put his own name on the title page, and receive the royalties. Sidney Moss would be undisturbed; he had great recuperative powers and many strings to his bow. But he would thereafter confine himself to commerce.

The party was only two days out of Elm Grove before trouble came. And it stemmed right from the head of the column, from Elijah White himself.

Already the travelers had discovered that White loved regulations, down on paper. Every male over eighteen had to provide one horse or mule, or one wagon; he had to possess a gun, three pounds of powder and twelve of lead, with suitable flints or at least a thousand caps. For every male there had to be thirty pounds of meal or flour, fifty of bacon, and suitable proportions for the women and children.

All this was well and good. But White insisted upon a code of laws. Morover, he insisted that they be enforced by reprimand—White personally officiating—or by fines or, in extreme cases, banishment from the brigade. He did his level best to prohibit swearing, obscene language, or lolligagging which might lead to immoral conduct. Things looked dark indeed for the Indians of Oregon, although they did not yet know that such a stringent sub-agent was on the way.

Nonetheless, the party had borne up until the way turned left from the Santa Fe Trail northwesterly toward the Kansas River crossing. At that night's encampment White thought of something else. There were a good many dogs with the train, and it seemed to him that they might all go mad on the plains. Or their night howling would attract marauding Indians.

White's new regulation was that all the dogs must be shot at once.

The howls of the dogs had been nothing to the cries of their masters and mistresses when this order went out. Next morning, in a pouring rain, White tried to enforce the fresh commandment. Twenty-two dogs were dispatched, some clumsily, and the din and excitement heralded the downfall of White as a leader. As women and children wept, wounded mongrels yelped, and the hardier drivers swore, White pursued his project with the aid of such doghaters as he could find.

It was the beginning of a division of wills that would persist almost the whole way across the continent. And there were portents of the long storm. At this encampment one family lost a child. The parents, too saddened for adventures now, turned their wagon for home. Always the first death in a wagon train brought the whole caravan to a realization that the way west was not the flowered path of immortals on an outing. That night there was little visiting among the campfires, and no games or singing. Next day the merry whistling had stopped; tight-lipped drivers urged the horses and cattle on behind the Pennsylvania wagons.

When in mid-June the emigrants refused to re-elect White, choosing Hastings as the new captain, the breach widened between two factions. Lansford Hastings was no stickler for rules, but he governed hard without them, which was almost as irritating to these freed souls as White's prissy regulations. By June 23 the party was marching in separate columns. Bissonette, the chief at Fort Laramie, strongly advised that the owners of the prairie schooners get together before they went on into hostile Indian country.

His tender concern extended no further. He charged the emigrants a dollar for a pound of coffee or sugar, or a pint of flour. And at Laramie many of the party exchanged wagons and ox teams for horses, to the advantage of the fort. Bissonette was not encouraging about the possibility of getting wagons through to Oregon.

A mile or so from the fort they encountered Jim Bridger and that taciturn Irishman, Thomas Fitzpatrick. Bridger was heading east with one of the last packets of furs, and the gangling Fitzpatrick was looking for work. The previous spring he had guided the Bidwell train to California, and now he agreed to lead the White-Hastings party to Oregon for five hundred dollars. It looked as if he was in business again for a while.

They were fortunate to run into Fitzpatrick. Not only did he know the trails; he knew how to handle Indians.

In mid-July, on the Sweetwater, death struck again. Adam Horn accidentally discharged his rifle and killed a young man named Bailey. They wrapped the body in a buffalo robe and buried it on the dismal plain. There was no clergyman in the party, and White volunteered for the funeral discourse. In the course of his "brief, solemn lecture" he said, "Let us pray" and was both pleased and astonished when every man, woman and child dropped upon their knees. "It was," White thought, "the most solemn funeral by far that any of us ever attended or probably ever will."

As soon as the annoying Sioux were left behind, the party divided again. The almost wordless Fitzpatrick shrugged. He was being paid to show the way, not to try to make peace among foolish white men. The guide pushed on, and White and others followed close on horseback. Hastings, in charge of the heavier gear, followed as best he could. At the Green River he could hold his wing together no longer; most of them chopped up their wagons to make pack saddles and firewood. Rainstorms made the going miserable and the encampments at nightfall worse.

Yet, miraculously, they reached Fort Hall almost together. There even the most stubborn decided against taking wagons further. Besides, the chief factor made them attractive offers. He would sell them supplies for half what they had paid at Laramie, and take in payment what was left of the wagons.

The weary band recuperated at Fort Hall for a week or ten days, then White and his cohorts pressed on ahead. At the crossing of the Snake the man who had accidentally killed Bailey paid the penalty of drowning. Past Fort Boise they slopped through the Burnt River Canyon and into the Grande Ronde Valley that had seemed so beautiful to Narcissa Whitman on a spring day six years before. The Blue Mountains were crossed in two days, and at the foot of their western slope Elijah White hired an Indian to lead him post-haste to Waiilatpu. Fort Walla Walla and a transfer to the down-sweeping Columbia was his combined and immediate goal—but he had important mail for Doctor Whitman and associates.

Every night, by the light of the campfire, the imperturbable Sidney Moss wrote a little more of *The Prairie Flower*. He had not yet seen the Willamette, but he knew how its leafy banks should be for a young man:

It was a lovely day in the spring of 1843. On the banks of the romantic Willamette, under the shade of a large tree, I was seated. By my side—with her sweet face averted and crimson with blushes, her right hand clasped in mine, her left unconsciously toying with a beautiful flower, which failed to rival her own fair self, sat Lilian Huntley.

The novel was destined to be incompletely autobiographical. On the banks of the Willamette the author would not marry "Lilian Huntley" but a buxom practical widow who knew how to run a dining room annex to his hotel.

Thus, paradoxically, the pragmatic businessman wrote his novel by night, and the schoolteacher Medorem Crawford kept a journal. The entry on the evening of September 14 began a theme that would be repeated, again and again for four more years, in the diaries and letters of the pioneers:

Doctor Whitman has a very comfortable house, and is farming to a considerable extent . . . I was never more pleased to see a house or white people in my life. We were treated by Dr. and Mrs. Whitman with the utmost kindness.

Elijah White, who got there first, was astonished at Whitman's progress, but not envious. His ambitions lay in another direction, and he hardly had time to inspect carefully a plantation that now consisted of the old house, the spacious mission house, a two-story building for wayfarers, a blacksmith shop, the gristmill and extensive fields. Although he was the new agent for Indian affairs White wasted little time among the Cayuse. He wanted to get to the Willamette and establish the seat of his authority.

He handed Whitman the packet of letters and quickly filled him in on events in the East. If the missionary opened at once the letters from Boston he must have been an inattentive listener.

It is probable that White told Whitman what he had every intention of telling the Willamette settlers, and what subsequently he did tell them. The United States would extend its jurisdiction and protection to the Oregon country; and what better proof than his own presence there in official capacity?

White may—or may not—have known President Tyler's attitude toward Oregon, which was precisely this: "I looked exclusively to an adjustment by the forty-ninth parallel, and never dreamed for a moment of surrendering the free navigation of the Columbia." Unless, as the President confided to his son two years later, Britain through her influence with Mexico would obtain for the United States "the greater equivalent of California."

Certainly Elijah White did know one general but vital fact: things were yeasting in the Far West, and particularly in Oregon. That generality he certainly impressed upon Whitman, who beneath a stolid exterior was always susceptible to excitement.

Such news and impressions as White brought could only strengthen Whitman in his belief that his policies for the mission, and especially for Waiilatpu, were right. We can imagine, then, the impact of David Greene's letter which White had brought.

The Prudential Committee had resolved on the twenty-third of the February past "that the Rev. Henry H. Spalding be recalled, with instructions to return by the first direct and suitable opportunity; that Mr. William H. Gray be advised to return home, and also the Reverend Asa B. Smith . . . that Dr. Marcus Whitman and Mr. Cornelius Rogers be designated to the northern branch of the mission, and that the two last named be authorized to dispose of the mission property in the southern branch of the mission."

What must have struck Whitman harder than any blow of Tilaukait's was that last part of the order. Sell out Waiilatpu!

Greene and the committee, of course, did not know that already the Smiths and Rogers had left the mission, and that Gray was on his way out. The two parts of the resolution now relevant involved the fate of Spalding and his wife, and of the mission property Narcissa called "our home."

Whitman, like the rest, had been expecting severe censure from the Board. But the extent of this action was stunning. By swift messenger he sent out the alarm. Elkanah and Mary Walker got the news at Tshimakain as they sat down to breakfast on September 20. Walker and Cushing Eells left the same day for Waiilatpu, and the long journey was punctuated with gloomy discussion. Eells felt that the mission was doomed and wished that he had remained in the States. But Walker could not bring himself to believe that all was lost.

Spalding had the shorter journey from Lapwai and was at Waiilatpu when Walker and Eells arrived on the twenty-sixth. They found the air of the mission house charged with electricity; obviously there had been recriminations. Although the Tshimakain visitors reached Waiilatpu at ten in the morning the missioners did not fall to business until that evening.

And then, curiously, they did not attack the basic problem. They began the sessions with a discussion of Gray's case, which actually had been decided already by Gray himself. The next day's meeting got nowhere, and by the morning of the twenty-seventh Eells, Walker and Spalding were ready to abide by the decision of the Prudential Committee.

At breakfast, informally, Whitman dropped his bombshell. Suppose he rode east and submitted their arguments in person before the committee?

Eells was appalled at the idea of Whitman, already broken in health, attempting the journey unprotected in the middle of winter. Walker had still another concern; he felt that perhaps Whitman should not desert his post. He was mindful, too, that the Methodists had been criticized for Jason Lee's long perambulation across country.

Spalding seems to have blown up completely at the doctor's suggestion. Doubtless the idea of letting Whitman ride east to save his post galled Spalding's sensitive pride. There were harsh words, and it was with difficulty that Walker and Eells persuaded these old antagonists to sit down and discuss the issue in formal mission session. But the meeting was managed, and Whitman won them over to a resolution signed by all three. Walker, Eells and Spalding resolved "that if arrangements can be made to continue the operation of this station, that Dr. Marcus Whitman be at liberty and advised to visit the United States as soon as practicable to confer with the committee of the A.B.C.F.M. in regard to the interests of this mission."

But the resolution was signed with doubts, and Whitman was aware of this. Walker particularly wanted to send a letter with him, presenting his own views to the Board. Whitman promised to give them time to return to their stations and prepare letters that he would take to Boston. The doctor also seems to have agreed to go to the Willamette first, probably to find a caretaker for Waiilatpu. But Walker knew well Whitman's impatience. As he started north for Tshimakain he said, "Doctor, do not start until you are sure you are ready."

Narcissa knew Husband's impetuosity even better. She flew to her own writing desk the next day, a Friday, and wrote home "in great haste. My beloved husband has about concluded to start next Monday to go to the United States . . . He wishes to reach Boston as early as possible so as to make arrangements to return next summer, if prospered."

Next day she prepared another letter, this one for her parents, saying that it had been Friday that "dear husband" had fully made up to leave the following Monday. She wrote: "He goes upon important business as connected with the missionary cause, the cause of Christ in this land, which I leave for him to explain when you see him . . . He has for a companion Mr. Lovejoy, a respectable, intelligent man and lawyer, but not a Christian, who expects to accompany him all the way to Boston, as his friends are in that region, and perhaps to Washington."

The acquisition of Lovejoy as a companion may have given Whitman excuse to cancel his promise to wait for letters from his associates. Elkanah Walker would be considerably upset when he found that the doctor had crossed the Blue Mountains by the time those letters reached Waiilatpu, a day ahead of the agreed time.

Why Asa Lovejoy should have wanted to face that transcontinental journey so soon again, and in winter, has puzzled many. He had not given up his intention of settling in Oregon, and had no interest in missionary work. He did not know Whitman well, and the doctor's persuasive powers would have had to be miraculous indeed to persuade him. Lovejoy was thirty-four, no adventurous youth. The clue seems to lie in his profession; he was a lawyer, and Whitman intended to go "perhaps to Washington" at a time when high officialdom was agog over Oregon. It would be simply an ironic twist that Whitman's greater energy would outdistance an exhausted Lovejoy.

But once Lovejoy had said yes there was no time to find someone to take charge at Waiilatpu. Walker may have wanted Whitman to go to the Willamette to make a selection personally, but now the hurrying Whitman assigned that chore to Gray, who, under the circumstances, must not have relished it.

In her frantic rush to get Whitman's things together Narcissa forgot to pack his comb, his pencil and journal. Days later she would find in a cupboard the pocket compass he had meant to take along. And she forgot to tell him to buy some spectacles for her in the East; she could only hope that he would remember how badly she needed them.

Whitman left Waiilatpu on October 3. The disgruntled Grays left next day for the Willamette. Narcissa was alone now except for Helen Mar and Mary Ann, the memories of Alice Clarissa, and the sullen Cayuse, who wondered where the doctor and Lovejoy were going—and why.

If she had been invited to Tshimakain or Lapwai she had refused; if Eliza Spalding or Mary Walker offered to stay with her a while, she had declined.

And one Cayuse watched with veiled eyes as the Grays' overloaded cart passed the Indian village.

H. L. Davis

THE KETTLE OF FIRE

The kettle of fire story was told to me at different times during the summer when I was eleven years old and working at typesetting for a patent-inside weekly newspaper in Antelope, Oregon, though it didn't end with the telling and, I think, has not ended even now. The man who told it to me, a rundown old relic named Sorefoot Capron, held the post of city marshal except when there was somebody loose who needed to be arrested, and also managed the town water system, because he was the only resident who had been there long enough to know where the mains were laid. He used to drop in at the newspaper office sometimes when things were dull around town, which was often, to borrow a couple of dollars to get drunk on, and he would kill time by digging up experiences from his youth while he waited for the editor to show up and open the safe.

As he told it, he had run away from a respectable home in Ohio in the early 1860s, out of disgust with his parents because, after he had beaten his brains half out winning some prize in school, they had merely glanced coldly at it and reminded him that he was almost a half-hour late with his milking. The war was beginning then, but the enlistment boards turned him down because he was only fourteen and slight of build even for that age. He castigated his itinerary on west to St. Louis, where he supported himself during the winter by gambling at marbles and spit-at-a-crack with the colored youngsters around the stockyards, and by running errands for a Nevada silver-mine operator named Cash Payton, a heavy-set man with a short red beard, a bald spot on top of his head like a tonsure, and a scar across the bridge of his nose from having mistimed a fuse, who was hanging around waiting for the Overland Mail route to reopen so he could freight some mining machinery west over it.

He had two partners who were waiting in St. Louis with him, one a blocky little Cornishman with bow legs who talked in a chewed-up kind of bray, the other a long-coupled German with a pale beard and gold earrings, which in those times were believed by some people to be a specific against weak eyesight. They were both pleasant-spoken men, though hard to understand most of the time, but Cash Payton was not the kind of man to let his good-nature stop with mere pleasant-spokenness. He took a special liking to young Capron, believed or let on to believe all the lies he told about being homeless and an orphan, and made plans to take him west with the mining machinery as soon as the road got opened up. When it turned out that the road was apt to stay closed for several months longer, he arranged to sign youg Capron on as a herder and roustabout with a train of emigrants from Illinois and Missouri who were organizing to sneak past the frontier outposts and head west for a new start in unspoiled country, and also, though none of them brought the point up, to get themselves somewhere out of reach before they got picked up in the draft.

Travel across the plains to Oregon was forbidden at the time, because the military posts along the emigrant route had been abandoned and there was no protection against Indian raids, but the train managed to work its way out into open country while the border garrisons were busy with some rebel foray, and it rolled along on its westward course without any sign of trouble until it struck the Malheur Desert, not far from the line between Oregon and Nevada. It had moved slowly, and summer ends early in that part of the country, so it struck bad weather and had its horse-herd stampeded by Snake and Bannock Indians, who also killed a couple of night-herders by filling them full of arrows. The emigrants had hired some mountain man to steer them through the bad country, but the killings made them scared and suspicious, and they talked so loud and pointedly about hanging him for treachery that he picked up and pulled out in the night, leaving them stalled without any idea where they were or any draft-animals to haul them anywhere else.

It was a doleful place to be stuck in with bad weather coming on: merely a little muddy water-hole at the bottom of a rock-gully with nothing in sight anywhere around it but sagebrush and greasewood and rocks. They had vinegar to correct the alkali in the water, but several of the women got sick from drinking it, the dead sagebrush that they picked up for fuel was so soggy they couldn't get it to burn, and when they tried starting it by shooting a cotton wad into it they discovered that all their powder had drawn damp and got unusable except what was in the guns. They didn't dare squander that, and some of them opposed shooting of any kind for fear of drawing more Indians down on them, so they held a meeting and decided, since young Capron was not of much use to them and had nobody depending on him, to send him down toward the Nevada mining settlements for help, if he could find any. In any case, and whatever he found or did, he was to bring back an iron kettle full of live coals that they could start a fire in damp wood with.

It was a risky mission to put off onto a youngster, and several of the men, all elderly and in no danger of being let in for it themselves, dwelt with some sarcasm on the idea of selecting anybody so young and inexperienced for a job that they were all willing to offer advice about but not to undertake in his place, but nobody came up with anything better, and as far as young Capron was concerned he didn't in the least mind being picked for it. He was tired of the whole pack of them by then, and would have welcomed anything, dangerous or not, that could serve as an excuse to get away from them. He was not especially uneasy about the risks, or about the chance of finding any fire to bring back. His only difficulty, all through the time when they were arguing back and forth about sending him, was trying to decide whether to come back and expose himself to them again even if he did find it.

The strain and solemnity of starting settled that for him. He knew, even before he had finished saddling up and had climbed on the saddlepony they had caught up for him, that he would have to come back. They had made him wait till after dark to start, and he couldn't see any of the men around him, though he knew that they were all there. From the ground, he had been able to make out their figures against the sky, but looking down at them from the saddle was like trying to keep track of a foam-streak after it had been swept under in a deep rapid. One of them reached out and clattered the kettle-bale over his saddle-horn, and he heard them all draw back to leave the way open for him. Except for that, they were all silent. There was no sound in the camp except for the herd-ponies shifting to keep warm, and a child blubbering listlessly in one of the wagons, and the choking sound of a sick woman trying to vomit. A curious apathy comes over people facing death when they know it and know what form it will take, even when they still go through the form of refusing to admit that they know anything about it. Afterward, when the reality begins to show itself, they are likely to fall into a panic and do things too revolting to bear telling or thinking of. Young Capron knew that he had to get back with the fire, and that if he failed to get back with it before they reached that point it would be useless. Saving the lives of people who had made themselves unfit to live would be work wasted, and possibly worse than wasted. It would not help merely to keep on going, either; that would mean carrying the sounds of the camp along with him, the woman choking, the child blubbering, the silent men shuffling as they drew back in the dark, through all the years that he could reasonably expect to live, and maybe even beyond them. He had to find fire, and he had to get back with it while they were still able to hold themselves together. They might have been wrong and selfish in picking him, and they might be hard to like or live with, but there was nothing else for it. With that in his head, and with the kettle on his saddle-horn and a sack of food strapped on the cantle, he rode out between the wagons into the sagebrush.

Getting out of the gully into open country was slow and precarious work. The Indians turned out to have an outpost line drawn all the way around the camp a half-mile back from it, and he had to keep to the draws and move cautiously, leading the pony and inching along in places a step at a time, to dodge them. The pony saved him once, by balking and refusing to move even when spurred. He got off and crawled ahead to investigate, and discovered that he had been riding straight into a watch-post at the top of the ridge. The Indians had dug a hole and covered it with a blanket to keep the warmth in, with a headslit cut in the middle to look out through. It took him over an hour to back-track, find the pony in the dark, and circle around it. Afterward he heard dogs yapping in the Indian camp, and he put in another two or three hours edging around that, dismounting and putting his ear to the ground every dozen yards or so to keep from running into squaws out rummaging firewood.

Toward daylight the desert around him looked clear, and he dropped down into a creek-wash and slept in a little thornberry thicket while the pony filled up on salt-grass around a mudhole, but when he got saddled up to start off again he saw mounted Indians casting around in the sagebrush for his trail a couple of miles away, so he kept to the draws, crawling and hauling the pony along by main strength where the thorn-brush grew heavy, until almost noon. Then he mounted and struck up a long lope and held it, stopping only to rest for an hour when he struck a waterhole, all day and most of the night and all through the next day, with no sleep except when he forgot and dozed in the saddle and no food except a sage-hen which he knocked over with a rock and ate raw. Toward nightfall he made out some scattering pine timber with shadows that looked palish blue as if smoke was coloring them. He headed for it, hoping to find some camp that was burning charcoal for the Nevada mines, or possibly a dead tree smouldering from being struck by lightning. Night came while he was still a couple of miles away, but he kept going because, in the darkness, he could see that it was a real fire, and that the reddish pine trunks lit up and darkened as it flickered back and forth across them.

He dismounted, playing it safe, tied the pony to a boulder and hung the kettle from his belt, and crept forward on his hands and knees, keeping the sagebrush clumps between him and the light and stopping behind every clump to sight out the ground before inching on ahead. It was a good thing he did, for he saw when he got close that the fire had men around it. The light was too fitful and uneven to show what they looked like, but he could make out a wickiyup behind them, a round-topped basketwork structure covered halfway down with skins and tattered pieces of old canvas. It was enough to make him hug the ground and peer through the tangle of sagebrush instead of looking around it. Only Snake Indians built basketwork wickiyups, and the Snakes were the most warlike of all the tribes in that part of the country. He felt pleased at being able to remember about wickiyups at such a time, and started looking for more signs that the men really were Indians, ignoring whatever evidence there was that might have hinted at anything else.

The fire itself was a clear sign that they were Indians. It was not the kind of towering holocaust that white travellers always set going when they were camped for the night in wild country, but a wan little flicker of only three or four small stocks, so puny and half-hearted that he wondered how its light could have been visible so far out in the open desert. It was not nearly big enough for the men to keep warm by, but it seemed what they wanted, for they kept piling ashes on it to hold it down, and once one of them picked up a stock that was beginning to blaze up and quenched it by sticking it into the dirt. Only Indians would have gone to so much trouble to keep a campfire low, and when the man who had quenched the stick stood up to rake the coals back together young Capron saw that he was wrapped in a blanket and that there was a gleam of something whitish as he turned his head that looked like an Indian headband.

There might have been other signs if he had looked for them, but they were not needed, and he didn't dare wait any longer. The smallness of the fire had led him to miscalculate his distances, and his pony was tied close enough so that they might hear it if it started stamping or pawing. There was nothing to hold back for, anyway. Indians were Indians. They had not wasted their time arguing about killing the emigrant train's two night-herders and running off its livestock, and the train needed fire worse than they had needed wagon-horses. He rummaged out his pistol, poked it carefully through the middle of the sagebrush clump, and waited till the man with the blanket stood away from the fire so he would have the light to sight against. He drew for the center of the blanket a handbreadth below the man's shoulders, levelled up till the foresight filled the back notch, and let go. The smoke of the black powder filled the tangle of sagebrush like gray cottonwood down settling from a wind, but he lay and glared through it and through the smoke still dribbling from the pistol muzzle without even noticing it.

The man stood motionless for a long second while the blanket slid from his shoulders and piled around his feet. Then he swayed, flapped his elbows and tipped his head back as if getting ready to crow, and fell face-down across the fire and plunged the whole camp into pitch darkness. He must have died falling, by the slack-jointed thump his body made when it hit in the ashes. If he had still been conscious he would have tried to avoid the fire, and he didn't; he merely let go all holds and whopped down and gathered it to his bosom like a hen covering her chickens from a hawk.

The other men jumped up and legged it for cover. Young Capron could hear brush cracking and dead branches ripping at their clothes as they galloped off into the timber. He waited till the light from the dead man's clothes taking fire showed him that he had the camp all to himself. There was something faintly worrisome about the smell of the clothes burning. It was like wool, and Indians never wore anything except cotton cloth and buckskin. Still, it might be from a corner of the blanket burning, and there was no time to speculate about it, whatever it was. He scrabbled in the dead sagebrush needles for the kettle, had an awful moment of thinking he might have lost it, and then found it by the clatter it made against his pistol, which was still clutched in his hand. He grabbed it and scrambled up and ran in, flubbing the pistol into his holster between strides, and rolled the body clear of the ashes and stirred the blackened embers together and began scraping dead pine needles from the ground to pile on them. They were almost out. He had to pile on small twigs and fan up a glaring blaze to keep them from dying on him, knowing that every twig that caught would make him an easier target for the men who had taken to the timber, and not daring to stop feeding in more sticks to make it flame up stronger.

Ministering to the flame and strained between dread when it gained and panic when it lost, he did some wondering about what the dead man looked like, but when it finally took a solid hold and burned high enough to see by, he decided that he would rather not know, and moved back into the shadows and sat with his back to it, except for one moment when some sound, possibly of tree limbs rubbing together, made him glance around to see if it had moved. There was no sign that it had, but he didn't turn away quite fast enough to keep from noticing that what he had taken for an Indian headband was a bald spot and that a stiff beard down one side of the face had been burnt to a pale gray ash that the draft from the fire kept crumbling into powder so that it looked, in the slanting light, as if it was twitching.

The sight was unnerving, though he had hard work to hold back from looking at it again, and its significance was not much help, either. Indians did not have beards or bald spots. The smell of wool had been the man's flannel shirt scorching. He had been white: possibly some Indian trader, or gun-peddler, or mining promoter; possibly somebody with political influence, and friends, and relatives; even possibly—

There was no use running possibilities all the way up the string. It was done, and there was no help for it and no use in thinking about it. It was not even certain that there was anything about it to regret. There were white men in the country who needed salting worse than most of the Indians, and a man shacked up in a Snake Indian lodge in that remote corner of the desert must have had some business in hand besides organizing classes in Bible study or quilt-piecing. Still, shooting him had been overhastiness, and young Capron was sorry about it, and scared. He scooped half the fire into the kettle, though the bigger pine sticks in it had not yet burned down to coals, and hung it on a dead tree-limb and ran for his pony. He was thankful that he had his errand to hurry for. Without it, his excuse for hurrying would have had to be something less dignified; fear that the two men might be creeping up through the trees to bushwhack him, fear that if he stayed any longer he would not be able to hold out against looking once more at the dead man's face.

The fire on the ground had burned low when he rode back, but the pitch-knots in the kettle were flaring up so the pony refused to edge within reach of it, even with spurring. Finally he got down and covered the kettle with a piece of bark, and then rode past at a trot and grabbed it from the limb before the bark had time to take fire. He moved up in the saddle, raked the pony down the ribs, and lit back into the desert with the kettle out at one side and the flame from the bark caressing his hand and arm as vengefully as if the dead man had prayed it on him for a parting retribution.

When he got a couple of miles out, he reined up to let the knots burn lower, but he heard hoofbeats from the trail behind, so he merely dumped a couple of the hottest knots out into the sagebrush and shoved on. Afterward, looking back at the glare they were making, he could have kicked himself for leaving so plain a marker for the men to steer by, though the truth was that it didn't matter much. Uncovering the coals he had kept made them flare high enough to be visible two miles away, and when he tried holding the kettle low they scared the pony into a paroxysm of rearing and pinwheeling that threatened to scatter all the fire out of it.

He had to go back to holding the kettle at arm's length before the pony would move ahead at all. It looked like trying to flag a steamboat, and the foolishness of it started him to reflecting bitterly on the things he should have done and had lacked the sense to think of till too late. He should have hunted out and stampeded the men's saddle-horses while he was waiting for the fire to get started. He should have picked greasewood for the fire instead of pitch-pine. He should have covered the kettle with dirt instead of bark. He should have used his brains instead of letting them run to imagining things that merely scared him. He should have kept his nerve, figured things out ahead, made himself into something steadier and more far-sighted than he ever had been. He should not have been in such a hurry to play the hand Providence had dealt him to establish his future on. It would have been better if he had held it back and tried to change the spots on the cards by making faces at them, or possibly by crying over them. A man had to live up to what he was, weaknesses and all. Finding out about them was probably not worth shooting a man for, but it was a gain. The kettle had returned him that much for his trouble, at least.

He held the pony to a high trot for a couple of miles, and then pulled up to let it catch its wind. He could no longer hear hoof-beats back of him, so he took time to pull off his coat and wrap it around his hand as a protection against the heat from the coals. Then a rock clattered back in the distance, and he knew the men were still coming, and closing the range. The pony heard it too, and he had to rein back hard to keep it from breaking into a run and getting windbroken. It would have been easy to lose them if his hands had been free: he could merely have walked the pony down into some gully and laid low till they passed. The kettle killed that possibility; they could line him in by the light from it, no matter which way he turned or what track he took. He thought of covering it with gravel, or with a sod from some mudhole, but decided against that for fear of smothering the fire completely.

At the end of six or seven miles, he realized that it was not far from going out all by itself. The coat wadded over his burnt hand had kept him from noticing how much the kettle had cooled down. One welcome part of it was that the light had got too weak to be visible at a distance, but he was too much afraid of losing the fire to take comfort in its debility. He slowed to a walk for awhile, and then turned sharp away from his course down a low draw, dismounted and tied the pony in a thicket of giant sagebrush, and felt his way down the slope hunting for dead roots that could be used for kindling. There was nothing dry enough until, in the low ground where the draw widened out, he bumped into some stunted junipers. Juniper wood is too light and porous to be much use as fuel, but the trunks were run through with dead streaks from which, by gouging with his knife, he managed to pry loose a handful of splinters that would take fire easily, even if they didn't hold it long.

The kettle was cool enough to touch by the time he finished collecting them, but with careful blowing they condescended to flicker up so that he could lay on heavier fuel from the dead branches. When that caught, he rammed the kettle down into a badger hole, piled whole branches over it to make sure the fire would last, and went on down the dry watercourse to find hardwood that would burn down into coals. The light from the branches glared like a haystack burning, and he had no trouble finding greasewood roots and a dead chokecherry tree and loading himself up with chunks from them. The flame behind him filled half the sky by then, so he circled back cautiously and hid under a low-branched juniper fifty or sixty yards from it, in case it drew anybody to come investigating.

It happened quicker than he had counted on. He had got himself settled among the juniper boughs, which smelled bad, and was smearing his face with wet dirt to blend with the shadows when two men came down the slope from his trail, stopped where the sagebrush thinned out, and stood watching the fire and shading their eyes against it. They were a hundred yards away, and they looked unhumanly tall in the roar of the firelight, but he could see that they were white men. They had on ordinary work clothes, and they wore hats and had their hair cut short. That was nothing much; he had expected that they would turn out to be white, and he was not afraid of them except for a slight feeling of strain inside him. It gouged harder to see that one of them was blocky and reddish and bowlegged, and that the other was tall and thin and pale-bearded, with earrings on which the light sparkled when he moved his head. Young Capron would not have noticed the earrings at such a distance if he had not been expecting them. The men were the sawed off Cornishman and the tall German who had been Cash Payton's partners. He had liked Cash Payton better than both of them—better than anybody else, as far as that went—but he had liked them. Because he had shot Cash Payton, he dared not move for fear they would pick out his hiding place and kill him. They stood peering across the firelight into the junipers, the German wagging a long army cap-and-ball revolver and the Cornishman holding a rifle as if he was fixing to rake hay with it, all primed and set to open up on anything that moved.

They loomed up against the shadows like clay pipes in a shooting gallery. If they had been strangers, if the firelight had not outdone itself to show who they were beyond the possibility of a mistake, he could have cleared his way back to the emigrant train with two cartridges, besides acquiring possession of two unjaded saddlehorses which he could have used very handily. What they had been doing camped in the timber so far from anywhere he didn't try to guess. Nothing to their credit, likely, or they would not have gone to so much trouble to run him down. Catching Indian children to sell as slaves in San Francisco was a flourishing business then, and if it was that, they deserved shooting for it. So did Cash Payton, except that points of ethics no longer counted. All that did count was knowing that the man who had befriended him and kept him alive over a whole winter was lying dead back in the pine timber with half his face burned off, all because of a scary young squirt's clubfooted foolishness. Bad or good, right or wrong, he had deserved better than to be shot down from cover when his back was turned. Young Capron shut his eyes and buried his face in the dirt, wondering, to end a painful train of reflection, whether he could ever smell juniper boughs again without getting sick, as in fact he never could, in all the years afterward.

When he looked up, the men were leaving, probably having realized the sappiness of standing in the full glare of the fire when the man they were hunting might be lurking somewhere close to take advantage of it. The tall German stopped at the edge of the sagebrush and examined the caps in his revolver to make sure they were all in place. That meant that they were not giving up, and that they would probably post themselves somewhere along his trail, figuring to knock him over when he came back to it. If it had not been for the shooting they would have been glad to see him and, if they could, to help him. If it had not been for the fire kettle there would not have been any shooting. Of course, he could leave it where it was and ride after them and let on not to know anything about it, so they would blame the shooting on somebody else. They would probably take his word for it: foreigners were trustful about things they didn't understand very well, in contrast to Americans, who were always the most suspicious in matters they knew the least about. He could go with the two men and be safe, and be rid of the emigrants and their snivelling and domineering for good.

The only trouble was that he couldn't bring himself to do it. It would mean that Cash Payton had died for nothing, for mere foolishness, because a streak of light hit him in the wrong place. The only way to make his death count for anything was to get the fire back to the train. He shook loose from his seesawing and went into the tall sagebrush for his pony.

The fire had burned down when he came back with the pony, and the juniper boughs were falling into coals that the stir of air fanned into flaky ashes. It was hard to lose time building them back, but he had to have some kind of fire that would last, and the pony would hold up better for being left to graze and rest a little longer. He piled on the greasewood and wild cherry, waited to make sure it caught, and then lay down upwind from the junipers and slept until the glare of the new fire woke him. He fished the kettle out with a forked tree-limb, left it to cool while he caught and bridled the pony, and scooped it full of new coals and tried to mount with it.

The pony had recuperated too well. It shied back and forth so that he had to put the kettle down to keep from being yanked off his feet. He tried covering the coals with ashes, but the glow still showed through, and the pony fought back from it till he set the kettle back on the ground and climbed aboard without it. He rode past it and tried to pick it up from the saddle, but the pony shied off so he couldn't reach it. Finally he found his forked tree-limb, circled back, and hooked the kettle at long range and hauled it in. Even then it took all his strength on the reins to keep the pony from pinwheeling and running away from the heat and light following along even with its off-shoulder.

He had held his feelings back too long, probably. He was crying by the time he got the kettle hoisted up and felt the heat on his burned flesh again. He got angry with himself for crying, and his anger made him forget about the two men waiting for him somewhere along the trail ahead. He remembered them after he had ridden a few hundred yards, and swung back along the draw on a wide circuit to keep clear of them. Half the coals in the kettle had got spilled out in his manipulations with the forked tree-limb, and he had no idea how he would manage about renewing them when they burned low again, but there was no use killing snakes till they stopped hibernating. He put it out of his mind, along with what seemed a lifetime of other useless reflections and apprehensions, and rode on.

The coals burned low about daylight, when he was crossing a long level plain on which even the sagebrush grew so thin that he was in plain sight of anybody two or three miles way in any direction. Sagebrush roots burned out almost like wadded newspaper, but there was nothing else, and he got down and gathered an armload of them and nursed the fire back to life. They were damp, and the smoke from them rose in a whitish column that could be seen for miles, but at least the open plain made it impossible for anybody to sneak up on him. It was about fifteen miles across, and he could see anything that moved on it. A man on horseback would have loomed up like a steeple, even at the edge of it.

Nothing came in sight. The plain was lifeless except for horned toads. With the daylight, the pony had got over its fright of the kettle, and it struck up a trot when he remounted, as if it was as anxious to see the last of the place as he was. The plain broke into a long ridge, speckled at its base with little rusty junipers and with a tangle of mountain mahogany marking the line of a dry gully. He halted and broke some of its dead boughs for fuel, since they were hot and slow-burning. They took away his anxiety about the fire for the moment, and it began to be brought home to him that he had circled into country where nobody had ever been before. A herd of antelope came out of the junipers as he passed, looked after him with their back-tufts twitching with inquisitiveness, and then followed along after him, edging downwind to catch his scent and then moving in to gawk at him from such close range that he could have hit them with a rock. The pony watched them uneasily and stumbled over so many rocks and roots trying to keep out of their way that he was halfway tempted to do it, except that it would have meant having to stop and dismount to find something to throw.

Beyond the ridge, he lost them. The ground levelled off into a long expanse of naked earth, pocked and honeycombed with sage-rat burrows. It must have been a mile across, and the country around it for a half-dozen miles was stripped as bare as if it had been plowed and harrowed. There were sage-rats all over it. Some sat up and stared at him as he passed, and then dropped almost under the pony's feet and went on about their business, whatever it was. Some scurried for their holes as if scared, but then they sat up and stared too, and finally sauntered back where they had come from, evidently feeling that whatever was happening at the pony's level was no concern of theirs, and that, when all was said and done, the proper study of ratkind was rats. There was nothing anywhere near their ground that could be used for fuel to keep the fire up, and the ground itself was treacherous because the pony kept breaking through it where they had tunnelled it for their nests.

They were not much company. The worst of it was not their strangeness and preoccupation with themselves, it was the loniness of the country that made young Capron adapt himself, without being aware of it, to their values and scale of living. A few more miles of them, he felt, and he would find himself growing feeler-whiskers, squeaking, and rearing up on his hind-legs to watch himself ride past and try for a second or two to figure out what he was. He turned down a dry gully to get clear of them and the waste they had created, and same to a long scarp of low gray cliffs, broken into rifts and ledges for its entire length. Every rift and every ledge was occupied by great pale-gray owls. None of them moved as he rode past. They sat straight and impassive, hooting to each other briefly sometimes with a hollow sound like blowing into an empty jug, their blank yellow eyes staring past him into the sun without seeing it or him and without knowing or caring what he was. They could see objects only in the half-dusk or in the dark. Nothing that passed in the sunlight made any impression on them.

The cliffs fell away, and the gully spread out into a wide flat covered with stubby clumps of old weatherstained rye-grass. The ground between the clumps was dark and watersoaked, but it was covered so densely with jackrabbits that it looked gray and moving like a spread of water. The jackrabbits moved sluggishly, some of them waiting till they were almost under the pony's feet and then dragging themselves barely out of the way and settling down again. Their trouble was one that usually hit jackrabbits in the years when they had run themselves down by overbreeding. They were swollen with wens from bot-flies, and so weakened by them that they couldn't have moved fast if they had wanted to.

A curious thing about it was that though disease had undermined their instinct for self-preservation, it had left their appetites unimpaired, or only a little slackened. They were still able to crop all the green sprouts out of the dead rye-grass clumps, and they had not lost their interest in copulation, whatever might have happened to their ability. They were not noticeably energetic about it, but they stayed with it faithfully, working as the pony picked its way among them at the absorbing task of perpetuating their kind, bot-flies and all, and regarding nothing else as deserving of notice.

The flat fell away into a long rise and fall of stony desert, and then to a broad grass-slope that reached down to a bright-green little alkali lake, with dark wire-grass in the shallows and patches of willow on the damp ground back of them. The slopes and the shallows were covered solid with wild geese, mottled like a patched quilt with their different colors—brown Canada geese, white snow-geese, dark little cacklers, blue honkers, ringnecked black brant—rocking placidly on the bitter water or crowded solid along the swell of short grass overlooking it. Young Capron would have liked to avoid them, but the fire was low in the kettle, and there was dead wood among the willows that would make good coals and no way of getting it except to ride straight through them.

Of all the forms of life the country had put him up against, they were the worst. They held their ground till he could have reached down and touched them, and then rose with a horrible blast of screeching and banging of wings, darkening the sky overhead and spattering him and the pony and the kettle and the fire in it with filth to show how much he had upset them by turning out to be something they had not been expecting. Then, as the next flock went squalling and clattering up with a new shower, the one behind him settled back onto the grass as unconcernedly as if nothing at all had happened, as no doubt, in the tablets of their memory, nothing at all had. They should have quieted down and gone back to resting when he dismounted and went to work preparing the dead willow limbs for his fire, but they seemed unable either to stand him or to let him alone. Every few minutes, though he moved as little as he could and the pony scarcely stirred out of its tracks, some of them would stalk close to him, rear up and look him over again, and then let out a horrified squawk and put the whole flock up to spatter him with filth all over again. It was not hostility so much as indignation. They were outraged with him for being there, without having the ghost of an idea what he was doing or the slightest interest in finding out.

Getting clear of the wild country took a long time. He had circled farther than he realized, and crossing the long swells of ground beyond the lake took up the whole afternoon, counting two or three times when he had to skirmish up dead limbs of cottonwood and service-berry to stoke the kettle. There was one more small flurry of wild life, a little creek bordered with short grass that was being stripped off by huge wingless Mormon crickets. They were slippery for the pony to step on, but there was nothing else to them except appetite. Some little darkish rattlesnakes picked languidly at them around the edges, without any great show of interest in doing it. Young Capron spurred away from the place, feeling with some self-pity that a man had to fall low to be siding with rattlesnakes, but wishing them well even in wanting to be rid of them for good.

He would have liked to keep going when it got dark, but the pony was sunken-flanked and laboring on the slopes, so he turned into a little stand of cottonwoods and unsaddled and turned it out to graze. He found some half-dead wild plum and dumped the coals from the kettle and built up a fire with fuel from it, first dead sticks and then bigger green ones, which burned slower but made long-lasting coals. When the fire took hold, he ate some salt pork that the emigrants had given him, downing it raw because cooking wasted it, and spread out on a patch of dampish ground and slept.

Something brought him awake along in the night. He didn't know what it had been, but he could tell by the waning fire that he had slept for several hours, and he noticed that the silence around him was deeper than it had been when he was going to sleep. Building the fire back, he realized that what he missed was the sound of the pony grazing. He piled kindling into the kettle for a light and went out to see what had become of it. The grass showed where it had been grazing, but it was gone. He tried farther out, remembering gloomily that Indians always ran the horses off from a camp that they were getting ready to jump, and found a shallow mudhole that had been trampled all around by horses. The tracks were fresh, which disturbed him for a minute, but a smoothed-down place in the mud where they had been rolling showed that they were running loose. Not all of them were Indian horses either; some of them were shod, and the calkmarks were big enough to have been made by wagon-teams, possibly from the emigrant train, not that it mattered. The pony might have been scared off by some cougar stalking the herd, and it might still be hanging around. That didn't matter either. All that mattered was that the pony had gone with a loose horse-herd, and that there was no use trying to get it back on foot and burdened with a kettle of fire that it had been scared of from the beginning. One from one left nothing, no matter what had been responsible for it.

He ate salt pork again, hung his saddle and bridle from a tree-limb, filled the kettle with new coals and cut a stick to carry it by, and started on afoot without waiting for daylight. In some ways, travelling was easier with the pony gone. There was no worry over having it snort or stamp or whinny at the wrong time, or over having to find grass or water at the stopping places, or having it shy and fight back when he tried to mount, and being able to carry the kettle close to the ground made it less easily seen at a distance. More than that, he was freed from the temptation to throw it away and head out for himself. Without a horse and without food enough for another day, the emigrant camp was the only place he could go. Having to concentrate on one thing instead of seesawing between lurking alternatives made everything simpler: not easier, but easier to summon strength for.

In the afternoon, plodding down a wide valley that opened into draws where there was small wood and water, he found the first sign that he was nearing human beings. It was not a brightening one, merely a dead horse spread out on a patch of bare ground with some buzzards lined up waiting for the sun to burst it open, but it did show that he was headed right and that he was making distance. It turned his thoughts to the emigrant camp, and he began to notice, thinking of the emigrants waiting for him, that the dead sagebrush tops were drying out and that the ground underfoot was strewn with little chips of black flint. He refired the kettle and hurried on, driven by fear that the emigrants might have run into the same thing near their camp, that they might have found dry kindling and lighted a flint-and-steel fire for themselves. Thinking of that possibility and discovering what his own feelings about it were opened a new area of self-knowledge to him, and not an especially comforting one. He tried to think how much suffering and fear and despair they would be spared if they had thought of trying it, and could get no farther than the reflection that it would make his own suffering and fear and despair useless: a man dead, and his pain, terror, weariness, humiliation and hunger all gone for nothing. He took more consolation from thinking that if his knowledge of the emigrants was a sign of anything, they wouldn't have sense enough to think of hunting for flints to start a fire with, even if they had the courage to venture far enough out to find them.

It was humiliating to realize that his values had all been turned upside down, when he could welcome seeing a dead horse with buzzards around it and be downcast to think that people he knew might be keeping warm and cooking food and drying out their gunpowder, but the fear held on in spite of him. When he looked down from the last rise of ground on the Indian camp he had skirted around in starting out, he saw a smoke rising from beyond it that appeared to come from the emigrant train, and it set him shaking at the knees so that he had to sit down to keep from collapsing. It was near sundown by them, and when it got dusk he crept through the sagebrush and discovered that it was not from the wagons at all, but from the hole where the Indian watchpost had been on the night he left camp. The hole had been abandoned, it appeared, and the Indians had made a smudge of damp sagebrush roots in it to scare the emigrants into staying where they were. He took time to pile wet earth on the smudge, to keep the emigrants from finding out how easy it would have been for them to get fire if any of them had thought of it, and he felt relieved and uplifted in spirit to think that none of them had.

The camp seemed dead when he came stumbling down into it, but after a few minutes he began to hear sounds from the wagons: children whimpering with the cold, a man praying in a loud monotone under a wagon, the sick woman still trying to vomit. He remembered that the sounds were the sweetest music he had ever listened to. No ninety-eight-piece orchestra in the land could have come within flagging-distance of them. Even after so many years and so many changes, remembering it still stirred him inside, something like jumping off a barn-roof after swallowing a half-dozen humming jews'-harps.

That was all of the story. He used to build up different parts of it at different times while he sat waiting in the printing offce for the editor to arrive, but at the first telling he told it all straight through, and he ended it, as he was right to do, with the concluding emotion instead of stringing it out into the subsequent events that dulled it all down. I asked what had happened afterward, and he said nothing worth telling about. The emigrants had scraped up nerve enough to go out and run in their teams, or most of them, and they were so pleased with themselves for doing it that they forgot all about his fire that had given them the necessary courage. Then they had moved on, and finally they had come out at a river-crossing that took them into the old Barlow Road. They were not worth much, on the average, any of them.

"They made me pay for the pony I lost," he said. "And the saddle and bridle, too. Took it out of my wages, what little there was of 'em."

"It don't sound like you'd got much out of it," I said. At the time, it didn't seem to me that any story with such a grazzled-out ending was worth spending all that time on. "It sounds like everybody had come out ahead except you."

"That was what they all thought, I guess," he said. "They're welcome to their notions. None of 'em come out as far ahead as they thought they had, and it's the only thing I've ever done that I got anything out of that was worth hellroom. It's the only thing I'd do over again, I believe, if I had to. Not that I'll ever get the chance. Things like that don't happen nowadays."

He was wrong about that, of course. Such things change in substance and setting, but they go on working in the spirit, through different and less explicit symbols, as they did through the centuries before emigrations west were ever heard of, and as they will for men too young to know about them now and for others not yet born. There will always be the fire to bring home, through the same hardships and doubts and adversities of one's life that make up the triumph of having lived it.

Mother of H. L. Davis, 1928.

H. L. Davis

1928 view of Davis Home, The Dalles, Oregon

Albert Richard Wetjen

From *FIDDLERS' GREEN* (1931)

Chapter 2, Which Introduces Ben the Bosun

Tommy Lawn set his peaked cap at a jaunty angle and flicked a black speck from the two gold bands that encircled his cuff.

"That reminds me," he observed. "Swiveltongue Saunders did say something about a fellow being turned into a gull when he died. Do I have to be a gull? You can't do much with a girl when you're a gull."

"No, no!" said Ben the Bosun. "You've got it all wrong."

"I always did think Swiveltongue Saunders was a liar," agreed Tommy with increased cheerfulness. "But he was an interesting old boy. The only man I ever knew who could make a rose knot."

"There ain't no manner o' doubt he wus a liar," observed Ben the Bosun. "You don't 'ave t' be a gull at all. The thing came about this way.... We found that none of you gentlemen, an' th' fo'c's'le 'ands too, for that matter, could stop frettin' an' botherin' about what was goin' on aloft. Seemed like you allus wanted t' know what ships were sailin', an' from where an' where to. Wanted t' know what was doin' on salt water. There was a lot o' breaking out at nights because of that, an' men and wimmin aloft was gettin' scared out their wits with so many 'ands from th' Green drifting about. It got so bad Old Nick made a complaint and it 'ad t' be stopped. 'E said men and wimmin were gettin' too good for 'is own business, since gettin' scared out their wits made 'em behave. Something 'ad t' be done about it, that was all. Th' Old Man decided at last to arrange f' all skippers, what was eligible, to 'ave an albatross, and all th' rest, what was eligible, to 'ave a gull. If your papers are good, ye'll get a stormy petrel. They goes farthest an' see most. If your papers ain't so good, ye'll maybe get a puffin or somethin' that doesn't travel much. An' that's a cruel 'ardship. Some of 'em only gets penguins and they don't see nothin' at all."

"Well, Bosun," said Tommy Lawn, "you're not very clear but I suppose I'll learn the ropes. Maybe you had the same trouble

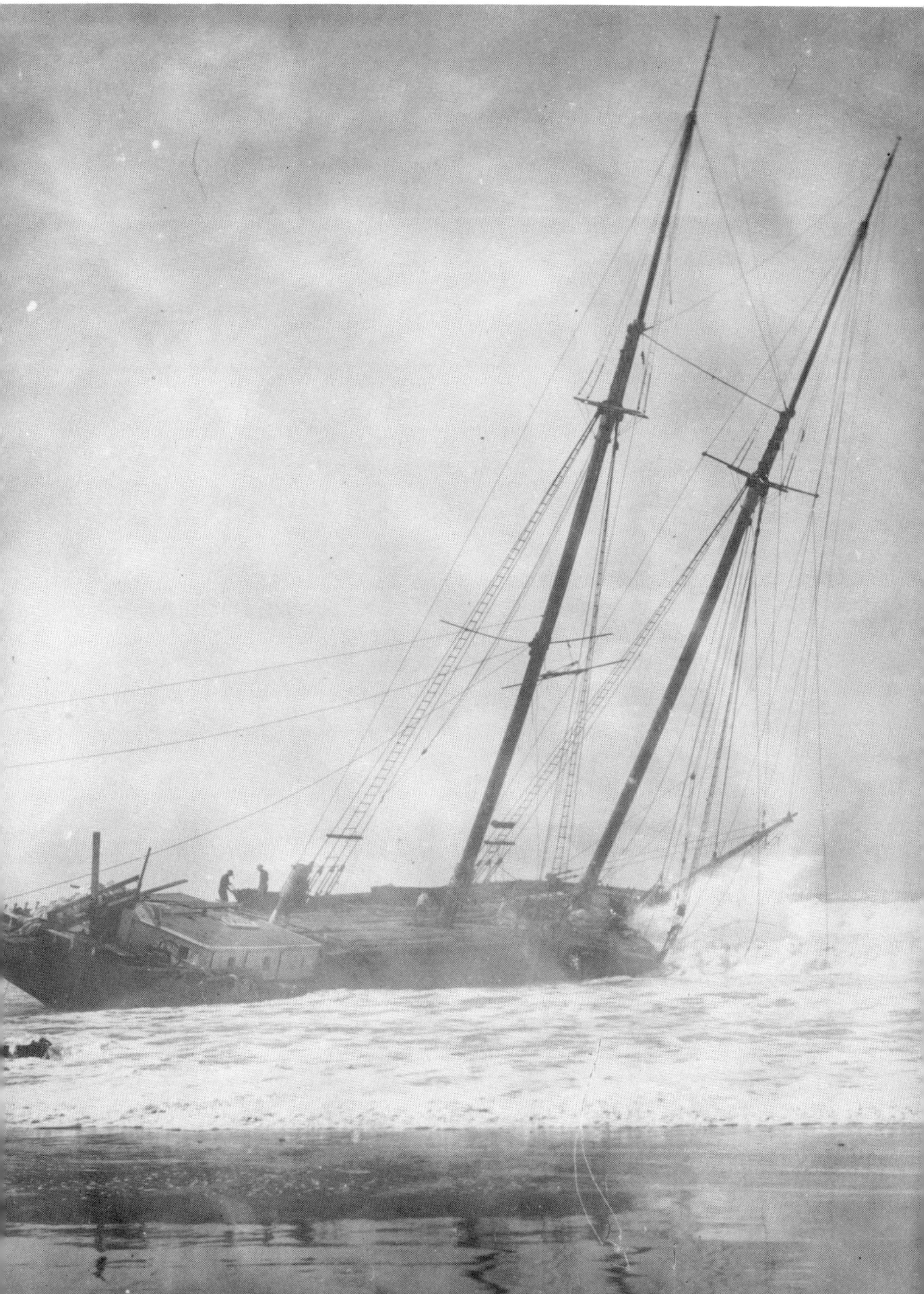

when you drifted down. Where did you serve your time?"

Ben the Bosun coughed and looked somewhat more important than he had done before.

"That was 'fore you were born and when th' *Merry Dun* was still in commission. . . . I was with Hudson in the *Half-Moon* when we cleared from th' Texel and sailed to th' ice pack of Novaya Zemlya, to find a passage to Cathay. That was afore we went to th' west an' the skipper was set adrift with me an' some others. The *Merry Dun* picked us up when th' shallop sank, and th' Old Man made me Bosun. We 'ad sailors them days."

"That's a regular wail from all you old warts," said Tommy Lawn disrespectfully, and in spite of a tinge of awe he felt at being with a man who had served under Hudson. "The best sailors were always in the old days. I think it's a lot of rot. What the devil!"

"Well, you young fellers gets things mighty easy to what we 'ad," said Ben the Bosun, looking annoyed. "I don't know what sort o' charts ye'd have nowadays if it wasn't fer skippers like mine. Bad grub an' water, an' we 'adn't compasses an' sextants an' chronometers such as there is now."

"Oh, we'd get along," said Tommy Lawn. "The trouble with you old boys is you think the world stops as soon as you take a watch below."

Ben the Bosun might have said something further on the subject but just then they came to a vast expanse of flat, reddish rock from which grew tufts of barnacles, and in the middle of which stood a big fat gray crab who waved his pincers and shouted hoarsely, "Is he eligible?"

"What the devil's wrong with him?" Tommy demanded. "What's he want to know?"

Ben the Bosun coughed deep in his throat and looked severe.

"Them as has bad papers," he explained, "too bad even for the Locker, are shut out of th' Green. Th' Locker is where them goes what 'as pretty bad papers, but th' worse ones don't get anywhere at all. They jest wander up and down with the Tides out 'ere until th' crabs get them. If they're too bad for th' crabs, Old Nick sends for 'em, but we ain't got th' same ideas of being bad as Old Nick 'as, and some we turn out 'e thinks are too good for 'im and 'e leaves 'em for th' crabs."

"You're a pleasant bunch down here," said Tommy stiffly, but he was feeling a little sick and wondering whether his papers were good enough. He didn't want to be kicked out for a lot of crabs to eat.

" 'Ere we are," said Ben the Bosun at last, and they stopped before a huge bulkhead that rose up through the greenness farther than the eye could reach. Confronting them there was a door, and over the door was a bell, and each side of the door there was a big porthole. Ben the Bosun reached for the long lanyard fastened to the clapper of the bell and he struck it sixteen times. Tommy saw that engraved on the bell's face was the name of the ship it had come from, as was the custom, and the name was "THE ARK."

"Yes," observed Tommy, staring up. "Swiveltongue Saunders said that Noah was the first one to board the *Merry Dun*."

"Swiveltongue Saunders was a liar," said Ben the Bosun comfortably. "There was lots on th' *Merry Dun* afore Noah was taken off the *Ark*. They jest use 'is bell because 'e was the first Great Legend among th' shellbacks. 'E was th' first to polish it, an' that's a job what all New Hands 'as t' do after being found eligible."

Tommy Lawn scratched his head and said nothing.

"It's th' only bell what's struck sixteen times," added Ben the Bosun; "which means a New Hand 'as arrived. That's eight bells t' show 'e's finished one watch an' eight more t' show 'e's starting another."

"That's where you're wrong," interrupted Tommy. "All ships strike their bells sixteen times on New Year's night. At least, we always did on my ships. You send the Old Year below with eight bells and bring the New Year on deck with eight more."

Ben the Bosun appeared embarrassed for a moment. He tugged at his white side whiskers, spat, and frowned portentously.

"There's been a lot o' complaints about that," he admitted at last. "It's against all the Rules, Regulations and Articles. Sixteen strokes was reserved fer Noah's bell. And Noah's bell was th' only one what 'ad sixteen strokes until th' Man Who Flogged the Dolphin made up a yarn that it was a custom on all ships. Something'll 'ave t' be done about it, that's certain!"

"Well," said Tommy, "that's interesting. I remember Swiveltongue Saunders told me once about the way bells came to be struck on shipboard. There used to be a boy told off to stand by the sandglass which took just half an hour to run empty. He'd strike a gong when he turned the glass, to let all hands know half an hour had gone by. When he turned it again, he'd strike the bong twice, and so on up to eight times, when the watches changed and he'd begin at one again. Queer old ducks, weren't they? . . . And say, who the deuce is the Man Who Flogged the Dolphin? We used to say that Swiveltongue Saunders did that but . . ."

There was no time to continue just then. One of the ports beside the door was flung open and a seamed, leather-colored, villainous-looking face, with a patch over one eye and a huge scar running from the left temple to the ugly chin, appeared to view. The solitary eye glittered at them for a moment and then a voice bellowed:

"Name *an'* rank?"

"A New Hand," answered Ben the Bosun, hitching up his belt and scratching his bare stomach. "Open 'er up, Bill, an' be right smart about it."

The other rumbled deep in his scrawny throat, scowled at them and then abruptly closed the port.

"Cheerful sort of bird," Tommy observed, his irrepressible spirits bubbling over, for he had an idea he was going to enjoy himself, especially if the girls were good-looking. The things he remembered Swiveltongue Saunders had told him about the *Merry Dun* made his mouth water. And he supposed that even if the *Merry Dun* was out of commmission, Fiddlers' Green would be organized on much the same lines. What more could a sailor want?

" 'E was a pirate under Lafitte," said Ben the Bosun gruffly, referring to the doorman. "Doesn't like me at all. Doesn't like anybody, for that matter. Doesn't like 'isself. . . . Most of th' pirates we couldn't let in 'ere, for fear they'd sack the place and run off with th' Daughters. You know what pirates are! Worse'n sailors! Old Nick took most of 'em but this feller was a shade better 'n the others so 'e was allowed jest inside th' door and given th' berth permanent when th' old doorman resigned. 'E'd got tired of th' job and became th' Keeper of th' Lost Ships."

Tommy Lawn chuckled.

"I don't know much about pirates Bosun, but I can tell you what a real sailor is. He's a guy who'll lend you his last cent, give you his shirts, pants and shoes; lend you his liquor and cigarettes; fight for you and with you, and maybe let you take his girl out for the evening. But you just relieve him two minutes late on a watch and he's as sore as hell!"

Ben the Bosun grunted but otherwise betrayed no sense of humor. The door was opening at last, with a tremendous creaking and squeaking of massive hinges, and Tommy Lawn was secretly a little relieved, for an unbelievable number of crabs had begun to amble towards him from hidden crevices in the rocky floor behind him. And he remembered that he had not yet been found eligible.

The Pirate stood with one bare brown foot on the brass-shod storm step of the door, staring suspiciously at Tommy. He held a great scarred cutlass in one hand and there were a brace of pistols thrust into his dirty red sash. There was also a somewhat bloodthirsty look in his solitary eye and he seemed to have an annoying habit of licking his lips as if in anticipation.

"Name *an'* rank?" he bellowed at last. "Name *an'* rank?"

"Tommy Lawn, second mate!" snapped Tommy with a sudden dislike. Besides, he wasn't afraid of the cutlass. And Ben the Bosun put in sharply, "I'll answer for 'im!"

The Pirate scowled, tucked his cutlass under one arm, blew his nose between his fingers and jerked a strip of parchment from his great red sash. He stared at the parchment for a moment, running a horny thumb up and down it and muttering audibly to himself. And then he shook his head until the big gold rings in his ears swung heavily, and he stared at Tommy Lawn again with his solitary eye glittering and cold.

"Yew ain't down fer t'day," he announced suspiciously, and putting the parchment back in his sash, he seized his cutlass with a significant swish and tested the edge on the hairs of his arm. It sheared them like a razor and Tommy buttoned up his coat.

"Don't try and start anything with me!" he said, in his best second mate manner, though he was wondering how he would get in under that heavy bright blade. He decided a kick in the stomach would be best, followed possibly by a right to the Pirate's jaw. There wasn't any use being a bucko unless you could figure things out like that. But it soon became obvious there would be no fighting.

"He's a year afore time," said Ben the Bosun, pushing forward and growing indignant. "I'll answer for 'im," I said. The *Bramcar* struck th' ice afore time and went down. Something's wrong with the bergs."

The Pirate seemed to deflate considerably. He scratched his unshaven jaw, stared at Tommy as if in deep thought, and then, frowning thunderously, he put his cutlass back under his arm and stood clear of the doorway, jerking his head in an invitation to enter. Ben the Bosun stepped inside, followed by Tommy Lawn, who felt a slight prickling at the back of his neck when he heard a hoarse chorus go up from the assembled crabs: "Is he eligible? Hey! Is he eligible?" Fortunately the door slammed shut just then or they might have swarmed inside. Tommy Lawn wiped his forehead and settled his peaked cap at a jauntier angle. He felt ready for anything now.

"I don't like th' way them schedules is always gettin' busted," grumbled the Pirate darkly, and still muttering to himself he followed the two of them down a long alleyway until they came to another and smaller door with a big brass ring handle, such as are found on the cabin doors of steamers. "Something oughta be done about them schedules," said the Pirate, halting and ready to retrace his steps. "Last week it was th' currents got mixed, and we 'ad them two ships collide outside Papeete 'arbor. Now it's th' damned ice. I'm goin' t' report to th' Old Man about it. No sense keepin' th' door the way things is."

"You ain't any sicker than I am," said Ben the Bosun, spitting profusely. "Report all y' like."

The Pirate went away, muttering and grumbling to himself.

" 'E's not allowed any further," explained Ben the Bosun with a superior sniff. " 'E ain't much class. If 'e got a look inside th' Green, there's no telling what might happen. Likely 'e'd be off to Old Nick's to see 'is pals, and then they'd all come back here for th' loot an' th' Daughters. Old Nick can 'ardly hold his guests, as it is. 'E's always 'aving mutinies and fights." He coughed and carefully brushed his whiskers. "This is th' Old Man's room an' you'd better be careful. None o' them funny remarks about us old warts."

"I've been to sea long enough to know how to speak to a captain!" snapped Tommy. "Go ahead, Bosun!"

Ben the Bosun knocked on the door, quietly opened it and went in, with Tommy Lawn treading softly at his heels and feeling not at all as cocksure and confident as he looked and spoke. Still, he managed a deep-sea swagger and squared his shoulders for whatever might come next in this remarkable place.

Daisy Belmont.

George MacDonald

from *FIFTY YEARS OF FREE THOUGHT*

An Editor in Snohomish (1945)

When my wife and I arrived there in the summer of 1891, the town of Snohomish, Washington, was not to be called a quiet hamlet. It was full of people, all moving. A desperado with a hotel hack seized us at the station, outside the business belt, and set us down in the center of population. While we gave admiring attention to a rider who managed his loping horse with a single line around the animal's jaw, C. H. Packard, editor and publisher of *The Eye*, who had induced me to come to Snohomish from New York, rushed up and named us.

Packard had selected a room for us at the Maple House, a hotel hanging over the river, and to the Maple House we went. We saw that Main Street was closely companied for a little distance by the Snohomish river. Houseboats lined the shores.

After being introduced to the printers on the following morning, I inquired which type was dead and "threw in a case." It lay before me to learn what was news in this town and where to look for it, and then to divide my time between gathering it and putting it in press. Mr. Packard wrote a paragraph for *The Eye* introducing me as the new city editor. He did not forget to name certain well-known publications, *Puck*, *Judge* and so forth, to which I had contributed. The city editor, when city editing, went to the justice's court, or to the superior court, or to a meeting of the city council, or to the opening of a new store or café, or he might absorb an item from observation or interview, and returned with the proceeds to the office. He there turned his notes into copy, and helped to put them into type; he proved the galley with a towel wrapped around a planer, read and corrected proof, transferred the matter from the forms and locked them up, put the forms on the press, and perhaps took a turn at feeding. Before I became accustomed to press work, I spoiled a set of rollers by starting the

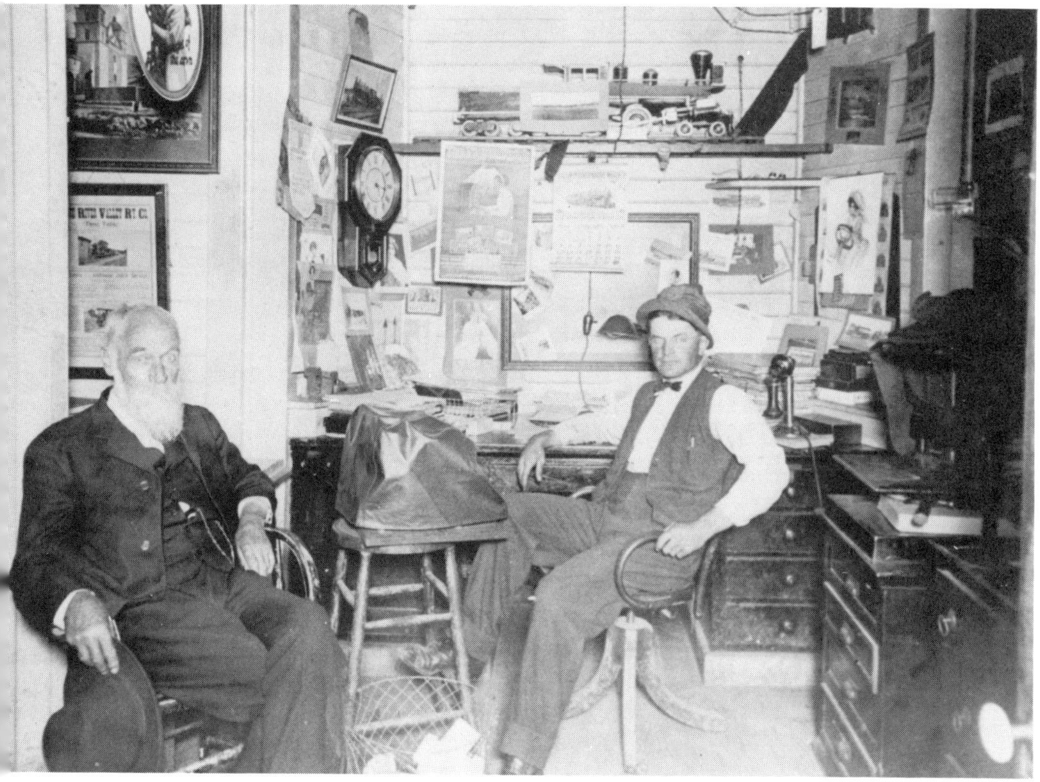

Dil Ibellis, one armed hunter.

Rose,
love of Minnie Tower,
Oct. 1882.
A highly cultivated lady
and a talented singer.

Man
with cycle.

press when they were lifted at one end. The sentiments that Packard managed to contain regarding a man, drunk or sober, who would start a press without looking at the rollers, did him honor. . . .

There was in our city another paper, the *Daily Sun,* upon which Packard looked with disfavor. The picture of its editor formed in the mind from the way Packard spoke his name fitted the man himself pretty well when one came to see him. He must have met with disappointments in life that had disillusioned him, for he had a saturnine countenance, a harsh laugh, and the morose outlook of a cynic. He was thought, in *The Eye* office, to be fit for treason, stratagems and spoils, and suspected of being on the outlook for opportunities for practicing them. Before I had ever laid eyes on the man, Packard one day said to me: "Here, Mac, is something on Frank Mussetter that I want you to write up." I asked: "What infamy has Mussetter been up to now?" and Packard replied: "Why, God damn it—" and then outlined in expletives the character of Mussetter. Our contemporary, it appears, had suppressed or misstated facts of public interest in order, as it was our place to allege, to curry favor with a certain low element and put *The Eye* in wrong. Hence I wrote the editorial, unconsciously using fighting language, and our afternoon edition gave it circulation. The consequences were set forth in the next number of our publication, in an editorial which read:

"A fierce-looking individual, loaded with several inches of adulterated hydrant water and a big revolver, which he said he had borrowed especially for the present crisis, awaited the senior *Eye* man's return from breakfast last Saturday morning. The distinguishing features of the combination were those of Frank Mussetter, editor and reputed owner of our at times luminous contemporary. Mussetter was evidently riled. He reads *The Eye* and thus keeps thoroughly posted on local and domestic affairs, although the scarcity of news and original editorials in his own paper might lead subscribers to doubt it. As we said before, Mussetter was riled. It might have been *The Eye*'s scoop in exposing a priestly scandal and the *Sun*'s supposed connection with the affair, but he didn't say so directly. Placing his good right hand in his pistol pocket, he inquired in a fierce, double-leaded voice fortified with beer if *The Eye* had a gun. Being informed that the chief engineer of this great moulder of public opinion was not in the habit of having such dangerous things in his possession when inside the city limits (*vide* Ordinance No. 4), Mussetter cautioned us to procure a weapon. He said he had come to shoot us; that he had borrowed a gun from Charlie Cyphers with that object in view, and he proposed to use it. He was informed that he would probably never find a better opportunity than now presented; also that he was making a damfool of himself. *The Eye* man explained that he was not a shootist, but would try to accommodate him with all the satisfaction he wanted in any other way. Mussetter averred that both he and his paper had been greatly hurt (and we don't doubt it) by *The Eye*'s articles, the truthfulness of which he did not deny; and that he would be satisfied with nothing short of shooting us. However, he graciously concluded to postpone the killing, and gracefully withdrew, remarking in a four-to-pica tone of voice, that he would surely open fire the next time he met us, and that we had better be prepared to meet our God, or words to that effect."

Siwash Indians lived in wickiups along the banks of the Snohomish river, and paddled up and down the stream in dugout canoes. "Canoe" brings to mind a kind of small and light craft, generally employed for idle uses, such as taking a girl out on the Charles river in Massachusetts. I have seen a Siwash canoe probably eighteen feet long and of four-foot beam, that carried the load of a moving-van, including the family. The Siwashes were savage as to their mode of life, but peaceable and friendly toward their fellow men. So far as I could make out, they had solved the problem of living without labor. With so many salmon in the stream they did not have to work; they went fishing.

Nevertheless civilization was in the process of absorbing them. Younger men went out as farmhands; the old men and women were most numerous in the wickiups. A government reservation at nearby Tulalip drew many away from the streams. Early settlers who, according to ancient history were deserters from British men-of-war had found their way up the rivers around Puget Sound and lived with the Siwashes, squatting on the land or buying it from the natives. The white men bought their Indian wives of fathers, brothers, or perhaps of husbands. The sale of a girl by her father to a man who said he wanted her for a wife was upheld by the courts as legal in this country, which in 1891 had been a state for only two years.

A young man settling there on a farm seventy years ago could make no better investment of his money or spare stock than to buy a wife with it, for the Indian women were good helpers about a place, and the children could be worked as they grew up. How many wives some of them bought I am not interested to know. The federal law that was passed for the abolition of polygamy in Utah in the '80s did away with the plural wife system among these old settlers in Washington, who were expected to acknowledge the wife they had taken first and discontinue the others. They obeyed the law by establishing the senior spouse as wife. As regards the rest, it was said that to avoid inflicting hardships on them they were retained in the family as maids. None of the so-called squaw-men lived inside the Snohomish city limits; they were ranchers. One of them, when his elder wife died, moved into town and married white. But he kept his ranch, and how large a population of secondary wives and their children the ranch maintained you could only judge from appearances. The man kept a general store in town. I saw one day a troop of mounted Indians galloping through the streets, and inquired of an older resident whether this was a massacre. He said no, it was only So-and-so's family going to his store for provisions. . . . Some of the best-looking girls in town were half or quarter Indian. . . .

The first year was the hardest, for *The Eye* was a Republican paper, and took sides in politics. Although I had been voting the Republican ticket since 1880, when it came to writing editorials I simply didn't know how. A book in *The Eye*'s library, entitled *A History of the Republican Party*, was the source of all I wrote in defense of the GOP. By good luck the need for these editorials ceased; Packard espoused the cause of Populism and wrote with such zeal that *The Eye* thereafter was never short of timely political matter.

The Eye was a good paper too. We brought it out as a triweekly, filled with local and county news, and every issue had a real editorial; and all that had been in the tri-weekly went into the weekly edition, where the accumulated editorials made a full page, as in the best city papers. No man in the county had a better reputation for honesty and squareness than Packard. His probity was unimpeachable.

The Press is said to be for sale. I never heard of any schemer trying to buy the opinion of our paper, and I was myself corrupted but once. That was when a man just starting a game down the street and mistakenly supposing I was going to make an outcry over it, took me aside and said that as *The Eye* had always used him well, he would like to show his appreciation. He was opening a little place, he said, to give the boys a chance to get action on their money; and while it was not the kind of proposition that competed for advertising space, still the Press ought to be supported by all good citizens. Then to my surprise he passed me a twenty-dollar gold piece.

As the first proffer of a bribe in my newspaper experience it produced in me a hitherto unknown reaction. On the spur of the moment one was not sure what one ought to do with the money or the base wretch offering it. While I mulled over the situation he invited me to step inside and see his little roulette layout. And now my course became clear. I changed the twenty into silver dollars and, picking number 27, told the man who turned the wheel to let it spin. He complied and announced "little 2-0." The other plays which I then tried were like the first one, and in half an hour I walked virtuously forth, carrying with me none of the wages of corruption. . . .

During my city editorship of *The Eye* I made an excursion to a "future metropolis" which the prospectus called Ocosta-by-the-Sea. The attractive name was the gift of Tacoma realtors interested in adjacent lands. The promoters organized a committee to entertain the gentlemen of the Press. By error, invitations were sent to the newspapers in Seattle and Snohomish, promising transportation, hotel accommodations, and entertainment to editors and their wives "as free as air." The city editor of *The Eye* and Mr. Sanger of the *Snohomish Sun* answered the invitation by letter. The committee in rejoiner gave them to understand that railroad trains were waiting for them to hop aboard. But the conductors declined to pass the editors and their wives on the strength of the committee's promises; so each of the editors paid $20.20 for carfare. The further "hospitality" of the committee was enjoyed at an average cost of $15 per editor and wife. Ocosta, when reached, we observed to be a marsh, with raised wooden walks, to which the appearance of being lined with trees had been given by spiking evergreens, or small saplings, to the stringpieces of the walks every ten or fifteen feet. The editors stopped, looked, and gave judgment. Said Mr. Sanger: "We have walked into the jaws of a big fake."

The committee had made provisions for fifty guests, and six hundred strangers were present. The committee compromised by selecting for its hospitality the newspapermen from Tacoma and points south, which did not include the Seattle and Snohomish editors. . . . I never went back to see how Ocosta-by-the-Sea came out. After what I said about the place in *The Eye*, I couldn't look for an invitation to return, except to explain myself.

Nearer home, however, I witnessed the transformation of a wilderness into a city. Downstream a few miles from Snohomish there used to be a landing place called The Portage. Between the Snohomish river and the waters of Puget Sound lies a peninsula. Mud and sand flats at the mouth of the Snohomish river interfere with navigation. For that reason, at this place a few miles downstream from Snohomish city, freight and passengers formerly were taken overland to deep water on the Sound side, which was Port Gardiner. The Portage and Port Gardiner are now no more. When I reached those regions in 1891 a land company had bought the peninsula to start a city on. The ground had to be cleared by uprooting and burning stumps, and the first time I saw the place it was smoking. A few weeks later a wide planked thoroughfare a mile and a half long bearing the name of an avenue ran lengthwise the neck of land, and there being no buildings as yet, merchants carried on business in tents. They christened the place Everett, after a future New Jersey politician named Colby, whose father was chief promoter.

Word soon went out that the Great Northern Railroad, then under construction by James J. Hill, would have its western terminal at Everett. They built a wharf and advertised that whalebacked ships from Duluth or Superior, in Wisconsin, would soon make port there. It was going to be the first city of the Sound, with Seattle second. Everett never fulfilled ten per cent of its ballyhoo. Nevertheless, in a remarkably short time it had a resident, maybe, for every stump that had been pulled, or a population of 7,000, twice that of Snohomish, while the Everett Land Company controlled county politics and patronage. . . .

Until the city of Everett was built up, just a few miles away, Snohomish had been the county seat and the center of traffic for the region. Now business departed. The hotels emptied, houses became vacant, the merchants lost their trade, labor was idle. The election went against *The Eye*, which without the city printing must take in its sign as official city paper. Advertisements disappeared from its pages or were run free to economize on composition and boiler plate. Lawyers and lodges, moving away, withdrew their cards. The character of the population changed and fewer knew or cared for *The Eye* as the historic county paper. Two other journals survived in Snohomish: *The Democrat*, which fed on public pap, and *The Tribune*, which had been bought by a couple of enterprising young men who knew what sort of a paper such a town as Snohomish was destined to become, a village of families, would read.

In past times, if I said to Justice Griffith, our best source of local news: "Have any items of news come under your judicial cognizance today?" he was likely to reply, "You may say that out-of-town relations bummed a Sunday dinner off our local society leader, Mrs. Barnum, yesterday." That was just the kind of news Packard and I overlooked, and it was the sort, less cynically worded, that the young fellows of *The Tribune* featured. A woman could not go for a horseback ride on the Pilchuck road without getting her name into *The Tribune*.

Conducting *The Eye* was a two-man business no longer and likely to become less so. I communicated with my brother in New York, who said that *The Truth Seeker*, which he then edited and on which I had worked, stood in need of my services. I then let Packard know that I was leaving. He fain would have condoled with me over the outcome of my venture into country journalism, but I wouldn't dole. I felt like repeating to Snohomish and its remaining people the formula of the departing guest: "I have enjoyed my visit very much, and it was kind of you to have me."

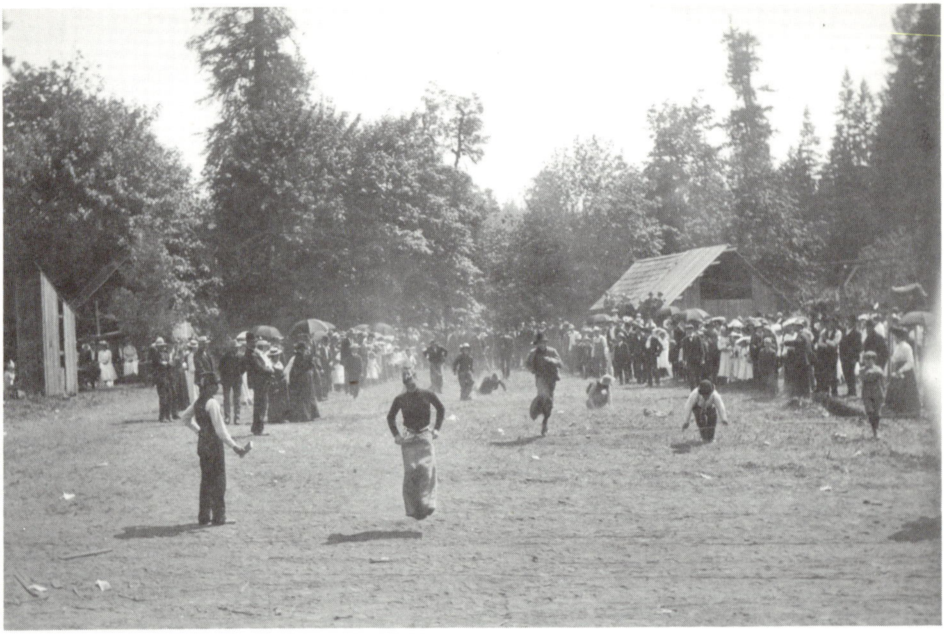

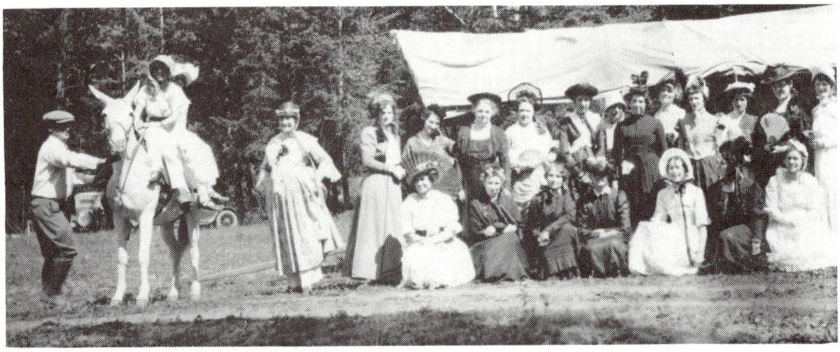

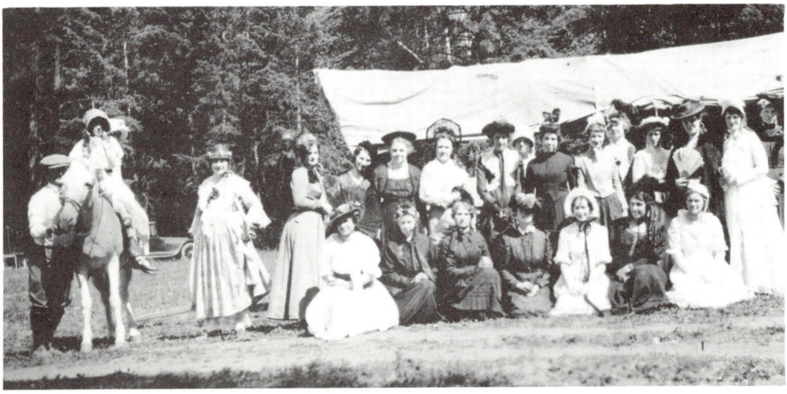

Nard Jones

Chapter 21: "Pioneer Picnic"

From *EVERGREEN LAND* (1947)

Nobody can understand the State of Washington who has not attended a Pioneer Picnic. Perhaps it is better to say "participated in"—for it is difficult, if not impossible, to view one of these gatherings merely as a spectator.

The one in the little town where I lived was styled the "Annual Reunion of the Pioneers" and popularly known as "the Pioneer Picnic," but they have different names in different towns. The basic characteristics are identical, whether they come as strawberry festivals or pow-wows, potlatches or rodeos. There is a simple program involving both white men and Indians, and somewhere in the program honor is paid to the pioneers. Usually such pioneers as are left merely sit on the platform behind the speakers. It has been proven unwise to allow them to speak for themselves, for they become garrulous and play hob with the schedule which, more often than not, is fitted for a local radio station. When the radio came, the old pioneer lost forever his chance to tell his tales, and I am sure that this has hastened the demise of the race. Surely more than one old gentleman, in the sickness of an evil winter, has simply thought it not worth while to stay on for one more Pioneer Picnic if he was not to be allowed to talk.

But some still sit quietly on the platform, wearing their badges, and in these latter days they are often so deaf that they cannot hear the compliments being paid to them. Around this simple framework of celebration are garlanded other activities which have little to do with pioneers and pioneering. There is usually a small traveling carnival complete with pitchmen. There is, weather permitting, a picnic lunch in the town park. There is a dance at night for the young folks and those who still feel young enough to dance.

But most of all there is incessant "visiting." There is visiting on the curbs, in the middle of the street that holds the carnival, in the stores, and on the benches of the park. Small children yammer and smear their faces happily with ice cream and all-day suckers while their parents visit—which is to say, while they trade news.

For there was, and is, a savor in the gossip traded at a pioneer picnic, a savor that is not in the printed pages of the town's weekly newspaper, not in the wall telephone at home, and certainly not in the newsreels and the radio and the dailies of near-by cities. The newsreels, the radio, and the city dailies speak of folks beyond the county line and they are of small interest in a visiting bee.

And you cannot visit by telephone and by reading the weekly. Somehow you cannot visit by paying calls, for there is something about a "call" paid in a small western town that freezes the tongue and curiosity a little. Women, and men, too, for that matter, visit best at a pioneer gathering.

Visiting means giving and getting the specific news you want, about the specific people you like or love, or envy or despise. Visiting means how did Mary Nichols come out with her fifth child, for Heaven's sake; and how many bushels did Ed Graham get off his north forty; and is the cannery paying high enough for peas, do you think, to make it worth while to change over from alfalfa or hops; and do you think the lumber mill is going to start up again, or is that just talk, and would you want Joe to go back there to work again if it did? Visiting is do you think there is anything to what they say about Virgi Denson's girl running around wild in Tacoma, and is it true that Ben Lomond isn't drinking like he used to and isn't it a godsend to Betty if he's really not?

For a pioneer picnic is, after all, the quilting bee and the corn husking. It goes beyond those—it is the old "rondyvoo" of the mountain men. And it goes still beyond that. It is the potlach of the Indians of the North Coast, too.

In fact, Seattle in the simple teens of the century, had a pioneer gathering which it called the Potlatch. These were the days when people spoke unashamedly of "the Seattle Spirit" which was a heritage from a "Great Fire"—one of those conflagrations which seem to be a necessary part of the early history of all frontier cities. The moving spirits of the Potlatch were "Tilikums" which is the Chinook word for friends. The Potlatch was a gay business, with the whole town turning out and everybody wearing "the Potlatch bug" on their lapels and shirtwaists, and fine parades by the "Tilikums" who dressed all in white for the occasion. I was young in those days and perhaps I idealize it too much, but to me the magic word "Potlatch" brings the same thrill to the breast as Mardi Gras does to a man from New Orleans. But the Potlatch died out during the first World War and it has never come back except once, for something had changed. Seattle had become too self-conscious, perhaps.

But the rest of Washington State does not hesitate to celebrate the Indians and the pioneers, and the Pioneer Picnic which I remember goes on today much as it did in the middle Twenties when I took part in it with Gail Williams. It seemed to Gail and me then that we were the leaders in the whole affair, and that we had staged it for the particular benefit of the two of us. As we look back on it now, it does not seem that this was an error.

Between Gail Williams today and that town and its Pioneer Picnic there are four years at Whitman College, almost as many at Harvard, and several years in the East before he returned to the Evergreen Land, as all of us do sooner or later. There are a wife and a young son, and a considerable pattern of toil at the bar. Yet I find that the pioneer picnic is as clear and real to him today as it is to me, which is to say as clear as if it had happened day before yesterday.

"You remember," he says, "how you got sick in the barber's chair when Frenchy Reynaud put lemon cream on your face, and you had to run for the back room?"

I remember. The first thing you did, on the first morning of the Pioneer Picnic, was to go to Frenchy's shop and get a haircut and a shave, although you did not need the latter very much. Then, because it was picnic time, you got a Boncilla facial. There was nothing dudish about getting a Boncilla facial. Harvest hands and mill hands got them because soap and water did not take the dust out of the pores (French said) and when the Boncilla "mud" got to drying you could just feel the stuff drawing dirt out of your pores. Your nose felt as if it was drawing up to a peak. Besides, a Boncilla facial cost a dollar and it was important to Gail and me to establish ourselves among the younger bloods of the town.

After the Boncilla would come some lemon cream and it was this that had made me ill. The reason was a dark one which Gail still likes to recall.

A part of every Pioneer Picnic is a little drinking, simply because it is a time of celebration. We were very young and no self-respecting bootlegger or Finn moonshiner from the Blue hills would have sold us anything even if we could have afforded it, which we could not. However, we had taken steps to prepare ourselves, months before the picnic that year.

I had stolen an earthen crock from my father's hardware store and this we smuggled into the old barn behind our house. The barn was not used any more and it seemed safe. Into the crock we put the juice of wild raspberries and considerable sugar together with, I think, three quarts of water and a cake of yeast. Our directions indicated that this concoction would, if stirred each day, turn into a wine which would be at least potent enough for our inexperienced heads.

It was of course a great secret, and so we had to do some talking about it. A couple of older young men heard our veiled bragging about "some stuff coming up for the Picnic" and they must have seen us sneaking into the barn regularly for the stirring. Also, they must have been familiar with our recipe, for with Machiavellian cunning they stole the crock on the very day before the wine was to have been strained into something potable!

With the Picnic only a few days away we were faced with an emergency. We met it, too. We had observed that the reservation Indians often got drunk on vanilla extract and that this sometimes happened also to white men of low standing. We knew that vanilla extract, while strong enough to do the business, was harmful as well. But we reasoned that if the extract were watered down and sugared up it would become harmless and perhaps even palatable. Certainly it would intoxicate us, and that was what we were after. The fact that only Indians and itinerant harvest bums drank extract did not concern us. After all, we did not intend to drink the stuff publicly.

It was somehow decided that Gail was to purchase the vanilla extract, but when he went to the store and asked for it Mr. Pope said, "You sure that's what you want, Gail? Your ma just bought a bottle of it yesterday." Mr. Williams displayed that quick thinking which has made him a boon to the legal profession of Washington State. "Gosh," he said, "I guess it was *lemon* extract she told me."

That was how we came to water down and sugar up lemon instead of vanilla extract. Now that we had got it we figured that lemon would be better anyhow. But it did not taste very good, and it burned our lips some. For a few minutes we thought we were intoxicated, but I doubt this now. All I know is that when Frenchy doubled lemon cream on my face I got very sick and had to run for the back room.

It was probably fortunate that the lemon extract did not work out, for Gail and I were on the program. He had two spots on the program because he was an elocutionist—one of the very last of the tribe, I suppose. He had taken lessons in Portland and could recite whole pieces of prose and poetry by heart, and on the Picnic program he recited parts of Walt Whitman's *O Pioneers!* At the suggestion of Mr. Robe, the high school principal and program chairman, Gail would leave out the verse that begins "Raise the mighty mother mistress." Gail and I could never see anything in it to be left out, but I think that Mr. Robe figured that when Walt got to raising his voice ecstatically and confusedly about a mighty mistress it was time to be cautious. Gail himself left out "Lo! the darting bowling orb!" which was just as well. I think the old pioneers were a little puzzled by the whole thing, but they liked it. At the end of each verse when Gail would bear down hard on *Pioneers! O pioneers!* they would beam and look proud behind their whiskers.

What Gail and I did together was a blackface act stolen from an old minstrel show. As I recall it, this puzzled the pioneers even more than Whitman's praise, but we would get a reasonable reaction out of the audience which sat on wooden benches under a tent. This still surprises us, when we think about it, but in that decade there were movies only once a week (with hard benches, too) and of course they were silent movies. Even so, at the Pioneer Picnic today you could never get folks to sit under a tent to hear a joke like one I remember. I hope that the setting down of it may erase the shame I have felt all these years:

"Did you hear what happened to Farmer Brown's bull?"
"No, I didn't. What all happened to Farmer Brown's bull?"
"He got run over by the train. Had a big lawsuit."
"You don't say!"
"They sure did. At the trial—at the trial the engineer said he stuck his head out of the cab and saw the bull comin' out of the alfalfa."

"Yeah. Then what happened?"

"Then he say he saw the alfalfa comin' out of the bull!"

But our consciences were light in those days, and being on the program gave us a standing which we could not otherwise achieve. We were not large of frame, or perhaps of courage either, and we could not accept the challenge of the carnival wrestlers like the Rayburn boys from up on the mountain. The Rayburn boys always challenged the wrestlers and they won so often that after a while the wrestlers would just not set up their show in our town.

Sometimes, though, we could enter a street race and this would bring us from three to five dollars and the sweet sound of encouragement and applause. Gail ruined the first suit of long trousers he ever had that way. He got across the finish line first but then he sprawled and he ripped the trousers right through both knees. It was the first day of the picnic and it meant that for the rest of the celebration he had to get back into knickerbockers and it was all very humiliating for him and satisfactory for me. I did not win a race that year but I preserved my trousers.

Perhaps we should have given a little more thought to the old pioneers and what the celebration was for. But I guess it was enough for them to wear red, white and blue ribbons on their coats and sit on the platform. It was enough, probably, to walk through the crowds and be smiled at and treated with deference. At least they seemed to be enjoying themselves, and they were bound to have a good time at the picnic lunch in the park. For there the women would ply them with fried chicken and potato salad and soft warm cake that did not need much chewing. It would be not just the women to whose lunch they "belonged" but it would be women from other picnic parties all around the park. I can hear Mrs. Herman Goodwin now, with her bright smile and her happy voice, saying: "Oh, there's old Mr. Newcomb. I'm to take him some of this tomato aspic. He liked it so much last year." I am filled with dismay nowadays when I see the diets on which doctors put old men who are not quite old enough to have been pioneers. I never heard of a Washington pioneer going on a diet until he was on his death bed. And I never knew any of them to be ill after a Pioneer Picnic.

The high spot of the picnic lunch would be Joe Payant's band, playing in the band stand, and Clark Wood's solo *Asleep in the Deep*. Dark, smiling Joe Payant was—and, I hope, still is—proud of his Indian blood, as he should have been. He was a wheat farmer in those days, but he had a band that played for dances and special events like the pioneer reunion. He got money for those, but not very much, and he would play all night long at a farm house dance, at a "shivaree" or a housewarming, for nothing. When the big canneries came to Washington and some of the farmers changed from wheat to peas, Joe changed over, too. He had never made a complete success of wheat somehow, but he took to peas, as they say in the county, and peas took to Joe. Last I heard of him he was making a lot of money, and he had an interest in a cannery of his own, and when he came into town of a Saturday he was greeted with, "Here comes the Pea King." I hope he has as much fun now as he did in the Twenties when he had the band. It was a small orchestra really—but it became a band when it played out of doors. At least that is the way Joe explained it to me once.

Clark Wood, the soloist, was publisher and editor of the weekly newspaper, but he liked better being called a soloist or the best horseshoe pitcher in the State, or the best fungo batter.

The Pioneer Picnic in that town seems to go without Gail Williams and me, but I don't see how it could go on without Clark Wood. He and men like him are an important part of every pioneer gathering· and I suppose that now they are by way of being pioneers themselves although they do not remember crossing the plains. So I ought to tell a little about Clark.

Clark set the type on the paper, and ran the flat-bed press, and washed down the forms with gasoline afterward. He got the news and he carried the paper in little bundles to the post office for mailing. I guess he was about the laziest man that ever lived, too, and he would not deny that. He rather gloried in it. He said he could make a thousand dollars a month if he had the gumption to get on the bus and travel to Walla Walla or Pendleton to get the advertising, but he couldn't see spending so much energy. So he just traded local advertising for groceries and wood and maybe a suit of clothes once a year, and free hair cuts at Frenchy Reynaud's barber shop. He took in enough cash on subscriptions to get to Walla Walla to a ball game or a show once in a while, which was all he wanted. Years ago he tried working on a big city paper, and he made quite a name for himself—but it wasn't long before he came back to the country weekly. When folks asked him why, he said, "Too damned much work on a big paper."

"What I need for the good of my soul," he used to say in the singing bass he used when he was orating, "is to use some big black headline type with words like TERRIFIC CATASTROPHE in them. TERRIFIC CATASTROPHE ENGULFS TOWN. Then there's *debacle*. There's a lovely word! I've been getting out this rag for more than forty years and never had an opportunity to use the word *debacle*."

I think that goes to show that Clark is a great newspaper man of a kind much needed now when they are no longer numerous. Most fellows feeling as he did would have gone ahead and used the word somehow—even if they had to write an editorial to get it in. But not Clark. He would never set up the word *debacle* until we had one, even if we never did have one, and that was that.

Then one day of an unusual spring we had a flood in the town. It drowned some people in the Blue hills and it tore into the town and did considerable damage and left mud two feet deep. I met Clark after the paper had come out the following Friday, and he was cussing and kicking himself all around the horse trough at the intersection of Main and Water streets. "I'll be a double-barreled nickel-plated vacillating varlet with a giraffe for a grandfather!" he said. "I'll be damned if we didn't have a *debacle* and I forgot to use the word in the goddamned story!"

I don't know whether Clark was a good bass singer or not, because I am no judge of those things, but he was always satisfactory. You could hear him in church, and at the Pioneer Picnic his voice would certainly fill the park. As a matter of fact, you could stand over in Main street, behind the carnival tents, and hear him doing *Asleep in the Deep* way above Joe Payant's band.

In the interests of absolute truth it ought to be said that the particular pioneer gathering I have been describing was just a little bit south of the Washington State line, but at least half the folks taking part were from the Washington side, and the pioneer gatherings are all pretty much the same in the Pacific Northwest whether they take part in Washington or Oregon or Idaho. There is a story I have been hearing recently which is attached to New Hampshire and Vermont, referring to the terrific winters, and perhaps the yarn did originate there. But when I heard it first some twenty years ago in the town of Ephrata it went like this:

It seems that John Barnes's farm had been right close to the Washington State line for years on end and he had always thought of himself as an Oregonian. Then one day they made another survey of John's farm and it turned out that it was in Washington instead of Oregon. "Well, I'm mighty damned glad to hear that," John Barnes said, "because I don't think I and the old lady could have stood another one of those damned rainy Oregon winters."

I suppose you could divide the pioneer gatherings into three classifications. There are those which take place in the water towns or on the rivers, and with these there is usually an Indian canoe race and maybe a log rolling contest. Then there are those which take place in the inland farm counties, and with them there may be pony races. Sometimes the men wear cowboy hats and begin to raise beards for weeks before the celebration. Finally, there are those which take place in the mountain lumber towns, and in these there may be a parade with a team of oxen such as were used in the pioneer logging days before horses and tractors were introduced into the big woods. I have been unable to discover what is done with a team of oxen the remainder of the year, for they have no duties now and are more extinct than the bison—if there are degrees of extinction. But at pioneer gatherings they still reappear, these great slow-moving anachronisms of the old skidroad.

So do stage coaches, in some of the celebrations, and so do ancient hotel hacks, and sagging buckboards, and elegant fringed-topped buggies. And there is almost always on these days, a lovely little old lady riding in one of the buggies, holding a parasol and decked out in some finery of the Eighties that is obviously her own and not rented from a theatrical costumer's. Where the little old lady comes from is a mystery, too, and nobody seems to know where she spends the other three hundred and sixty-four days of the year. Once, along the crowded curbs, there were hundreds of people who knew her. Then scores, then perhaps a dozen. And now—no one at all. That is the sad thing about pioneer picnics. There must always come the gathering day when there is the last old lady or the last old man who crossed the plains in a covered wagon.

Of course, there will always be pioneers of one kind or another, and so I suspect that the pioneer celebrations will not wash out. "Things were mighty bad in Kansas, so your mother and I put your brother and sister—you wasn't born yet—into the old jaloppy and we started out for the coast. We were going to Seattle, but first I stopped at Ephrata and I worked on the old Grand Coulee dam. Then the second war started and we went to Seattle and I worked in the old Seattle-Todd shipyards. The town didn't have more than maybe four hundred thousand people, then, but it was sure exciting. And we built the new destroyers. I remember one day . . ."

Sure there'll always be pioneers, and they need not be more than thirty-five or so. "I can remember when we got the first air line direct from Seattle to New York. Leave in the evening and get in before the middle of the next morning. They had those old DC-4s—those old four-motor Douglas clunks. Everybody had to grunt to get 'em off the ground. I remember one day . . ."

But they won't be covered-wagon pioneers, and therefore they won't be quite the same. That is why Gail Williams and I do not go back any more to the particular Pioneer Picnic in which we took part. We have attended them elsewhere in the State, assisted perhaps by Scotch rather than diluted lemon extract. We have gone to Walla Walla and Okanogan and Yakima, over the rim of the Cascades. We have returned to the annual Clambake and Pioneer Day at Port Townsend, and the pioneer gathering at Conconully, and the Makah Indian Festival at Neah Bay. Once we went to the Old Settlers' Picnic at Ferndale where, I remember, Gail won a kewpie doll at ring-toss and gave it to a middle-aged squaw who turned out to be intoxicated and followed him for the rest of the evening.

We have even tried celebrations, with and without Scotch, which do not have for their purpose the honoring of the pioneer but which worship the bounties of the lush land of Washington. The Apple Festival at Wenatchee, and the Strawberry Festival at Bellevue. We have watched the Salmon Derbies without number, although neither of us is lucky with fish.

But not in recent years have we ever returned to the Pioneer Picnic in the little town where Joe Payant fiddled and Clark Wood sang *Asleep in the Deep*. It would be rather bad if we went back, and found that all the pioneers had gone.

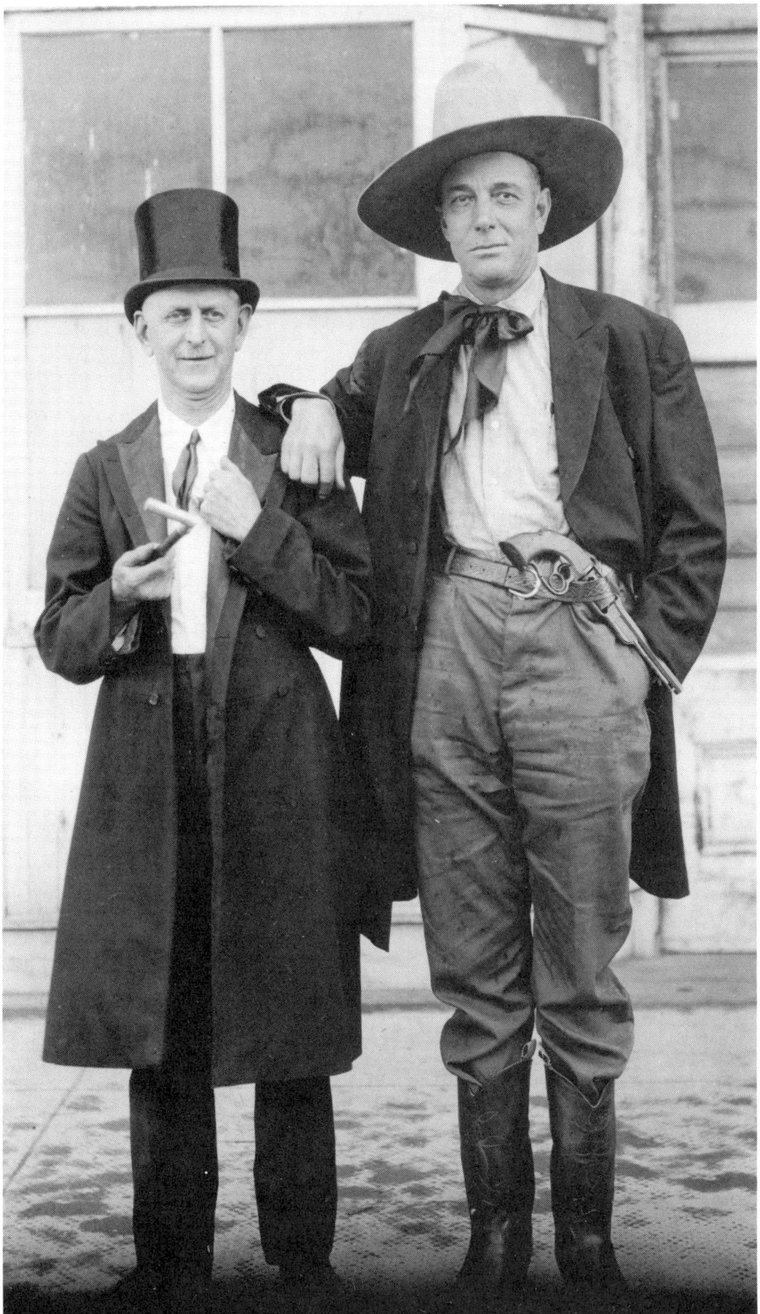

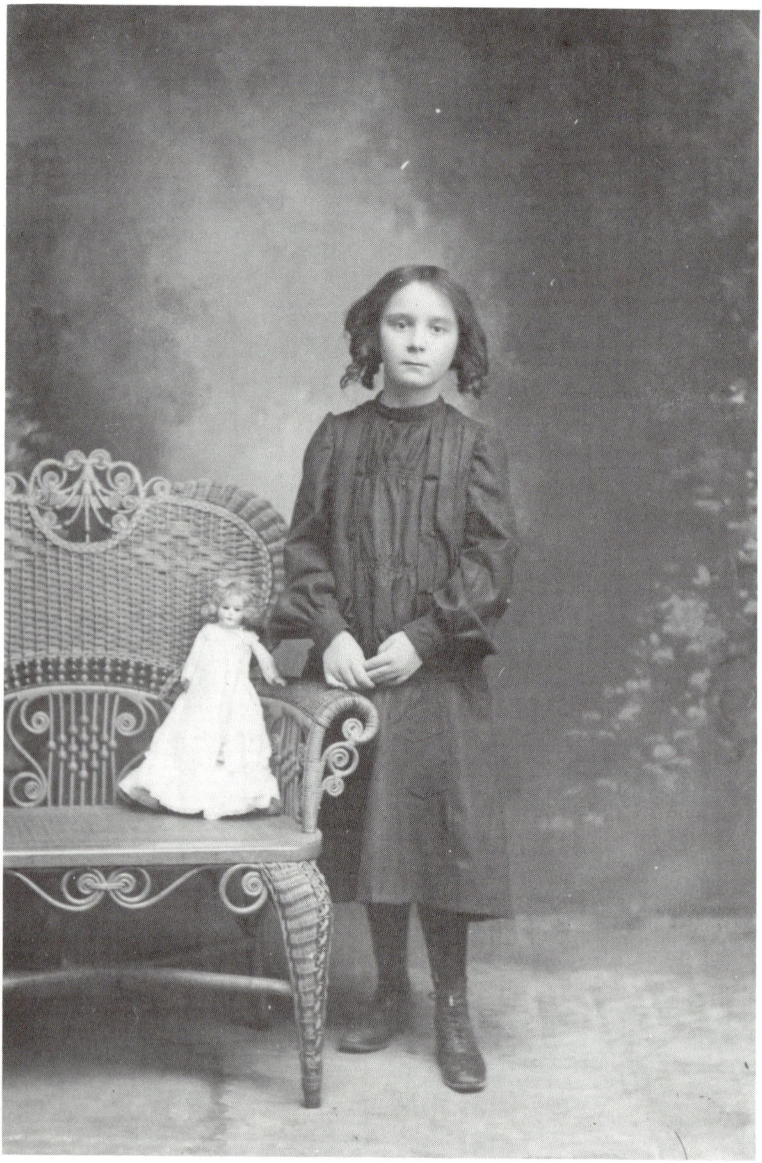

Chapter 14: "Reminds Me of a Story"

From *EVERGREEN LAND* (1947)

Not so long ago, when Seattle was a village, Dexter Horton, the banker, was walking down the street, making an occasional detour around a smouldering stump. It was a raw morning. A drizzling rain held down the stump smoke like a blue marsh fog. So Dexter Horton backed up to one of the stumps and lifted his coat-tails to warm himself.

In the very next moment he found himself sprawled several feet away, an embarrassing but not dangerous wound in his tattered backside. The heat of the stump fire had set off a cannon ball imbedded in the wood from the warship *Decatur* when she laid down a barrage on the Indians a few years before.

Horton told the story on himself, and it was repeated with great glee for half a century. Another story told on Dexter Horton is that his first money safe had no back to it, so that when he forgot the combination or was in a hurry, he could simply slide the strong box away from the wall. There seems to be some evidence to support the tale, but Horton's daughter denies it. "Do you," she demanded of a recent interrogator, "do you really believe that father was so stupid?"

But Seattle rather likes the story, and it does not detract in the slightest from the figure of Dexter Horton. I can remember that when my father and grandfather spoke of "the Dexter Horton Bank" there was always a slight deference in their tone; there was a respect there that was not present when they talked of another bank. Possibly Dexter Horton had been more pleasant than other bankers in the matter of a loan for some of their enterprises, but I think it is just as likely that they favored Mr. Horton because he had his moments of informality, even if he was a banker.

Washingtonians still like that kind of informality, although modern banking makes it less practical than of old. We still cotton to the picture of a banker who could be laid low by a delayed cannon-ball explosion and not hesitate to tell the tale. This is the same kind of admiration which prompted respect for the Clallam County farmer who found himself on the wrong end of so many lawsuits that he had some letterheads printed which said, simply: *Hezekiah Saylor, Defendant.* Men of the Evergreen Land, big and small, have never taken themselves too seriously, or their troubles either, and neither have they hesitated to take advantage of those strangers who do.

But sometimes the stranger is needlessly wary. I remember an afternoon at the Olympia Yacht Club when a nice young man from New York was being told of the fun in catching gweducks.

"What kind of ducks?" he inquired incredulously.

"G-w-e-d-u-c-k-s is the way Webster spells it," he was told. "But around here we call them gooey-ducks."

"I see. How are they caught?"

"Well, you hunt them with a shovel and a length of stove-pipe. What a gooey-duck really is, is a very large kind of clam that is found only around Puget Sound. It's got a neck four or five feet long, and the shell is maybe six inches in diameter. They weigh up to eight or nine pounds sometimes."

The New Yorker tried to get into the spirit of the thing. "Tomorrow," he said, "I will get myself a small shovel, and also a length of stove-pipe. On that stove-pipe I shall have lettered the device: *A gooey-duck or bust!*"

"But this is the truth," he was told. "You see, the clam burrows into the sand at low water. It'll go down five feet if the neck is that long. When you get after him he pulls in his neck and hopes you won't spot him in that four or five feet of sand. That's where the stove-pipe comes in."

"And after you get this kind of duck, what do you do with it?" asked the man from Manhattan.

"His neck goes into chowder and the rest you can slice into steaks. It's good eating. The tide is out at five o'clock tomorrow morning. Want to meet us at the beach?"

"Sure," said the stranger amiably. "I said I'd be there."

But, alas, he was not. He was not, because he was determined not to be taken in by one of our broad practical jests of the kind he knew obtained in the farthest reach. However, his hosts were waiting for him at five o'clock the next morning—simply because everything they had told him was true!

There have been Washington jests, however, which reach toward astonishing proportions. Take the Society for the Preservation of the Cigar Store Indian. It headquarters is in Bellevue, Washington, and it holds an annual breakfast meeting in the staid Union Club in Victoria, British Columbia. Its correspondence, which is international is carried on largely in the Chinook jargon.

The thing began innocently enough. Miller Freeman, Seattle publisher, happened to be a guest at the Overseas Press Club in New York and was asked to make a talk. He protested that he was not so much, that perhaps his sole claim to fame was the fact that he headed "the Society for the Preservation of the Cigar Store Indian."

It was a light remark on the spur of the moment, but the reverberations were heard around the world. Chapters have been formed in Dallas, in New Orleans, in Boston, in Detroit; they have been installed wherever men suddenly remember that of late they have not seen a cigar store Indian, the symbol of the days of their youth. The public relations departments of the big tobacco companies began to take such a lively interest that Freeman and two of his cronies, J. H. Bloedel and Dwight Merrill, took steps to protect what was fast becoming an organization of power and scope; they incorporated under the laws of the State of Washington! Almost daily now they receive telegrams from devotees in remote areas who have discovered a cigar store Indian and want to know what to do with it. There is no telling where it will all end—but it could have begun in few other States beside Washington.

"Bundles for Congress" was a jest begun in the Evergreen Land, but like many a joke it went too far; and, considering Washington's political record over the years, it came from the wrong direction. We are better off when we keep our broader gags to ourselves, because in the absence of constructive publicity it gives the State a screwball reputation. The publicans of the Evergreen Land may labor long and well without result in the nation's press —then along comes a swimming contest for pigs, and we are in the news. We are in the news, regrettably, with the bewildered porkers.

Washington in many quarters is identified with the legendary figure of Paul Bunyan, perhaps because Jim Stevens, Washington author, raised him from a myth to literature. But the giant lumberman is ours only by adoption; he really belongs to the Saginaw country and, before that, to the Scandinavian countries. But Paul has been taken up throughout the State, and not just in the timber regions. When I heard of him first it was in Whitman County, and so he was a wheat rancher, not a logger. He had Babe, the Blue Ox, but he used her to pull all his wheat into town in one big load, not to drag logs over the skid-road. He cut his wheat in a single day with a gigantic scythe, but he hired a harvest crew to thrash it, because that part of harvesting bored Paul. He cooked for the crew, and to grease the mile-long stove for flapjacks he tied bacon rinds to his feet and skated back and forth over the smoking surface. He was in all essentials the same Paul who logged in the Saginaw and later on Puget Sound, and I suppose his story was brought to the wheat lands by some early logger who had decided to try his hand at ranching.

I have heard of Paul, too, in the Big Bend cattle region of Washington, where of course he is disguised as a cowpuncher. He wore not a ten-gallon hat but a Stetson which could dip Lake Chelan dry in one swoop. But somehow the wheat Bunyan and the cattle Bunyan are not the genuine article. He belongs to the big woods.

And anyhow, Washington has never seemed to me the true harbor of the tall tale, except for our friendly kidnapping of Paul Bunyan. The tall story is the medium of expression for the plainsman, the river man, and the mountain man. We have to remember that the early settlers of the State's coast were often rather practical fellows and many were from New England. The first really permanent settlers in the eastern half of the State were missionaries. Gold seekers, soldiers, adventurers, men who could really lie like hell and freeze it over, were in a sense just passing through. Thus the tall tale which flowers beautifully in the mountain states and in some parts of California is a grafted specie in the Evergreen Land. Hastily I except from this generalization men of the deep woods, old Alaskans, and certain talented ranchers and miners in the arid regions east of the Cascades, all of whom have been known to build a tale at least as tall as Rainer.

But our best genre is the rough and simple anecdote of character, and of place. My good friend Jack Gose, a sagebrusher who now lives on the Sound, and who is an expert taster of tales and situations indigenous to the Evergreen Land, likes to tell of a public dinner in Bellingham. Unaccountably, it was attended by a Vinerian Professor of Law from Oxford University. Seated across from the distinguished visitor was a local patriot filled with equal parts cocktails and equal parts facts and figures about his home county.

"Beautiful country you have here," the Oxford man was unfortunate enough to remark across the table.

"No question about it," said the local man. "And do you know that last year the retail sales per capita in Whatcom County were seven hundred and three dollars?"

"Really!" said the Oxford man.

"Yes, sir. And you know why? Because this is a wealthy country you're in right here. Last year Bellingham handled seven and a half million pounds of bottom fish, three and a half million pounds of salmon, and a hundred and sixty-five thousand pounds of fish livers."

"You don't say!"

"I certainly do. That's a lot of fish. *And* livers. Look, you know what the mineral situation is around here?"

"I'm afraid I don't."

"Well, we got occurrences of gold, silver, copper—let's see, copper, lead, zinc, iron, limestone, talc, and moly—molyb—"

"Molybdenum?"

"Molybdenum, yes. What's more, Whatcom County is one of the six coal counties in Washington and it's got the biggest mine. Been producing coal since 1853, maybe since 1852, but I think it's 1853. And there are almost five thousand farms in the county."

"I dare say."

"Why, there's thirty thousand apple trees in the county, and seventeen thousand filbert trees. That's a nut."

The man from Oxford was beginning to look a little wild. His chair scraped back and he said, "If you'll pardon me—"

"Men's room?" said the Whatcom County native, getting up, too. "I'll show you where it is!" The last Jack Gose heard was the man from Whatcom explaining that seven million strawberry plants had been produced the previous year. He claims never to have seen the Vinerian professor again, not that evening, or ever.

Like most sagebrushers, Jack laments the passing of the old kind of Washington tale. Jack's uncle, old Judge Mack Gose, was a master of that kind of story. He could sit in the sun on the steps of the court house in Dayton, Washington, and tell them by the hour, and they all had a basis of fact somewhere in them. But

Judge Mack and most of his contemporaries are gone now, and the stories you hear in Washington are too likely to be the kind you can pick up on the radio, or from fellows who travel around.

The real Washington yarn is almost all in the telling and hearing; they are no great shucks in print. They need the nasal twang of the Northeast, or the high drawl of Missouri, or the accents of the Midwest, all of which may be heard in the Evergreen Land. The frontier days are still so close to us that we can be fond of a practical joke as wide and rough as Skagit County, and for the same reason we like our yarns to have some local color and tang.

We like to know the victim, even, or somebody very like him. In the Walla Walla valley they still tell stories about Pat Lyons although he died long ago; and, of course, there are often applied to Pat Lyons, actions and speeches with which he had nothing to do. They say he would not let his men wear high boots because it took too long to lace them in the morning. And they tell the story of how he came into town one day and picked up a Chinaman for a cook. Pat was never loquacious, and the Oriental was too new in the country for long speeches. But the story goes that, about a mile from the ranch, the Chinaman said: "My name is Lee. What is your name please?" Pat Lyons told him, and they say that the Chinaman rolled out of the buckboard and ran back toward town screaming, "Oh, oh, oh! I hear of you in China!"

You see. That is what I mean. A night club entertainer or a radio comedian would have nothing to do with a story like that. But if you knew Pat Lyons, or someone like him, and you were sitting on the steps of the court house listening and watching while Judge Mack told it . . .

Seattle, from Denny's Hill.

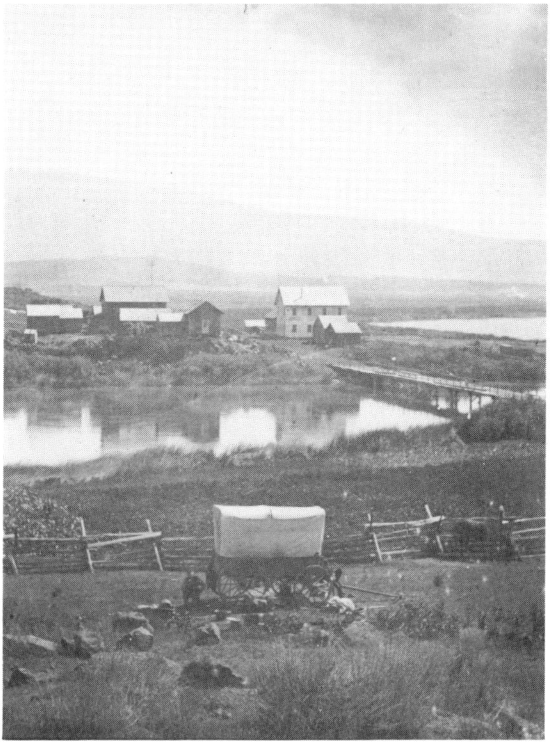

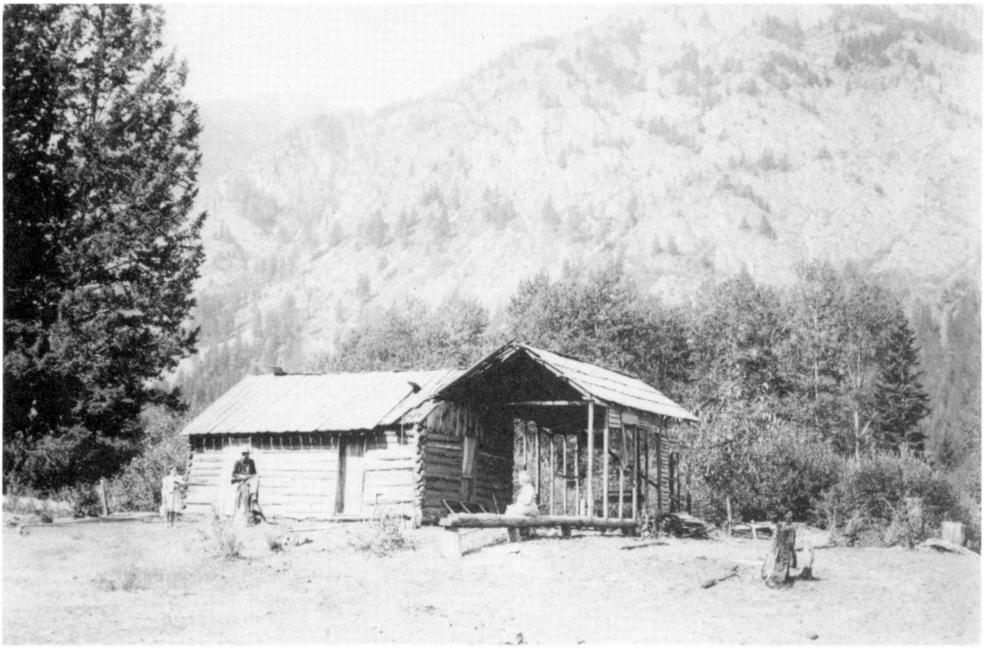

Trevett Monument and Indian burial site.

Recreation Camping, J. Minker family.

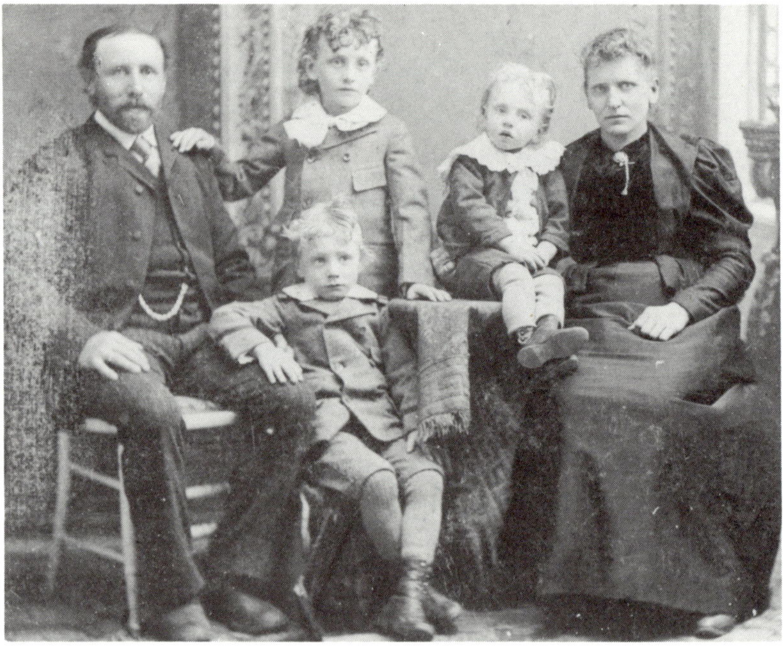

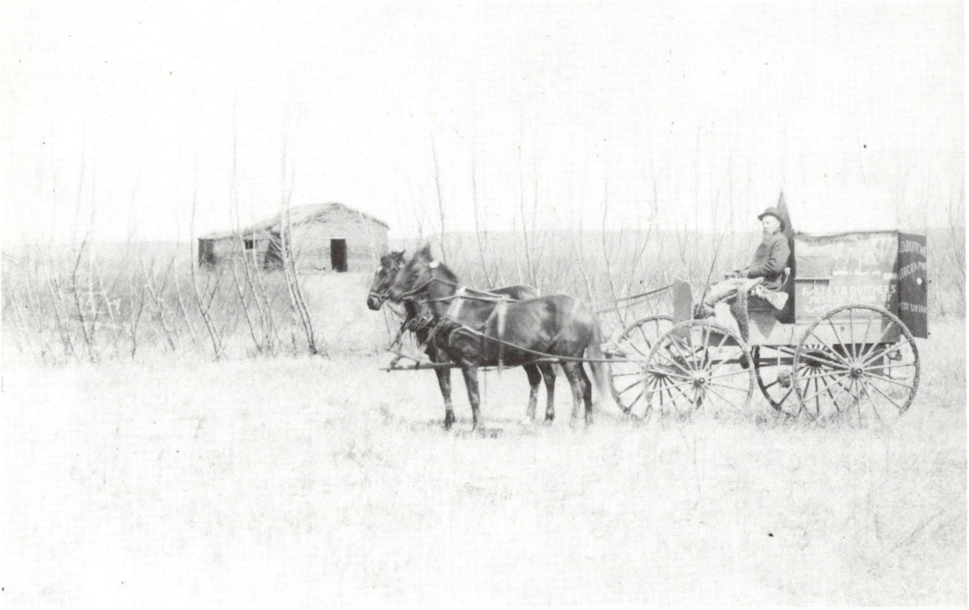

Sophus Keith Winther

From *MORTGAGE YOUR HEART* (1937)

II

It's no use trying to stretch old, rusty barbed wire, because the tension will make it snap. Even if it holds through the stretching, it may break when the staples are being driven. The sharp, rusty barbs, tearing through the hand that can't let go until it is too late, leave the fingers looking as though they had been stuck in a sausage-grinder. Even worse may happen. The red bump on Clausen's head, left where his ear should have been, was caused by a rusty wire that had been stretched too tightly. It had broken as he leaned over to drive in a staple, and, in recoiling, had taken off his left ear, not slick and clean, but torn in a hundred little shreds. Then blood poison had followed.

It's not a good thing to put a wire-stretcher on rusty barbed wire. The best thing to do is to make it fairly taut with a claw-hammer braced around the post. With good, new, double-strand barbed wire it is different. When the wire-stretcher is fastened to a well anchored post, the wire can stand all the power that a man can give to the pulley rope. It can be stretched until it sings, until the barbs, as sharp as dagger points, quiver along the line.

The atmosphere in Peter Grimsen's house these June days was as tense and sharp as new, barbed wire stretched to the last ounce of tension that it could stand. In man's memory there had never been a better growing season. Gentle rains had fallen all through May and now into the third week of June. The green wheat fields waved over the rolling hills. It was waist-high with long, bearded heads filling out rich, fat kernels. But weeds were growing, too. It was with great difficulty that the farmers had found enough dry days to get through cultivating corn the first time. The corn was rank, and in some places, especially in the rich low-lands, it was beginning to turn yellow. If another week of rain should keep the farmers out of the fields, the weeds would have the upper hand.

Every day, Peter Grimsen, walking out over his broad acres, watched the rich crops growing. He was often soaked to the skin, but inside he burned with a passion for a chance to get at these weeds. Never had he seen such wheat nor such promise in the corn. Here was promise for more than any year America had ever given him, and now when victory was almost within his grasp, it seemed as though he would lose again, as he had so often lost before.

The rain beat in his face. The water and mud squashed in his shoes at every step, but still he kept going. Beating in his blood was the love of his corn and wheat, the love of work for a great harvest. He glanced back to the house and barn. Three sons there, ready to put the cultivators into the field. Horses a plenty in the barn, all fat and strong, ready for the work that needed to be done. Even the milkweeds were getting so thick they seemed from a distance to cover the whole ground.

"By God, we'll cut the milkweeds," he said, and turned back to the house. When he reached home it was raining stronger than ever. In the house, the boys were either lying down or leaning their chairs against the wall. "You four—out into the field and cut milkweeds!" he said.

The rain blew against the window as if to punctuate his words. "Out, I say! Is this the home of a great landowner that my sons shall lie around like lords, eating and drinking, while the corn is choked to death by weeds? Never in my life have I seen anything like it. Day after day, you sit around the house reading, laughing, talking as though you were glad that it rained. Ten times in the night I wake and look out the window, hoping for a clear sunrise, and still it rains."

"Do we make the rain, maybe?" spoke Alfred in an ironical tone.

"Now, hell will break loose," thought Hans, but Meta was ready to lend a hand.

"Peter, what is it you are saying? Do you want the boys to go out in the field in weather like this? Why, they would be as wet as you are before they got past the cow barn. Here"—with a firm hand she took hold of his coat—"let me help you out of those wet clothes. No, don't stand there. Come into the kitchen so we can hang them up to dry by the stove."

In the kitchen the boys could still hear the conversation.

"I can't stand it any longer. You are here in the house. You don't know what the fields are like. I tell you, another week of this, and there won't be enough corn to feed the rats. You'll see how it will be. I had plans for this fall, and now every day this rotten rain is washing them away. Do I have to live all my days in the clutches of the merchants and the bankers?"

"No, Peter, of course not, but you can't send them out in weather like this. Why, we would all be the laughingstock of the neighborhood. You know that. What is the good of cutting milkweeds anyway, if it keeps on raining?"

"Oh, I suppose it's nothing to you either. Let it rain. What do you care about it!"

Meta let him continue until his loud voice subsided into a grumble. It was always best to let him talk it out in his own way. Soon he would be in dry clothes, and then she could give him something to eat. That would help.

While he changed his clothes, the three oldest boys left the dining room. Hans went upstairs, while Alfred and David went to the barn. Each had his own problems. The scolding from their father did not bother them much. They were so used to him and his ways that they did not even resent them. They had never learned to understand him, nor did they ever take him into their confidence. He seemed to be their natural enemy on any program that was purely their own. He always talked of how much he sacrificed for them, but his justification of himself was on such a high moral plane that it never seemed real or convincing to the boys. Their problems were of an immediate and specific nature. If they wanted the team and buggy for a trip to town on Saturday night, he would wonder why. Hadn't he been to town that day for the groceries? Was there anything that he had forgotten that could not wait till next Saturday? No, there was not. That much was clear then. If one of the boys should say that it was just for the fun of it, that they all wanted to go, his answer was often another lecture of the kind the boys hated because they had heard it so often. "So you want to go to town for fun. I should have my horses trotting four miles to town just for fun! What are you thinking about? Don't we have enough troubles without going to town for fun? You act as though I had nothing to think about but your fun. When I was a boy of your age, I would have had my ass warmed with an oak paddle if I had talked to my father about going to town for fun." And then, as if that settled all the problems, he said, "And now, if you are so restless you don't know what to do with yourselves, you can go down to the granary and begin fanning the seed oats."

What Peter Grimsen wanted for his sons was that they should grow up to be good workers and honest men. What they thought he wanted was that they should work like slaves and never have pleasures like other boys. There were times when they spoke openly of their bitter feelings toward their father. Two sets of thoughts lived side by side in this house in the corn field. While Peter sat by the window, gazing out over the rain-soaked fields, he thought of all the things he needed for his house and family. His sons at the same time thought only of his cruelty and lack of sympathy.

Sophus Keith Winther

John Reed

WAR IN PATERSON (1919?)

There's war in Paterson, New Jersey. But it's a curious kind of war. All the violence is the work of one side—the mill owners. Their servants, the police, club unresisting men and women and ride down law-abiding crowds on horseback. Their paid mercenaries, the armed detectives, shoot and kill innocent people. Their newspapers, the Paterson *Press* and the Paterson *Call*, publish incendiary and crime-inciting appeals to mob violence against the strike leaders. Their tool, Recorder Carroll, deals out heavy sentences to peaceful pickets that the police net gathers up. They control absolutely the police, the press, the courts.

Opposing them are about twenty-five thousand striking silk workers, of whom perhaps ten thousand are active, and their weapon is the picket-line. Let me tell you what I saw in Paterson and then you will say which side of this struggle is "anarchistic" and "contrary to American ideals."

At six o'clock in the morning a light rain was falling. Slate-gray and cold, the streets of Paterson were deserted. But soon came the cops—twenty of them—strolling along with night-sticks under their arms. We went ahead of them toward the mill district. Now we began to see workmen going in the same direction, coat collars turned up, hands in their pockets. We came into a long street, one side of which was lined with silk mills, the other side with the wooden tenement houses. In every doorway, at every window of the houses clustered men and women, laughing and chatting as if after breakfast on a holiday. There seemed no sense of expectancy, no strain or feeling of fear. The sidewalks were almost empty, only over in front of the mills a few couples—there couldn't have been more than fifty—marched slowly up and down, dripping with the rain. Some were men, with here and there a man and woman together, or two young boys. As the warmer light of full day came the people drifted out of their houses and began to pace back and forth, gathering in little knots on the corners. They were quick with gesticulating hands, and low-voiced conversation. They looked often toward the corners of side streets.

Suddenly appeared a policeman, swinging his club. "Ah-h-h!" said the crowd softly.

Six men had taken shelter from the rain under the canopy of a saloon. "Come on! Get out of that!" yelled the policeman, advancing. The men quietly obeyed. "Get off this street! Go on home, now! Don't be standing here!" They gave way before him in silence, drifting back again when he turned away. Other policemen materialized, hustling, cursing, brutal, ineffectual. No one answered back. Nervous, bleary-eyed, unshaven, these officers were worn out with nine weeks incessant strike duty.

On the mill side of the street the picket-line had grown to about four hundred. Several policemen shouldered roughly among them, looking for trouble. A workman appeared, with a tin pail, escorted by two detectives. "Boo! Boo!" shouted a few scattered voices. Two Italian boys leaned against the mill fence and shouted a merry Irish threat, "Scab! Come outa here I knock your head off!" A policeman grabbed the boys roughly by the shoulder. "Get to hell out of here!" he cried, jerking and pushing them violently to the corner, where he kicked them. Not a voice, not a movement from the crowd.

A little further along the street we saw a young woman with an umbrella, who had been picketing, suddenly confronted by a big policeman.

"What the hell are *you* doing here?" he roared. "God damn you, you go home!" and he jammed his club against her mouth. "I *no* go home!" she shrilled passionately, with blazing eyes. "You big stiff!"

Silently, steadfastly, solidly the picket-line grew. In groups or in couples the strikers patrolled the sidewalk. There was no more laughing. They looked on with eyes full of hate. These were fiery Italians, and the police were the same brutal thugs that had beaten them and insulted them for nine weeks. I wondered how long they could stand it.

It began to rain heavily. I asked a man's permission to stand on the porch of his house. There was a policeman standing in front of it. His name, I afterwards discovered, was McCormack. I had to walk around him to mount the steps.

Suddenly he turned round, and shot at the owner: "Do all them fellows live in that house?" The man indicated the three other strikers and himself, and shook his head at me.

"Then you get to hell off of there!" said the cop, pointing his club at me.

"I have the permission of this gentleman to stand here," I said. "He owns this house."

"Never mind! Do what I tell you! Come off of there, and come off damn quick!"

"I'll do nothing of the sort."

With that he leaped up the steps, seized my arm, and violently jerked me to the sidewalk. Another cop took my arm and they gave me a shove.

"Now you get to hell off this street!" said Officer McCormack.

"I won't get off this street or any other street. If I'm breaking any law, you arrest me!"

Officer McCormack was dreadfully troubled by my request. He didn't want to arrest me, and said so with a great deal of profanity.

"I've *got* your number," said I sweetly. "Now will you tell me your name?"

"Yes," he bellowed, "an' I got *your* number! I'll arrest you." He took me by the arm and marched me up the street.

He was sorry he *had* arrested me. There was no charge he could lodge against me. I hadn't been doing anything. He felt he must make me say something that could be construed as a violation of the law. To which end he God-damned me harshly, loading me with abuse and obscenity, and threatened me with his night-stick, saying, "You big—lug, I'd like to beat the hell out of you with this club."

I returned airy persiflage to his threats.

Other officers came to the rescue, two of them, and supplied fresh epithets. I soon found them repeating themselves, however, and told them so. "I had to come all the way to Paterson to put one over on a cop!" I said. Eureka! They had at last found a crime! When I was arraigned in the Recorder's Court that remark of mine was the charge against me!

Ushered into the patrol-wagon, I was driven with much clanging of gongs along the picket-line. Our passage was greeted with "Boos" and ironical cheers, and enthusiastic waving. At headquarters I was interrogated and lodged in the lockup. My cell was about four feet wide by seven feet long, at least a foot higher than a standing man's head, and it contained an iron bunk hung from the side-wall with chains, and an open toilet of disgusting dirtiness in the corner. A crowd of pickets had been jammed into the same lockup only three days before, *eight or nine in a cell*, and kept there without food or water for *twenty-two hours!* Among them a young girl of seventeen, who had led a procession right up to the police sergeant's nose and defied him to arrest them. In spite of the horrible discomfort, fatigue and thirst, these prisoners had *never let up cheering and singing* for a day and a night!

In about an hour the outside door clanged open, and in came about forty pickets in charge of the police, joking and laughing among themselves. They were hustled into the cells, two in each. Then pandemonium broke loose! With one accord the heavy iron beds were lifted and slammed thunderingly against the metal walls. It was like a cannon battery in action.

"Hooray for I.W.W.!" screamed a voice. And unanimously answered all the voices as one, "Hooray!"

"Hooray for Chief Bums!" (Chief of Police Bimson).

"Boo-o-o!" roared forty pairs of lungs—a great boom of echoing sound that had more of hate in it than anything I ever heard.

"To hell with Mayor McBride!"

"Boo-o-o!" It was an awful voice in that reverberant iron room, full of menace.

"Hooray for Haywood! One big Union! Hooray for strike! To hell with the police! Boo-o-o-o! Boo-o-o-o! Hooray!"

"Music! Music!" cried the Italians. Whereupon one voice went "Plunk-plunk! Plunk-plunk!" like a guitar, and another, a rich tenor, burst into the first verse of the Italian-English song, written and composed by one of the strikers to be sung at the strike meetings. He came to the chorus:

"*Do you like Miss Flynn?*"

(CHORUS) "*Yes! Yes! Yes! Yes!*"

"*Do you like Mayor McBride?*"

(CHORUS) "*No! No! NO! NO!!!*"

"*Hooray for I.W.W.!*"

"*Hooray! Hooray!! Hooray!!!*"

"*Bis! Bis!*" shouted everybody, clapping hands, banging the beds up and down. An officer came in and attempted to quell the noise. He was met with "Boos" and jeers. Some one called for water. The policeman filled a tin cup and brought it to the cell door. A hand reached out swiftly and slapped it out of his fingers on the floor. "Scab! Thug!" they yelled. The policeman retreated. The noise continued.

The time approached for the opening of the Recorder's Court, but word had evidently been brought that there was no more room in the county jail, for suddenly the police appeared and began to open the cell doors. And so the strikers passed out, cheering wildly. I could hear them outside, marching back to the picket-line with the mob which had waited for them at the jail gates.

And then I was taken before the court of Recorder Carroll. Mr. Carroll has the intelligent, cruel, merciless face of the ordinary police court magistrate. But he is worse than most police court magistrates. He sentences beggars to *six months' imprisonment* in the county jail without a chance to answer back. He also sends little children there, where they mingle with dopefiends, and tramps, and men with running sores upon their bodies—to the county jail, where the air is foul and insufficient to breathe, and the food is full of dead vermin, and grown men become insane.

Mr. Carroll read the charge against me. I was permitted to tell my story. Officer McCormack recited a clever *mélange* of lies that I am sure he himself could never have concocted. "John Reed," said the Recorder. "Twenty days." That was all.

And so it was that I went up to the county jail. In the outer office I was questioned again, searched for concealed weapons, and my money and valuables taken away. Then the great barred door swung open and I went into a vast room lined with three tiers of cells. About eighty prisoners strolled around, talked, smoked, and ate the food sent in to them by those outside. Of this eighty almost half were strikers. They were in their street clothes, held in prison under $500 bail to await the action of the Grand Jury. Surrounded by a dense crowd of short, dark-faced men, Big Bill Haywood towered in the center of the room. His big hand made simple gestures as he explained something to them. His massive, rugged face, seamed and scarred like a mountain, and as calm, radiated strength. These strikers, one of many desperate little armies in the vanguard of the battle-line of labor, quickened and strengthened by Bill Haywood's face and voice, looked up at him lovingly, eloquently. Faces deadened and dulled with grinding routine in the sunless mills glowed with hope and understanding. Faces scarred and bruised from policemen's clubs grinned eagerly at the thought of going back on the picket-line. And there were other faces, too—lined and sunken with the slow starvation of a nine weeks' poverty—shadowed with the sight of so much suffering, or the hopeless brutality of the police. But not one showed discouragement; not one a sign of faltering or of fear. As one little Italian said to me, with blazing eyes: "We all one big Union. I.W.W.—the word is pierced in the heart of the people!"

"Yes! Yes! right! I.W.W.! One big Union"—they murmured with soft, eager voices, crowding around.

I shook hands with Haywood.

"Boys," said Haywood, indicating me, "this man wants to *know* things. You tell him everything—"

They crowded around me, shaking my hand, smiling, welcoming me. "Too bad you get in jail," they said, sympathetically. "We tell you everything. You ask. We tell you. Yes. Yes. You good feller."

And they did. Most of them were still weak and exhausted from their terrible night before in the lockup. Some had been lined up against a wall, as they marched to and fro in front of the mills, and herded to jail on the charge of "unlawful assemblage"! Others had been clubbed into the patrol-wagon on the charge of "rioting," as they stood at the track, on their way home from picketing, waiting for a train to pass! They were being held for the Grand Jury that indicted Haywood and Gurley Flynn. *Four of these jurymen were silk manufacturers, another the head of the local Edison company—which Haywood tried to organize for a strike—and not one a workingman!*

"We not take bail," said another, shaking his head. "We stay here. Fill up the damn jail. Pretty soon no more room. Pretty soon can't arrest no more pickets!"

It was visitors' day. I went to the door to speak with a friend. Outside the reception room was full of women and children, carrying packages, and pasteboard boxes, and pails full of dainties and little comforts lovingly prepared, which meant hungry and ragged wives and babies, so that the men might be comfortable in jail. The place was full of the sound of moaning; tears ran down their work-roughened faces; the children looked up at their fathers' unshaven faces through the bars and tried to reach them with their hands.

The keeper ordered me to the "convicted room", where I was pushed into a bath and compelled to put on regulation prison clothes. I shan't attempt to describe the horrors I saw in that room. Suffice it to say that forty-odd men lounged about a long corridor lined on one side with cells; that the only ventilation and light came from one small skylight up a funnel-shaped airshaft; that one man had syphilitic sores on his legs and was treated by the prison doctor with sugar-pills for "nervousness"; that a seventeen-year-old boy *who had never been sentenced* had remained in that corridor without ever seeing the sun for over *nine months*; that a cocaine-fiend was getting his "dope" regularly from the inside, and that the background of this and much more was the monotonous and terrible spectacle of a man who had lost his mind in that hell-hole and who walked among us.

There were about fourteen strikers in the "convicted" room—Italians, Lithuanians, Poles, Jews, one Frenchman and one "free-born" Englishman! That Englishman was a peach. He was the only Anglo-Saxon striker in prison except the leaders—and perhaps the only one who *had been* there for picketing. He had been sentenced for insulting a mill-owner who came out of his mill and ordered him off the sidewalk. "Wait till I get out," he said to me. "If them damned English-speaking workers don't go on picket *I'll* put the curse o'Cromwell on 'em!"

Then there was a Pole—an aristocratic, sensitive chap, a member of the local strike committee, a born fighter. He was reading Bob Ingersoll's lectures, translating them to the others. Patting the book, he said with a slow smile: "Now I don't care if I stay in here one year . . ."

With laughter, the strikers told me how the combined clergy of the city of Paterson had attempted from their pulpits to persuade them back to work—back to wage-slavery and the tender mercies of the mill-owners on grounds of religion! They told me of that disgraceful and ridiculous conference between the clergy and the strike committee, with the clergy in the part of Judas. It was hard to believe that until I saw in the paper the sermon delivered the previous day at the Presbyterian Church by the Reverend William A. Littell. He had the impudence to flay the strike leaders and advise workmen to be respectful and obedient to their employers—to tell them that the saloons were the cause of their unhappiness—to proclaim the horrible depravity of Sabbath-breaking workmen and more rot of the same sort. And this while living men were fighting for their very existence and singing gloriously of the Brotherhood of Man! . . .

Then there was the strike-breaker. He was a fat man, with sunken, flabby cheeks, jailed by some mistake of the Recorder. So completely did the strikers ostracize him—rising and moving away when he sat by them, refusing to speak to him, absolutely ignoring his presence—that he was in a pitiable condition of loneliness.

"I've learned my lesson," he moaned. "I ain't never goin' to scab on workingmen no more!"

One young Italian came up to me with a newspaper and pointed to three items in turn. One was "American Federation of Labor hopes to break the strike next week," another, "Victor Berger says 'I am a member of the A.F. of L., and I have no love for the I.W.W. in Paterson,'" and the third, "Newark Socialists refuse to help the Paterson strikers."

"I no understand," he told me, looking up at me appealingly. "You tell me. I Socialist—I belong union—I strike with I.W.W. Socialist, he say, 'Workmen of the world, unite!' A.F. of L., he say, 'All workmen join together.' Both these organizations, he say, 'I am for the working class.' All right, I say, I am the working class. I unite, I strike. Then he say, 'No! You *cannot* strike.' What that? I no understand. You explain me."

But I could not explain. All I could say was that a good share of the Socialist Party and the American Federation of Labor have forgotten all about the class struggle, and seem to be playing a little game with capitalistic rules, called "Button, button, who's got the vote!"

When it came time for me to go out I said good-by to all those gentle, alert, brave men, ennobled by something greater than themselves. *They* were the strike—not Bill Haywood, not Gurley Flynn, not any other individual. And if they should lose all their leaders other leaders would arise from the ranks, even as *they* rose, and the strike would go on! Think of it! Twelve years they have been losing strikes—twelve solid years of disappointments and incalculable suffering. They must not lose again! They cannot lose!

And as I passed out through the front room they crowded around me again, patting my sleeve and my hand, friendly, warm-hearted, trusting, eloquent. Haywood had gone out on bail.

"You go out," they said softly. "That's nice. Glad you go out. Pretty soon we go out. Then we go back on picket-line."

HAZEL HALL

by Eleanor H. Matthews

In the 1920's the Northwest witnessed an awakening of literary interest that brought with it national reputation for several poets of the area, including Ethel Romig Fuller, Howard McKinley Corning, Mary Carolyn Davies, Walter Evans Kidd, Hazel Hall and Verne Bright. Their poems were published widely in prestigious magazines and anthologies. They knew each other, met frequently and shared their struggles and successes.

Hazel Hall stood a little apart from the others in this group of writers. Unable to walk from the age of twelve as a result of illness or injury, she could not join the casual groups that congregated at several Portland homes, especially those of Charles Oluf Olsen and his wife Elizabeth ("Bessie") and Charles and Ethel Romig Fuller. Confined to her wheelchair, she sat at her window in the family home at 52 Lucretia Street (now 104 Northwest 22nd Place), reading and doing fine needlework. In the poems of her first book, she speaks of her pleasure in embroidering baby dresses, bishops' cuffs, bridal linens:

> All my stitches, running fleet,
> Cannot match the tread
> Of my thoughts whose winged feet
> Race ahead.

Hazel Hall was born February 7, 1886, in St. Paul, Minnesota, and came with her family to Portland, Oregon, as a small child. According to her sister Ruth, her childhood was a normal one "except that she was especially sensitive and imaginative." Her formal education ended in the fifth grade, but her real education in life and its meanings continued through reading and ever-deepening observation of the lives around her and the strangers passing by on the street below her window.

Viola Price Franklin, who edited a memorial volume, *A Tribute to Hazel Hall* (Caxton Printers, Ltd., 1939) states that Hazel Hall turned to the writing of poetry because failing eyesight prevented her from continuing her needlework. Her first published poem, "To an English Sparrow," appeared in the *Boston Transcript* in 1916, when she was thirty years old. Soon magazines such as *The Bookman, New Republic, Century, Poetry, Harpers*, the *Yale Review* and *Voices* were printing her poems. Harold Vinal asked her to become a contributing editor of *Voices*.

Other honors came to her. In 1921 William Stanley Braithwaite selected "Three Girls" as one of his five best poems of the year and published nineteen of her poems in his ANTHOLOGY OF MAGAZINE VERSE FOR 1921. In the same year she received the Young Poets' Prize from *Poetry* and the *Contemporary Verse* award of the year. Later, Harold G. Merriam, editor of *The Frontier*, dedicated to her memory NORTHWEST VERSE, AN ANTHOLOGY (1931) and used eleven of her poems therein.

It is the testimony of her sister, Ruth Hall, rather than discernable echoes in Hazel Hall's work that gives us a brief list of her favorite authors: poets Edna St. Vincent Millay, Elinor Wylie, Emily Dickinson, Robert Frost, Vachel Lindsay, Sara Teasdale; prose writers Lytton Strachey, Katherine Mansfield, James Stephens, Virginia Woolf, Donn Byrne. At the time of her death she was studying a history of philosophy.

Hazel Hall preferred to write in conventional metrical forms and only occasionally used free verse. Rhymed four-line stanzas occur frequently; a few sonnets; and free verse stanzas of irregular lengths in which the thought rather than a fixed pattern dictates the form. A brief note preceding the table of contents of her first book, *CURTAINS*, states: "In certain of these poems I have blended metrical and irregular rhythms in an attempt to contrast monotonous motion, presented in even measures, with interruption which is expressed in freer forms."

CURTAINS (John Lane Company, 1921) is a very personal volume of verse. A reviewer for *Poetry* called it "the crystallization of a personality." In its poems, Hazel Hall declares: "Grey walls, my days are bound within your hold/Cast there and lost like pebbles in a sea"; she speaks of "the eternal winter here"; "Winter, spring, summer and fall—/Shadows fading on a wall"; "the sick sound/Of crickets on the ground" and "My spirit is a captive bird/That beats against its cage all day." A feeling of rebellion against impersonal fate breathes through many passages. The section called "Needlework" ends with the gray despair of "Late Sewing":

> There is nothing new in what is said
> By either a needle or a thread:
> *Stitch,* says a needle, *Stitch* says the thread;
> *Stitch for the living; stitch for the dead;*
> *All seams measure the same.*
>
> *Garb for the living is light and gay.*
> *While that for the dead is a shrouding grey,*
> *But all things match in a later day*
> *When little worm-stitches in the clay*
> *Finish all seams the same.*

Her second volume of poems, *WALKERS* (Dodd, Mead & Co., 1923), marks a distinct advance in technique and in her ability to look on life with objectivity and compassion. As their titles indicate, many of the poems are observations of people passing by her window: "Walkers at Dusk," "Disputed Tread," "Footfalls," "On the Street" are examples. But these poems are not simply surface observations: they delve into motivations, fears, interpretations. To Hazel Hall, we all wear masks which delude us with illusions of splendor and valor; for a youth, life is a friendly hound running at his side; to a hurrier, hours "are spaniels snapping at his feet"; pavement has "all the arrogance of stone"; a sigh is the worn remnant of "a heart's wild cry"; a very old woman drags stricken sound and shadow "behind her on the ground/Like broken chains"; a mature man "cannot clear/His thought from the restricting gaze/Fastened upon him from behind,/Where follow the gracelessly resigned/Figures of his yesterdays."

Most of what she sees in the passers-by is sober, even tragic; but in the children are happiness and hope: a passing boy is "incarnate laughter/Lifting from Time's deep lungs"; a school girl has eyes "like wide doors/Opening out on misted shores"; a child is unaware of the "relentless destinies" stalking. Only rarely does an adult smile in passing or seem to fix eyes upon a distant hope or a bright-seeming tomorrow.

In *WALKERS* sunshine and shadow take on deeper symbolism than in the first volume. Shadows are sinister: a frightened walker is pursued by her own self "close as a shadow"; ropes of shadow tether the night walker, breaking her progress; shadow casts ragged stains behind the very old. There is more shadow than sunshine in these poems, but occasionally appears "a smiling hour/Like a girl with blossoms in her hair"; in spring "feet have a song to sing/And every bird in the sky is mad"; the sun wraps a walker "with dangerous radiancy"; she sees even the sun "involved in its more slow/Manner of dissolution."

In place of the rebelliousness of CURTAINS, the tone of WALKERS is prevailing one of acceptance of fate and acknowledgment of the diversity of human experience:

> Pass on, seeker, seeking the touch of spaces.
> Many the ways of life, and many a one
> Is all too brief a fluttering of hours
> To serve our purpose here beneath the sun.

The poet is companied by thoughts of grief and mortality, but she is led to acknowledge that "there's a better way/To die than to die of sorrow." The baffling search for this better way haunts her lines.

Like Emily Dickinson, whose lyrics she admired, Hazel Hall was a careful crafter of her songs, searching always for the exactly right word, the precise metaphor to give her lines maximum intellectual and emotional impact. All the vigor of spring is packed into a single word when she writes of "leaves *spurting* from the bough." The uncertainties and new dignity of adolescence are underlined in the contrasting adverbs of "The past and future *gravely* arbitrate/And *gaily* compromise." The notes of a whistler in the night appear as "Bright disks of sound" and "Metallic petals falling." When a boy goes by, "An *elemental* trill/Echoes behind his feet," the adjective linking him to nature and to the long centuries of evolutionary development that have made him human and yet let him remain an untamed, primitive force.

CRY OF TIME (E.P. Dutton & Co., Inc., 1928) appeared four years after Hazel Hall's death, from poems collected by her sister Ruth, many of them written in the last few weeks of the poet's life. The mysticism characterizing her earlier work here deepens and strengthens, becoming the principal characteristic of the book. Louise Townsend Nicholl in her introduction to this final volume wrote: "Few artists can round their art this way, make its arc lie on the arc of the descending life itself . . . . Hazel Hall's last book deepens and furthers the exquisite mystic quality of the early work. In the quietness of her days she had reached out always for the intangible—now it is Time, and breath, and smiling space, which she has touched."

William Troy, reviewing *CRY OF TIME* in *The Bookman*, declared: "Her poems, read separately or as a whole, constitute one of the clearest, deepest and most individual testaments presented by any modern poet."

The influence of Elinor Wylie's taut, incisive lines is more apparent in the final volume, but these poems cannot be called in any way derivative: they are pure Hazel Hall, enigmatic, spiritual, deeply feminine, and charged with tremendous force.

> But sorrow does not die, sorrow only gathers
> Weight about itself—a clay that bakes to stone.
> When your own share of sorrow has worn itself to slumber
> Then every woman's sorrow is your own.

The anthologist Braithwaite compared Hazel Hall's poetry with that of the then highly popular Sara Teasdale thus: "She has the same perfected utterance of singing meters, the same intensity of moods, the same subtle intuition of comprehension, and a similar consciousness of the symbolic value of the simple and innumerable forms of nature and experience. But where these echo in the reedy, the piercing and poignant revelation of Sara Teasdale's subjective interests, in Hazel Hall they have an outspreading vision which embraces a universal significance."

Hardly any of the poems in CRY OF TIME are unrhymed. Often the lines are grouped in four- or eight-line stanzas with an a-b-a-b rhyme scheme. This is sometimes enlarged by a couplet, the rhyme scheme becoming a-b-a-b-c-c. There are also a few sonnets in the volume, their patterns being variants of the Italian form. Other poems also show her interest in experimenting with rhyme patterns.

In subject matter the poems of this last volume probe into the secret relationships of poet and reader; the meanings in the impersonal rhythms of the seasons, of day and night; the "quarrel of thought"; the never-ending struggle for courageous endurance; the old, old mysteries of life and death, the "inky blue of nothing

/ . . . like ashes out of space"; the existence of a heaven that remains to her "a riddle . . . /Or dazzle of snow." The significantly named "Hearsay," final poem of the book, ends on the wistful note of "Purple time drifting/Like sand where you sleep."

The impression of Hazel Hall as frail and delicate was strongly contradicted by her sister Ruth in a letter to Harriet Monroe, editor of *Poetry*. She wrote: "When anyone speaks of my sister as crippled, I always feel rebellious, because she gave the impression of such abundant health. She enjoyed living immensely—her days were never long enough for all the activities she wished to press into them. Except that she did not walk, she was in good health until about six weeks before her death."

Despite her cloistered life and early death, the work of Hazel Hall has had considerable impact upon her contemporaries and later writers. Her cleanly crafted lines, stripped of obtrusive ornamentation, her derivation of philosophical meaning from brief moments of observation, her deft handling of nature imagery used for symbolic purposes, all have found admiring emulators among poets of the last half century. Howard McKinley Corning wrote of her influence: "From the high quality of her wise and lyrical verses, from their cool intensity and exquisite craftsmanship, the poets of Oregon's dawning literary majority learned much. From her poems the region's new voices first recognized and appreciated the value of emotional restraint, and from the culture bed of her carefully textured lines the tree of knowledge grew. Her poetry was at once achievement and counsel, and an entire region listened well. Meanwhile, the discerning ear of America had given audience . . . . Few poets of any age contribute so much." Her works continue to be read in defiance of the creeping destructiveness of time. She is not a regional poet but a poet of time and space and the ever-seeking human heart.

Ada Hastings Hedges, in her sonnet "Farewell," has summed up Hazel Hall's enduring place in American literature:

> Spring is not lost, for this intense white hour
> Is yours forever—past our dark distrust;
> The cool white texture that you loved, the flower,
> The stainless bough will never turn to dust;
> Graven it is in memory so deep—
> Forever yours beyond this marble sleep.

From *CURTAINS*:

Night Silence

A great mouth, lean and grey,
Munching the sounds of day:
Last voices and the beat
Of weather and late feet.

Gently parted lips
Telling of high white ships
That sail the imaged seas
Of borrowed memories.

Inexorable lips shut tight
Over the tongue of the night . . .

Suddenly the sick sound
Of crickets on the ground,
Or the long shuddering bark
Of a dog into the dark . . .

Insinuations of vain
Forgetfulness of pain,
Taunts of old moonlights
And other sound-stung nights.

Two Sewing

The wind is sewing with needles of rain.
With shining needles of rain
It stitches into the thin
Cloth of earth. In,
In, in, in.
Oh, the wind has often sewed with me.
One, two, three.

Spring must have fine things
To wear like other springs.
Of silken green the grass must be
Embroidered. *One and two and three.*
Then every crocus must be made
So subtly as to seem afraid
Of lifting colour from the ground;
And after crocuses the round
Heads of tulips, and all the fair
Intricate garb that Spring will wear.
The wind must sew with needles of rain,
With shining needles of rain,
Stitching into the thin
Cloth of earth, in,
In, in, in,
For all the springs of futurity.
One, two, three.

From *WALKERS*:

A Boy Went By

He goes whacking a stick
Against a tree or wall,
Giving a stone a kick,
Or aiming at nothing at all.

And with his grin or stare,
The freckles on his nose,
His aimless, intent air,
An inimitable way he goes.

He, though in making, still
Is in himself complete;
An elemental trill
Echoes behind his feet.

Inviolate even after
Ages of dissenting tongues,
He is incarnate laughter
Lifting from Time's deep lungs.

Three Girls

Three school girls pass this way each day.
Two of them go in a fluttery way
Of girls, with all that girlhood buys;
But one goes with a dream in her eyes.

Two of them have the eyes of girls
Whose hair is learning scorn of curls,
But the eyes of one are like wide doors
Opening out on misted shores.

And they will go as they go today
On to the end of life's short way;
Two will have what living buys,
And one will have the dream in her eyes.

Two will die as many must,
And fitly dust will become dust;
But dust has nothing to do with one—
She dies as soon as her dream is done.

The Way She Walks

She walks with a gravely conscious tread,
As though she carries above her head
A banner whose flaming inscription runs
In charactery dazzling as the sun's.
And little old winds, like little brown elves,
Run at her side and talk to themselves.

If you look deep as she carries it by
You will see the red inscription's cry:
There is earth below, there is sky above,
And life is music and laughter and love.
You will see the winds, like little brown elves,
Wink at each other and talk to themselves.

The Singing

Song is unrest;
It lives in the blood,
It flames in my pulses,
It rhythms this flood
Of people passing.

Quiet may sweep,
Water-slow, down my fingers,
Though my blood will not sleep.

The street may be cold stone,
Yet people sing by,
For the reason they live,
And the reason they die.

Nakedness

She has a way of being glad,
Of being glad that she has feet;
Of saying she will not be sad
So long as there remains a street
To be welcome to her feet.

She says it with a parasol
And with a gown of rainbow plaid;
She boasts of it with heels; yet all
She tells is were she not so glad
It might be that she would be sad.

From *CRY OF TIME*:

Inheritance

Over and over again I lose myself in sorrow;
Whatever I have borne I bear again tenfold.
The death of sorrow is a sleep; a newer sorrow
Wakes into flame from ashes of the old.

They said that sorrow died and that a sorrow buried
Made your mind a dear place like a grave with grass,
Where you might rest yourself as in a willow's shadow,
And cold and clean, might feel the long world pass.

But sorrow does not die, sorrow only gathers
Weight about itself—a clay that bakes to stone.
When your share of sorrow has worn itself to slumber
Then every woman's sorrow is your own.

Submergence

The only loneliness is the wind's,
The only sorrow is the sea's.
Why must a heart ache all life long
To learn such simple truths as these?

Lonely hours burn out like candles,
And sorrow is a leaf swept by;
But the wind is lonely forever and forever,
And the sea must hush an eternal cry.

Any Woman

When there is nothing left but darkness
And the day is like a leaf
Fallen onto sodden grasses,
You have earned a subtle grief.

Never let them take it from you,
Never let them come and say:
Night is made of black gauze; moonlight
Blows the filmy dark away.

You have a right to know the thickness
Of the night upon your face,
To feel the inky blue of nothing
Drift like ashes out of space.

You have a right to lift your fingers
And stare in pity at your hands
That are exquisite frail mirrors
Of all the mind misunderstands.

Your hands, potent in portrayal,
Falls of its own weight to rest
In a quiet curve of sorrow
On the beating of your breast.

Flight

A bird may curve across the sky—
A feather of dusk, a streak of song;
And save a space and a bird to fly
There may be nothing all day long.

Flying through a cloud-made place
a bird may tangle east and west,
Maddened with going, crushing space
With the arrow of its breast.

Though never wind nor motion bring
It back again from indefinite lands,
The thin blue shadow of its wing
May cross and cross above your hands.

Slow Death

You need no other death than this
Slow death that wears your heart away;
It is enough, the death that is
Your every night, your every day.

It is enough, the sun that slants
Across your breast, heavy as steel,
Leaving the rust of radiance
To shape a wound that will not heal.

Enough, the crystal at your lips,
Wasting you even as it lies—
Vibrant there before it slips
Away, torn from your mouth like cries.

There will be now, as fumes from wood,
A passing, yet no new death's care.
You will know only the frustrate mood
Of breath tarnished to color of air.

Here Comes The Thief

Here comes the thief
Men nickname Time,
Oh, hide you, leaf,
And hide you, rhyme.
Leaf, he would take you
And leave you rust.

Rhyme, he would flake you
With spotted dust.
Scurry to cover,
Delicate maid
And serious lover.
Girl, bind the braid
Of your burning hair;
He has an eye
For the lusciously fair
Who passes by.
O lover, hide—
Who comes to plunder
Has the crafty stride
Of unheard thunder.
Quick—lest he snatch,
In his grave need,
And sift and match,
Then sow like seed
Your love's sweet grief
On the backward air,
With the rhyme and the leaf
And the maiden's hair.

Ernest Haycox

Chapter 11 of *THE ADVENTURERS* (1954)

Mark was back at the ranch in time for supper and found a dozen armed neighborhood men in the yard. The Shottler family, living over the ridge in the next small valley, had moved in with the Murdocks for the night. The Shottlers were man, wife and one daughter around seventeen—she a pale girl with intense, round eyes and a homely mouth.

"It's the wild man," explained Murdock.

Kerby seemed to be the head of the armed group. Kerby said: "We'll keep two on guard here all night. Meet here in the morning and we'll get on his trail. Shouldn't be no trouble about that."

"It's the wild man," Murdock repeated to Sheridan.

They were unsure of what it was and they smelled danger in it and the glitter of hunting was in their eyes. The women were frightened—or at least Mrs. Murdock and the Shottler women were. They believed in the wild man's terror; it was a werewolf memory springing up from a very old place. "I won't sleep," said Mrs. Murdock. "Two's not enough to stay here and watch."

"I'll be here too," said Murdock. "So'll Sheridan. That's four. By God, he ain't bigger than four of us."

"I don't know. He don't make any noise. That's the wolf part of him sneakin' along. Lily said he didn't make a sound. Lily said he had a monstrous face—that's what I always told you, Murdock. She said his mouth was split wide and his teeth were terrible things. That's what I always said but you said no, such a thing couldn't be."

Murdock turned to Sheridan. "Lily here"—pointing to the big-eyed Shottler girl—"was walkin' out back of her place this afternoon. In the timber. Well, she didn't show up and her folks got worried and went after her. They heard her screamin'. She came out of the timber damn near dead for scared. It was the monster thing, or whatever it is. She was walkin' along a trail when it jumped out of the brush in front of her." He stopped and he scowled and he looked at the girl. "What'd it do, Lily?"

Lily Shottler wore a vacant, sly expression and her tone was the tone of a child going over memory work. "It had claws. Maybe it was a man. Maybe it was an animal, I don't know. It jumped at me and that's when I screamed and ran back. I heard Pa hollering, and so did the monster. It turned back into the brush."

"Whud its face look like, Lily?" asked Murdock in his mildly curious way.

"Like a man's, I guess. But not like a man's either. I don't know. I was terrible scared. I didn't see well."

"There, Murdock," said Mrs. Murdock. "Now you believe me."

"Well, by God," said Kerby, "we'll track it down in the morning. Ira, you stay with me here tonight."

The rest of the crowd wandered away into the twilight, homeward bound. Mrs. Murdock went into her kitchen to put the meal on the table, Mrs. Shottler following. Sheridan observed Liza Murdock on the porch. She stood with a shoulder slouched against the two-by-four post and she shared none of the fright of the two older women. She had her eyes on Lily Shottler and her expression was disbelieving. Lily caught Liza's glance but quickly avoided it. Mrs. Murdock shouted out of the kitchen. "Come in— come in. I got the meal on the table and I don't intend it should get cold while you talk nothin' out there all night."

"It's a funny thing," said Murdock in his idle way. "It's only women that see him. Seems he's smart enough to stay away from men, don't it?" He grinned at Sheridan, and he gave Lily an up-and-down look and turned into the house.

After the meal Sheridan walked through the shadows with his cigar, toward the mill. He moved around the lumber piles, scaling the cut with his eyes; the smell of the drying lumber—the heavy odor of sap drawn out by the warm day and warm night—was an unseen fog around him, a pleasant thing in his nostrils. The earth was dry, the air brittle, and the smell of smoke lay about him. From the log deck he had a view of the hills far across the valley and saw the corrosive-yellow glow of a timber fire. Behind him was the scuff of light feet traveling; he turned and saw Liza coming on. She stopped in front of him, close to him. She said: "I know why you don't take me to town. You've got a woman there."

"No."

"Then you're afraid of me."

"No."

"Then you don't like me."

"Yes," he said, "I like you."

She stood silent, brooding over his answers. "You've got a woman there," she decided. "Is she prettier than I am?"

He put his hand on her arm. Her body stirred at his touch and she lifted her head until he saw the dim flashing of her eyes in the twilight. He turned her about, saying, "Let's walk back." She dropped her head and walked silently with him.

The neighborhood men were in the yard at seven next morning. Kerby got them together and made his speech. "We'll cut up the logging road to the timber. Then we'll spread out and beat the brush. First man to sight tracks, let him yip. Lily said she saw this thing back on that old trail. We'll edge that way—but nobody go beyond it and get the trail all chewed up." He looked at Sheridan. "If you're goin', where's your gun."

"You've got guns enough," said Sheridan.

They went over the short meadow, with Mrs. Murdock's half-screamed advice following Murdock, "Don't you get lost from the rest of 'em. Don't you do it." They scrambled up the rough hill, around the pitch-frosted stumps, through salal and vine maple and fireweed; they came to the logging road on the ridge and followed it, grouped together and full of talk.

"Too goddamned much noise," said Kerby. "Shut up—shut up."

When the logging road reached the solid timber, Kerby threw his arms out to either side, signaling for the crowd to spread, and the brush began to rattle and crack as men surged into it. Sheridan walked behind Kerby. Murdock, his breath hauling wind hard in and out, was behind Sheridan as they pursued the soft trail through the shadows. Kerby had his head down to read a sign. "There's Lily's feet and the old man's comin' after her—Shottler, I mean." Two hundred yards beyond, the hill having reached a level stretch, Kerby stopped. "That another set of tracks? Shoes? This creature wear shoes?" He went rummaging into the brush, slapping it aside with his impatient arms; he halted and bent down. "Here," he said. "He must've slept here, or waited here. Ground's got a sort of beaten look."

The other men came in and gathered around the beaten spot.

Sheridan watched the little flickers of expression around mouth and nose, the keening and the quickening of their appetites. Murdock stood aside, tired from the climb and showing no great amount of interest, but there was a younger man in this party—young Crabtree who had watched Sheridan with such close hostility during the purchase of the horse—who came to the beaten spot and watched others as they studied it.

Kerby went rummaging forward; he cut aside in the brush and he worked his way through it, and cursed at the vines. He came back, not satisfied. "We'll go toward Deer Creek Canyon. Spread out again. Yip if you see anything."

They left the beaten spot—all but the Crabtree boy. He stayed a moment longer, stooped over to read the ground. Then he rose full up, looked about him sharply, and trotted away.

Kerby walked through this with a spring-kneed speed. The other men were foraying through the trees, leaving the echoes of their travel behind them, calling back and forth. Murdock heaved out a painful observation. "By God, if anybody starts shootin', somebody's goin' to get killed. I'm gettin' old. It just came to me."

There was no more trail. Sheridan followed Kerby into a sunless reach of timber, over deadfalls, under the slanted archway of trees half fallen and lodged, through a dense patch of huckleberry higher than his head. Here and there daylight broke through as a single shaft of light in which dust turbulently boiled. They broke out into a knobby clearing made by some long-ago fire. Over to the left, a quarter mile or less, a shot faintly echoed, and was soon followed by a shot which rolled back in delayed, bouncing echoes.

"There," said Kerby, and clawed forward through the brush.

"That's mighty queer," said Murdock.

There was a second shot in that direction, and the underbrush crackled in a more lively way as men rushed toward a common center—downhill—through a swampy ravine's bottom, up another hill, over its summit to a breakaway edge. Everybody rushed this way and came panting in. Below them was a fire-swept flat cluttered with dead logs, and beyond was another hill. A third shot broke the clear morning quiet and suddenly Kerby pointed. "There he is."

On the face of that hillside, dark and small and wiggling, a man moved upward over the rough slope. Rifles came up at once to begin a potluck firing.

"How the hell you know it's him?" asked Murdock.

Kerby jumped in great stiff-legged surges down the slope, leading the crowd. Sheridan found himself fighting through the matchstick tangle of the logs in the flats, dropping farther and farther behind, and noticing that Murdock was considerably to his rear. He got to the foot of the slope about the time the guns began to shoot again somewhere at the top of the ridge. He dug in with his feet, pulling himself up the stiff pitch. He was stung on the hand by a wasp. Dust boiled up from the powder-dry earth and sweat began to roll down his face. The guns were still going off, one bullet screaming as it struck some small obstacle and went on.

Reaching the crest of the ridge he noticed the crowd in a semicircle slightly ahead. When he got up with the group, he saw the dense timber confronting them. They were shooting into this without much sense but, looking carefully into that darkness, he saw the edge of a body, or the motion of a hand behind a huge fir trunk, this marking the target at which they were all firing. Chips of bark sprang out from the tree as the bullets tore into it; the target disappeared behind the shelter of the trunk.

Kerby said, in a loud voice, "Jen—you start edgin' off to the left and I'll go the other way. We'll flank that goddamned tree. The rest of you don't move—and don't shoot at anything except that tree."

He hadn't gone more than ten feet when the human target behind the tree, no doubt hearing the strategy which was to uncover him, made a sudden rush away from the tree, angling deeper into the forest. Half a dozen guns cracked around Sheridan. He blinked his eyes at the sound of them, and for an instant lost sight of the victim. Then he saw the man, standing still with one hand propped against another tree. He had been hit and stopped. He could stand but he couldn't move. Another round of shots reached him and tore into him and fluttered him and shook him like a puppet; his arm slid from the tree and he dropped down.

Kerby said, "Careful now. Walk up slow." He pointed his gun at the fallen figure and he stepped on with flat-footed care, approaching as he would have approached a buck he wasn't certain was dead. He stopped a few feet away and he waited; the others came behind, making a half ring around the body.

Kerby said, "I think the bastard's dead."

"Well," said somebody, "put another in him and he'll be damned dead."

"Naw," said Kerby and stepped on to touch the body with his foot. It gave to pressure, without flinching or reacting; then Kerby reached down, caught a shoulder and heaved the figure over on its back. He stared at it and stood up; he turned to the men around him with an offguard expression which might have been chagrin or sudden doubt. "Why, by God, it's a man."

It was indeed a man; a small man of around five feet four, with not much meat on his bones and weighing certainly no more than a hundred and thirty pounds. It wasn't possible to tell his age, for he wore a black, untrimmed beard which left nothing visible except a small nose, a button of a mouth and a pair of eyes which seemed hollowed out by either hunger or fright. He was a man, and nothing else at all; a small man who had turned fugitive or hermit. The bullets had all hit him in the middle body; his coat was black-speckled with the shot which had torn through him; and blood gently swelled through the holes.

Murdock was the last to come up, so winded he couldn't speak. He put a hand on Sheridan's shoulder to have his own look at the body.

"Anybody know him?" asked Kerby.

Nobody said anything.

"Well," said Kerby, "that's the last women he'll scare." He looked around him as he said it; he said it without too much conviction, with defensiveness in his words. He met Sheridan's glance. "That's right, ain't it?" he asked. "I mean, you can't have something like that loose." Then he turned from Sheridan and said in his more natural way. "Well, we've got to get him out of here. That's goin' to be a hell of a job. A man on each leg and a man grab each arm."

Sheridan turned back without waiting for the rest, and made his way homeward. Murdock had also turned back and from the distant rear hallooed at him. "Wait for me, Sheridan." Sheridan disregarded the call and went on. It was late in the morning when he got to the Murdocks'. The women had heard the shooting and were all in the yard waiting for him.

Mrs. Murdock said: "What happened?"

"They got him," said Sheridan, watching Lily Shottler.

"What kind of a monster was he?" said Mrs. Murdock.

"Just a man. Pretty small—pretty thin."

"Then it's not the right one," said Mrs. Murdock. "They got the wrong one."

"No," said Murdock. "I guess they got the one you thought was a monster."

Lily Shottler said: "He had big teeth, didn't he?"

"No."

"They looked big to me!" Then she asked a quicker question. "Is he dead—did he yell or say anything?"

"Not a thing," said Sheridan.

"No," said Mrs. Murdock, "they couldn't of got the right one. The sheriff came by just a while ago. He started up there."

Liza watched Lily Shottler closely. The Shottler girl gave each one around her a quick glance and turned away. "I'm going home," she said and walked away.

It was another hour before the main party came into sight on the hill and straggled down its side, one group of four swinging the dead man between them, sometimes holding him up by his legs and arms, sometimes letting him slide. They dropped him in the road and stepped back, and all the group stood by. Another man presently showed on the crest of the hill—the sheriff on horseback—and let himself down. He called out: "You got him?"

"That's him," said Kerby.

The sheriff came up to the body. He bent in the saddle and took one short glance; he lifted his head. "You're sure he's the one?"

"Nobody else out there in them woods," said Kerby, his voice stiffening.

"Where's his claws, where's his wolf face, where's his fangs?" said the sheriff, quite softly.

"Well, hell, that was woman's talk," said Kerby. "But he must of been dangerous, hunting around for women like he was."

"His name," said the sheriff, "is Eb Price. He was a loony fellow with no harm in him. Ate nuts and raw wheat and didn't wear any shirt. Couple of years ago he disappeared from Forest Grove. Just wanted to live alone. There's your wild man."

Nobody said anything. The sheriff ran a hand across his face and shook his head. He stood in great thought, looking from man to man. "Maybe you damned fools will learn there ain't any monsters in Oregon. You've all fired your guns—and from the looks of him I'd say you all hit him. That could go hard. There ain't an open season on men in this county."

Kerby said, "By God, he might of killed some woman sooner or later."

The sheriff let out a long breath. He said wearily, "I suppose that's the verdict that'll come out of this." He nodded at one of the men. "You go get your wagon. We'll take the body into Forest Grove."

"Why me more than anybody else?" asked the man.

The sheriff let all of his accumulated exasperation go into an enraged shout, "Because I said so," and stared at the man until the latter turned away. He remained silent until the wagon came up and the body was put aboard—his silence lashing the crowd with its effect; and still in silence he followed the wagon away.

The neighboring men had little to say; and one by one they broke from the group and moved homeward. Sheridan noticed that young Crabtree had left the party earlier.

Houseboats and dock house along wide bend in Willamette River.

H. L. Davis

From *THE SELECTED POEMS OF H. L. DAVIS*

The River People

Gray and white sea-gulls, we own tight-rooted grass
Haired over with frost, and wild leaves that women rake
To cover their bulbs from frost—as when I watched and might
    ask,
Being a child, why she raked them, and why she laughed
At wild geese crying to pass the sharp apple-pruning smoke
Which shut them from the river. She wondered of the sea.
And that she taught me to make little of women, and of all but
    death,
Is not my debt. Yet in the hard fields of the river I build speech
Till I say: "When I saw the sea-tide I remembered how you lived
When I was a little boy. I helped you, and cleaned grass
From your wind-fallen apples, and I have seen the sea,
Which in that cold autumn you wished for—not level water,
But higher than your head and like a smooth hill
On which the grass turns the light. Wind presses a man's mouth,
And cuts furrows in that sloped water where dark combs run
And bloom white, and bloom like the black-barked limbs of ap-
    ples in rain.
As wild cattle break from the counting-pens, with what dust
The low-headed leaders raise blowing on the packed ground—
When the press lay their horns back and mount plunging with
    sharp feet,
And low quaking-asp-boughs whip them on the naked eyes."
And she: "We tasted of waves when we were children gathering
    mast
Under the myrtle-trees whose broad leafage takes
The bitter taste out of the air. They shook the ground."

And I: "Children on the beach play cattle with myrtle-nuts.
They are Finn and Russian children, who have white hair
And cross the mountains in fall to pick hops. They have cried
When the train passed the hopyards, from ignorance.
They graze cattle on the cliffs for milk. Their hay
Grows wild, seeds, but never ripens. Fine-petalled purple flowers
And late spotted snapdragons fall to the scythe."
        "Are they green all year?
We used to race before light when they were burning straw.
We called out for cold of morning. Is there never smoke
Raising the wild geese that glean our hulled wheat? No birds
Like ours that flock twitching the wheat-stems and their sharp
Changing ground when the smoke turns?"
         "Not those."
         "I'll keep here
And not owe my daughters, but lie against the black ground
Till sand come and weigh down my hands, until birds come close
Having long observed me. I know how much I came
Surely out of the round hills, those that are in grain
Or white stubble against winter; and out of that sound
Of blackbirds changing stand, let that return.
And you also, son, when you described the sea, took your words
Out of cattle-counting and out of river-hills rounded with wind."

            March, 1925

Seavy's Hopyard, near Eugene, 1900.

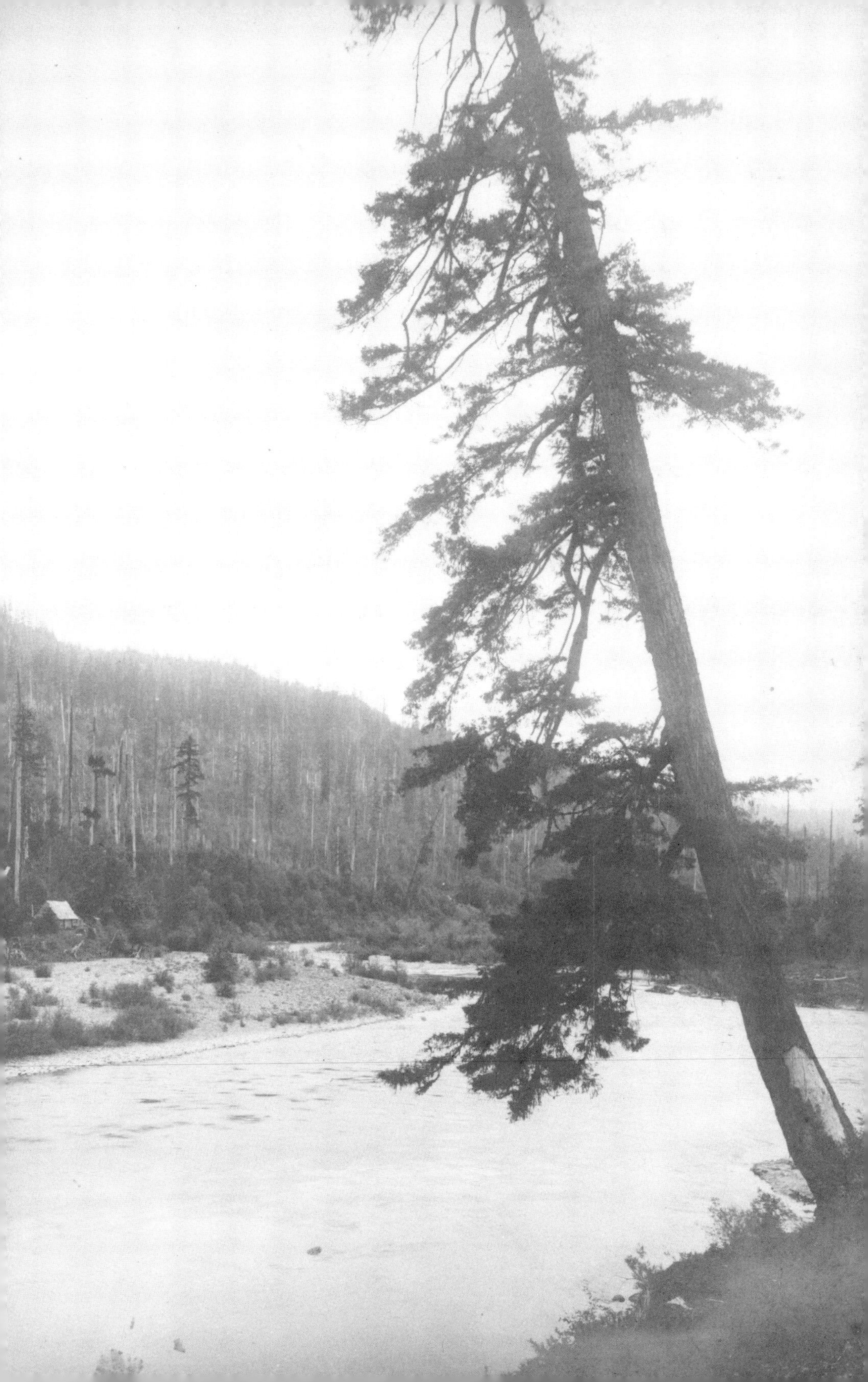

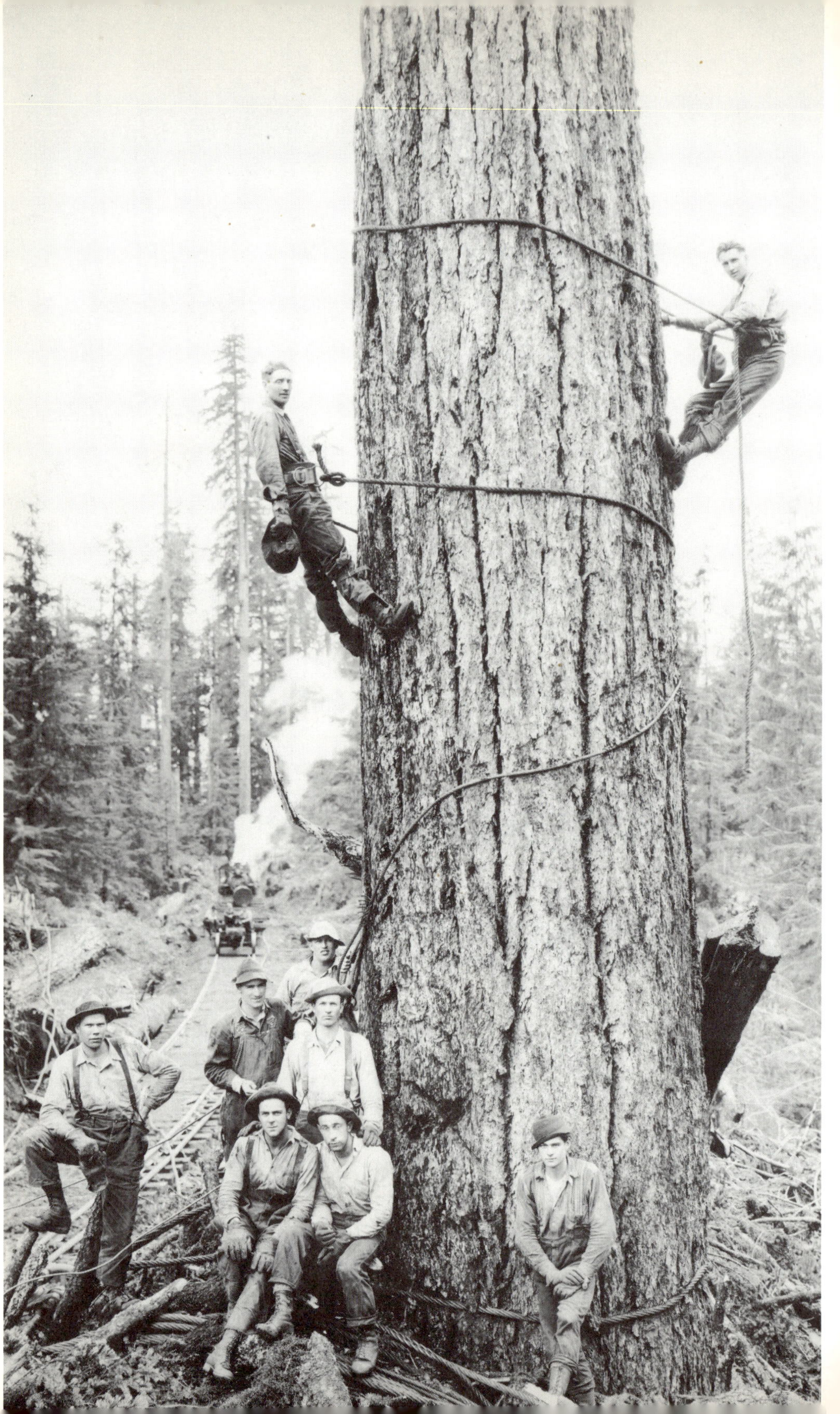

James Stevens

From *PAUL BUNYAN* (1926)

Oratorical Medicine

Before the second season in the Hickory Hill country there had never been a great sickness in Paul Bunyan's camp. The health his loggers constantly enjoyed was due to the skill of Johnny Inkslinger, who was physician and surgeon, as well as timekeeper, to the good and mighty Paul Bunyan. His surgical feats were marvelous. When ears were bitten off, for example, in the playful jousts with which the loggers amused themselves, it was no trick for Johnny Inkslinger to sew them on tightly again. And when a logger got his face walked on by calked boots the timekeeper would fill the resulting cavities with bread crumbs, slap on some red paint, and the victim of play would return to the frolic, happy and unmarred. But it was digestive ills which he understood completely; for Paul Bunyan's loggers like the laborers and farmers of to-day, had most of their physical miseries in the mysterious regions about the stomach. His knowledge was gained by the most arduous study and extensive research. The timekeeper wrote reports and figured all day, he dosed the loggers and operated on them in the evening, and the night long he read doctor books. His Sundays and holidays he spent among the wild creatures of the forests and seas, and these he studied shrewdly and patiently. He examined fleas, he explored whales, he once found the bones of a moose who had died of old age, and he tracked the animal to its birthplace, noting all its habits and methods of life on his way. His knowledge was monumental and complete, but he was content to remain a timekeeper in position and name.

In the second season on Hickory Hill the life of the camp went on as usual for a long time. For twelve hours each day the axes rang in the undercuts, the saws sang through bark and grain, and there was everywhere the death shudder, the topple and crashing fall of lofty trees. The blue ox placidly snaked the logs to the riverside, following the Big Swede, who, lost in dreams every trip always walked on into the water. The fumes and exhalations of the great cookhouse were never richer with delightful smells. In the evenings the bunkhouses were loud with gleeful roars as the loggers punched and kicked each other in their pastimes. As the work went on Paul Bunyan grew certain that this would be his greatest season among the hardwoods. His heart warmed toward his men. He planned for them feasts, revels, largesses, grand rewards. All his thoughts were benevolent ones as he directed operations. Then, at the height of his record-breaking season, Babe, the blue ox, got a misery.

It was a sly, slow, deceitful illness. It was first marked in the decline of his sportiveness and affection. It was his habit, when yoked and harnessed in the morning, to make for the woods at a roaring gallop. Always the Big Swede would grip the halter rope and try to hold the blue ox to a walk; always Babe would plunge on, dragging the Big Swede after him; and always the dutiful foreman would hit the ground once in every ninety feet, yell, "Har noo!" and then be yanked into the air again, for Babe would pay no heed to the bouncing boss. In the woods the blue ox always had to be closely watched, for he would chew up the trees in his jestful moments as fast as they were felled, and on the great drives he would prankishly drink the river dry, leaving the astounded rivermen mired in the mud of the stream bed. He was forever gouging the Big Swede with his sharp horns or tickling Paul Bunyan's neck with his tongue.

When this playful spirit of his slackened and he began to walk slowly to the timber each morning, it was first thought to signify the approach of maturity, with its graver moods. But when Paul Bunyan discovered him one day, standing with his front feet crossed, his head bowed, his cud vanished, and with tears rolling from his half-closed eyes, the great logger was alarmed. He called Johnny Inkslinger from among his ledgers and ink barrels and ordered him to drop all other work until Babe's ailment was diagnosed and cured.

Though he had studied all animals exhaustively, Johnny Inkslinger had never practised veterinary medicine, except in treating Babe's inconsequential attacks of hayfever and asthma. If he took the case he would be assuming a great responsibility, he told Paul Bunyan; he must have at least forty-seven hours to consider the matter. The great logger, having due respect for the scientific temperament, granted him this, so the timekeeper retired to his office.

Paul Bunyan waited patiently, despite the fears and anguish that smote him when Babe looked at him with beseeching eyes. Work had been stopped in the woods, and the anxious loggers spent most of their time around the stable. The cooks, remembering Babe's fondness for hot cakes and fried eggs, brought him tubfuls of them most delicately cooked, but he would only nibble at them politely, then turn away. Once indeed his old jestful spirit returned when the Big Swede came near him. He set his hoof on the foreman's foot, and at the anguished "Har noo!" he seemed to smile. But what a difference there was between that shadow of merriment and the one time gay bellow that always followed the joke! Paul Bunyan and the loggers were deeply touched.

Johnny Inkslinger finally announced in a scientific speech that he was prepared to examine and treat the blue ox. He was certain, above all, that this illness was not caused by indigestion, for Babe's stomach had always seemed to be iron-clad, invulnerable. When the hay supply ran low in the wintertime Paul Bunyan would tie a pair of green goggles over Babe's eyes and he would graze for weeks on the snow. He was fond of the wires that bound his bales of hay, and he had always eaten them without apparent injury. So Johnny Inkslinger ignored Babe's stomachs, but every other part of him, from muzzle to tail brush, was minutely scrutinized and explored. Nothing escaped observation. Six intrepid loggers with lanterns were lowered by ropes into his throat to examine his tonsils when he stubbornly refused to say "Ah!" But no diseased condition could anywhere be discovered.

Johnny Inkslinger was baffled, but he would not give up. For sixty-one hours he sat in the stable, watching every movement of the blue ox and making pages of notes about each one. And all of the time he was thinking with the full power of his scientific mind, bringing all his vast medical knowledge to the solution of his problem. Then, just as he had reached the darkest depths of hopelessness, a flashing idea saved him with its light. The idea did not spring from his science or knowledge; indeed, it seemed to be in opposition to them. It was a simple idea, simply inspired.

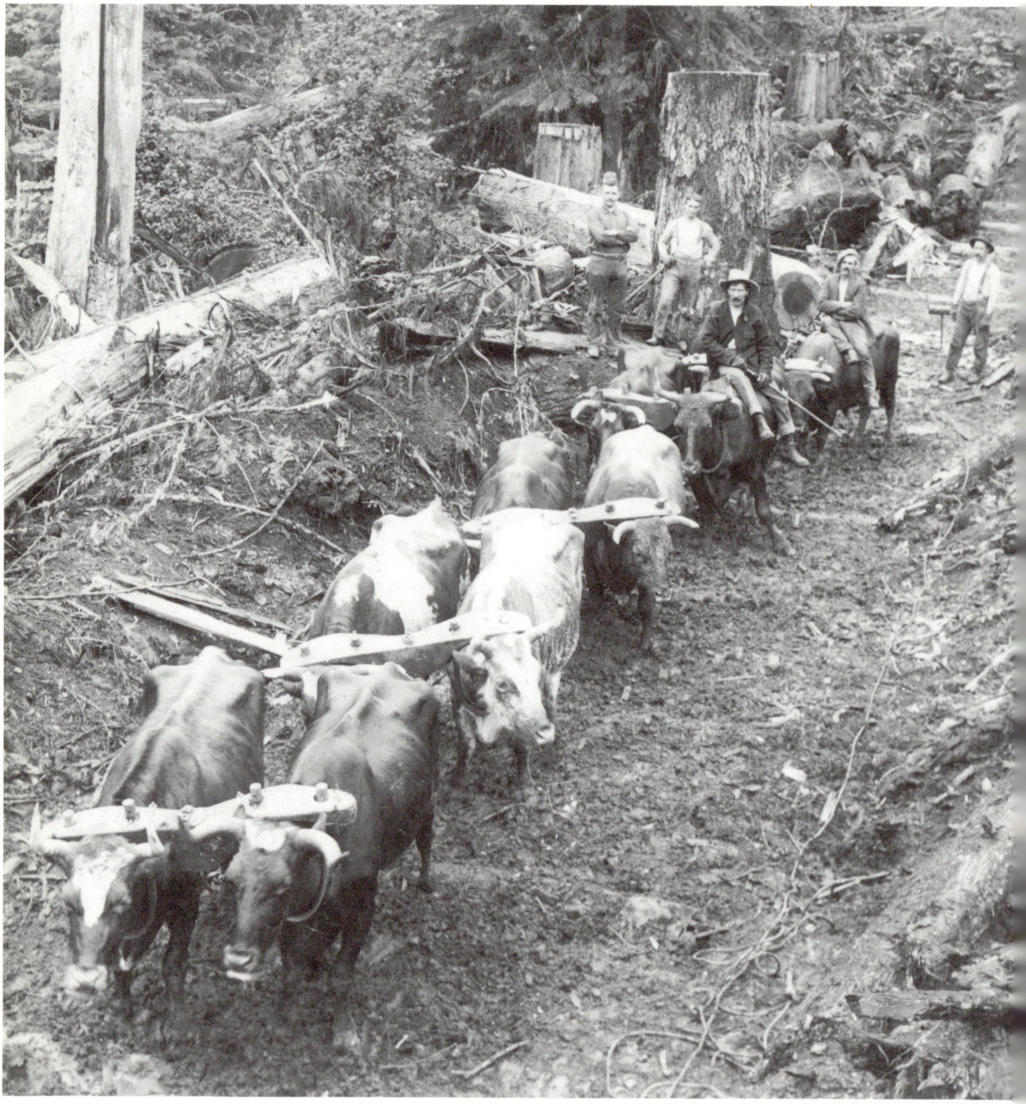

His gaze had been fixed for some time on the hump which the blue ox had on his back. It was such a hump as all ailing animals contrive, but, unoriginal as it was, it was yet the source of an original and startling idea, that the hump in a sick animal's back, instead of being the *result* of the sickness, was really the *cause* of it! Johnny Inkslinger jumped to his feet with a shout of joy. He saw in the idea, not only the salvation of Paul Bunyan's logging enterprises, but the root of a great fame for himself as a veterinarian as well. His jubilant calls soon roused the camp.

Paul Bunyan listened somewhat doubtfully as the timekeeper revealed his idea and plans. But he was not one to oppose a scientific man with mere logic, so he gave orders that the great treatment devised by Johnny Inkslinger should be carried out. For five days the loggers toiled, erecting a scaffold on each side of the blue ox. Runways were built from the top floors of the scaffolds to Babe's back. Then all was ready for the first treatment. For three hours loggers carrying pike poles, peavys, sledges and mauls climbed the scaffolds and extended in lines on each side of Babe's humped spine. Then Paul Bunyan grasped the horns of the sick creature, Johnny Inkslinger and the Big Swede seized his tail, the command, "Get ready!" was given, then, "Let's go!" Paul Bunyan said, and the army of doctors began the cure. All that day, through the night, and for seventy-six consecutive hours thereafter the loggers attacked the hump in Babe's spine, while Paul Bunyan, Johnny Inkslinger, and the Big Swede attempted to stretch it to its former shape by tugging on the poor animal's horns and tail. Babe mooed dolorously indeed while this treatment was being performed, and the tears rolled from his saddened eyes in foaming torrents. But he did not resist. Intelligent animal that he was, he knew that his friends were only trying to drive away his misery. And kindly of soul as he was, it was no doubt as much to give them the pleasure of success as to stop them from prodding, pounding and stretching his spine that he made a heroic effort to act as cured ox. Pretty deceiver! Once he had straightened his aching back, how lustily he began to devour bale after bale of bitter-tasting hay from his manger! How speedily he emptied tubfuls of hot cakes and fried eggs, while Hot Biscuit Slim, Cream Puff Fatty and the assistant cooks looked on and cheered! Never did Babe depart more friskily for the woods than on the morning he was pronounced cured. The Big Swede, hanging to the halter rope, only hit the dirt once in every mile and a half!

The work of logging was soon in its old routine, but Paul Bunyan was not satisfied. Babe could not hide his spells of trembling; he moved feverishly; his expression was haggard, his mooings hollow. Johnny Inkslinger, still flushed with the fire of his grand idea, was impatient with Paul Bunyan's worriment. But he could not quiet the great logger's fears. When it was noted that Hickory River would suddenly rise three or four feet above its normal level and as suddenly fall again, Paul Bunyan set a close watch on the blue ox and discovered that there were times when the hump in his back became greater than ever before, and that torrents of tears poured from his eyes in fits of weeping, thus flooding the river. Firmly, but without anger, Paul Bunyan ordered his timekeeper to devise another treatment.

Johnny Inkslinger reluctantly admitted his failure and again brought his powers of thought to consider the perplexing sickness of the blue ox. But he did not labor with the materials of his knowledge and science. He longed to glow again with the tickling heat of originality, to taste once more the sweet fat of his own ideas. So he sat and thought, awaiting inspiration, while his doctor books stood unopened on the towering shelves of the camp office. And at last he was rewarded by an idea that floated from mysterious darkness like a bubble of golden light. It was midnight, but his ecstatic shouts awakened the camp. The loggers, thrilled and alarmed, rolled from their bunks and ran in their underclothes to the camp office. A white-clad host soon filled the broad valley and covered the distant hills. Johnny Inkslinger then came out of the office, carrying a box that had held ninety-five tons of soap. He mounted this box and began to speak. His eyes flamed, his hair waved, his hands fanned the air. He was voluble. "Doctor or prophet?" Paul Bunyan asked himself sadly as he strode away, after listening for a short time. But the loggers were enchanted as the speech went on. Johnny Inkslinger ended each period with a mesmeric phrase, and after he had repeated it thrice at the ending of his speech the loggers made a chant of it. "Milk of the Western whale! Milk of the Western whale! Milk of the Western whale!" they roared, as they swayed and danced in their underclothes. The chant rose in thunders to the sky, it rolled over the hickory forests, and it shook the rocks of far mountains. It re-echoed for hours after the loggers had returned to the bunkhouses.

Paul Bunyan considered the situation bravely and calmly. He admitted no vain regrets that he had never studied doctoring himself. He pronounced no maledictions on his timekeeper's puzzling mania. He simply considered the plain facts of his problem: if Babe died the great logging enterprises would be halted forever; Johnny Inkslinger was the only man who had the science and knowledge to cure the sick ox, and if humored he might return to his senses; a change to the Western coast might benefit Babe, and the milk of the Western whale would surely do him no harm. So the mighty logger decided to move his camp to the West, and there let Johnny Inkslinger give him the whale's milk cure.

There was great rejoicing in the camp when Paul Bunyan gave orders for the move. The blue ox, seeming to realize that it was made for his benefit, acted as though he was in high spirits when he was hitched to the camp buildings and the bunkhouses loaded with loggers. He skipped and capered along the trail behind Paul Bunyan, Johnny Inkslinger and the Big Swede all the way to the Mississippi. But there he was attacked by innumerable squadrons of Iowa horse flies. He smashed them unmercifully with blows of his tail until the ground for miles around was strewn with their mangled bodies, but the carnivorous insects persisted in their assaults until Babe became blindly enraged. He lowered his head and began a furious charge that did not end until he reached Colorado, where he fell exhausted. The loggers had been made violently seasick by their bouncing journey over the hills, and Paul Bunyan was compelled to call a halt until they and the blue ox had recovered. While waiting, Paul Bunyan and the Big Swede built a landmark by heaping dirt around an upright pike pole, and the great logger was so pleased with the creation that he gave it a name, Pike's Peak.

The trip to the coast was made without further misadventures, and the loggers were set to work at once to build a whale corral, for Paul Bunyan wished to get the cure over as soon as possible, so that his stubborn timekeeper would begin to do some real doctoring. The loggers grumbled loudly at working with picks and shovels; such foreign labor demeaned them, they said. But the exhortations which 'Johnny Inkslinger delivered from his great soap box, and the alarming condition of the blue ox, who now made no effort to hide his sickness, but lay quietly, with closed eyes, overwhelmed their prejudices, and they made the dirt fly in spite of their dislike for shovels and picks. For nine days and nights they threw dirt like badgers, while Paul Bunyan and the Big Swede scooped it aside and piled it into big hills. Then the whale corral was finished, and Paul Bunyan sent the loggers to the bunkhouses. They were so sleepy and weary that they began to snore before they had put away their tools.

Paul Bunyan kicked a hole in the seaward side of the corral, and the waters of the Pacific roared into the basin. When it was filled he began his famous imitation of the bawl of a lonely whale, and so perfect was his mimicry that in less than an hour an approaching school of leviathans was sighted. They swam hesitatingly about the opening to the corral for a time, but as Paul Bunyan continued to call ever more cunningly and appealingly, they at last entered the trap. The Big Swede then got his stool and milk bucket, while Paul Bunyan scooped dirt into the corral gate. Johnny Inkslinger was called from the office, and all was ready for the first milking of a creature of the seas.

The Big Swede, who had been raised on a dairy farm in the old country, selected a cow whale that looked like a good milker, and Paul Bunyan, using all his wiles of manner and tricks of voice, soon had her playing about his hands. At last she was gentle and quiet, and, while Johnny Inkslinger held up her tail, the Big Swede came into the water with his bucket and stool and began milking with all the energy and skill that had won him the name of Sweden's greatest milker in his youth. With the vigorous pressure of his hands, the whale's milk was soon gushing into his bucket with such force that a dozen fire engines could not have equaled the flow. The gentled whale made no resistance, and the pail was soon filled with healthful, creamy milk. But just as the Big Swede was about to rise from his stool the whale's calf, who had been swimming angrily about, suddenly charged the great milker and upset him. His head lodged in the milk bucket; he was bent double; and before he could recover himself, the little whale had butted the breath out of him and had spanked him blisteringly with his corrugated tail. This incident frightened the mother whale, and she escaped from Paul Bunyan's hands; the Big Swede floundered about and yelled from the depths of the milk bucket; and the whole school of whales plunged about the corral in a wild panic. Worst of all, the first milking was spilled.

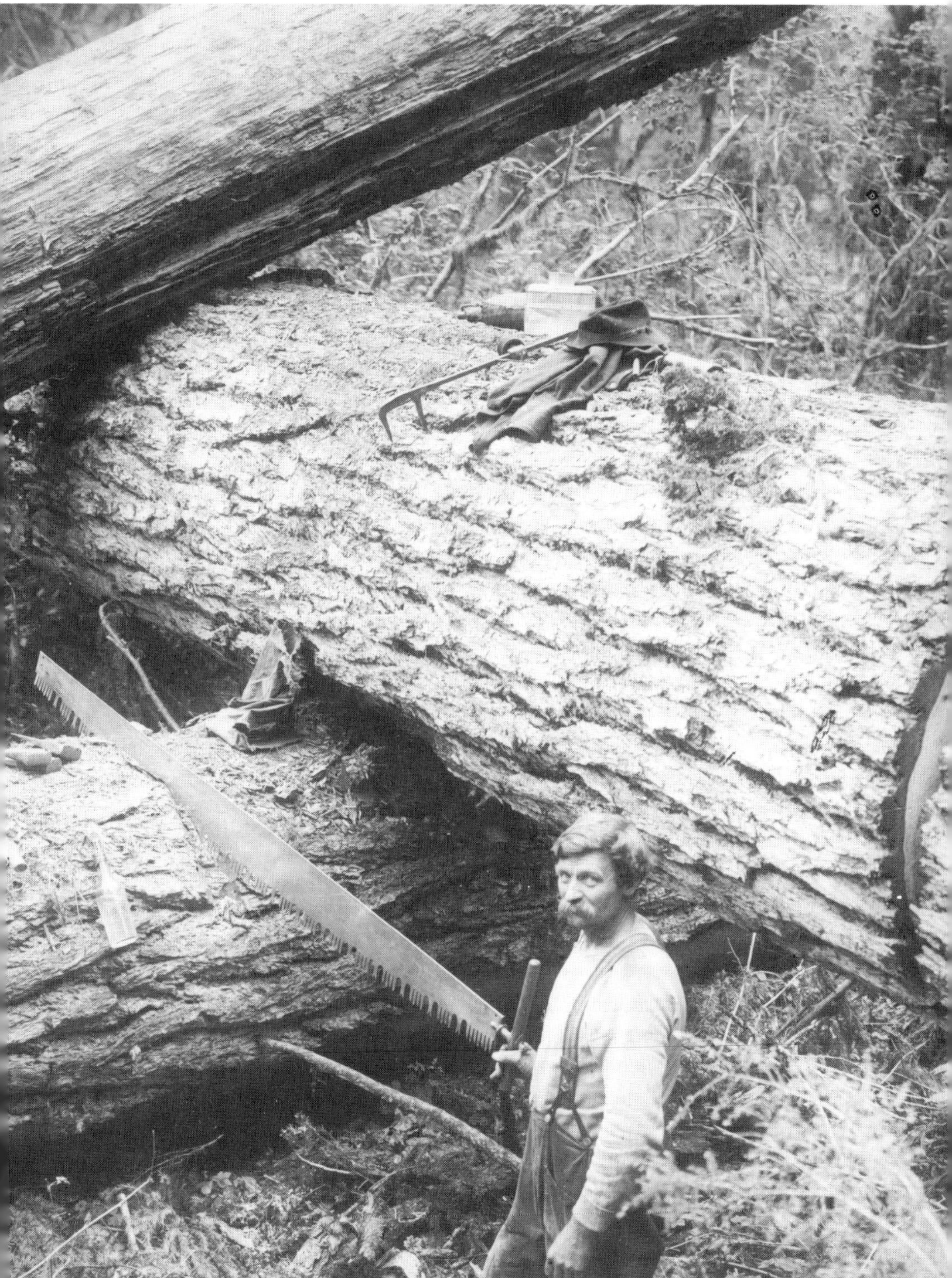

And indeed they were the whole day securing one bucket of milk. Not until Paul Bunyan thought of letting a whale calf suck his finger while the Big Swede was milking its mother were the sea-going dairymen able to get away from the corral with one milking. But at last the great milker limped to the shore with a foaming pail. He was breathing in wheezes, his clothes were in tatters, and the back of him, from head to heels, was marked from the tail blows of the little whales. He was the sorriest of sorry sights, but he had a feeble smile, nevertheless, in return for Paul Bunyan's praise.

Babe took his first dose of whale's milk resignedly and then closed his eyes again in weariness and sighed with pain. Paul Bunyan's emotions smothered his caution; he ventured to express his doubts about the cure. Johnny Inkslinger immediately ran to the office, brought out his great soap box and mounted it.

"It is a nature cure!" he cried in ringing tones. "It cures slowly because nature cures slowly, but it cures surely and divinely! It is a great cure because it is a great idea, a marvelous idea, a heaven-sent idea, an original idea, my own idea, and it is the idea that will save us all!"

Paul Bunyan looked for a moment into the glowing eyes of his timekeeper and sighed. He did not reply.

For a week the three milked the whales twice daily and dosed the blue ox, while the loggers slept away their weariness. Babe took the whale's milk meekly, but at each successive dose he swallowed more sluggishly, and after the fourth day he would not open his eyes while he drank. On the day the loggers came from the bunkhouses he refused to drink at all. Only an occasional twitching of his eyelids showed that life yet remained with him.

"He is dying," said Paul Bunyan.

Johnny Inkslinger mounted the great box which had held the ninety-five tons of soap and began to speak.

"Fellow loggers and Paul Bunyan," he began.

"This miraculous idea, this saving and transfiguring idea——"

"Silence!" commanded the good and mighty logger.

So compelling was the power of that grave and august voice that the loggers hardly breathed as it sounded, and the wind subsided until it made only the faintest whisper among the trees. Then Paul Bunyan made one of his great orations. He did not require a soap box, he made no fantastic gestures, and he spoke simply and smoothly. He reviewed his enterprises and the deeds of his loggers; he dwelt especially on the achievements and faithfulness of Babe, the blue ox. His plain sincerity held the loggers spellbound; for sixty-nine hours the speech went on, and they did not so much as move an eyelash. In conclusion, Paul Bunyan told them that Babe would surely die, and as logging could not be done without him, their last labor together would be to dig his grave. He did not blame Johnny Inkslinger, he said; the best of men may be led astray by their imaginings and fall into evil ways. He had been a great doctor once, and he was a noble scribe still. Then Paul Bunyan solemnly and warningly spoke of the shadowy workings of fate, and in somber utterance he portrayed the pathos of yearnings, the frailty of blessings and the ultimate vanity of all endeavor. In the last three hours of his oration his voice sounded as a tolling bell. Mournfully, mournfully, the moment marched on, and a darkness came over the hills and the sea. From the eyes of each motionless logger the tears streamed unchecked; they formed in puddles around each man's feet until all of them stood knee-deep in mud. When the oration was finished and they had extricated themselves and cleaned their boots, they made ready, and they left with Paul Bunyan for the North, where he had decided to dig Babe's grave. The Big Swede stayed with the dying ox, and Johnny Inkslinger hid himself in the shadows of his office.

For a long time he remained there in an agony of thought. Remorse tormented him, though Paul Bunyan had not judged him guilty. But he suffered most from the humiliation of failure. It was his first, but—the thought came like a blinding flash of light —had he failed—yet? His reservoir of ideas was inexhaustible; as long as breath remained in the blue ox he could try other ideas on him. Think now! It had become as easy for him to summon grand ideas as for a magician to conjure rabbits from a hat, and almost instantly he had one, a superb notion, a glorious thought!

Johnny Inkslinger rushed from the office and roused the Big Swede, who was sitting in apathetic sadness by the blue ox.

"Listen now!" commanded the timekeeper. "You are to sit here and repeat continuously in a soothing voice, 'You are well. You are well. You are well.' Do you understand? Well then—no questions now—do as I have told you and Babe's life will be saved. Do not fail, for all depends on your faithfulness! When I have returned with Mr. Bunyan I will finish the cure myself.

The timekeeper, exulting in the certainty that his method would positively restore health to the blue ox, then started out on the trail of Paul Bunyan and the loggers. They should quit their melancholy task and return to find Babe on the road to recovery. He would complete the cure, and logging should go on as before.

The Big Swede at once began to repeat the words, "You ban well," according to orders. For thirty-one hours they came from his tongue without interruption. Then his mouth got dry and hoarseness invaded his throat. The phrase was uttered with an effort. Then he had to resort to whispering in Babe's ear. And finally even his whisper failed him.

The Big Swede had once nearly choked to death after making a high dive into muddy earth, and he had only been saved by copious doses of alcohol. The new oratorical cures were not understandable to him, but he remembered the potency of alcohol in clearing out the throat, so he got up and ran to the camp office, where he found the great carboys of the medicine once highly prized by Johnny Inkslinger. Taking three of them under his arm, the Big Swede returned to the blue ox. He took a huge drink from one of them, and he was again able to go on with the treatment. For a few hours it was only necessary for him to drink once every thirty minutes to drive away the hoarseness, but it resisted stubbornly, and the periods between the drinks grew shorter and shorter. By the time the Big Swede had opened the last carboy of alcohol his brain was addled by the fumes of the liquor, and his heart was softened by its influence until it beat only with sympathy for the blue ox. He forgot what he was to say, and instead of repeating, "You ban well," he began to sigh, over and over, "Poor ol' sick feller. Poor ol' sick feller." Fortunately this horrid perversion of Johnny Inkslinger's idea did not last. The Big Swede's vocal cords finally gave out, the alcohol smothered his will and closed his eyes. He could not resist the fogginess that crept over his brain, and at last he fell over and began to snore.

Babe had lain motionless and silent while the Big Swede was treating him, but when the foreman fell he had knocked over the last carboy of alcohol, and the liquor poured over the nostrils of the blue ox and trickled into his mouth. He groaned, he stirred, his legs quivered. Then he sat up, looking eagerly about for more. He soon spied, through the open door of the office, the glitter of the other containers of liquor. Slowly, painfully, he staggered to his feet. His tongue lolling feverishly, he stumbled towards the office. A desperate swing of his horns crashed in the side of the building, a flirt of his hoofs knocked the tops from the remaining carboys, and in nineteen minutes he had emptied them all. A vat of Epsom salts was cleaned up in seven gulps, barrels of pills and capsules, and cartons of powders were quickly devoured; in half an hour there was nothing left of the old time medicines of Johnny Inkslinger but splinters and broken glass.

Then the alcohol began to surge through the veins of the blue ox. The frisky, exuberant spirit of his healthy days returned. He pranced and sashayed. He lifted his tail and bellowed. His breath came in snorts as he lightly pawed the ground. For a time he was content with such merry gamboling, frolicking and romping about, then he felt a sentimental longing for Paul Bunyan and his mates of the woods, and he started out to find them. But the alcohol mounted to his head, it dimmed his eyes, and he lost the trail. He wandered into the West Desert country and was caught in a terrific rainstorm. He toiled stubbornly on, though his befuddled senses had lost all sense of direction and he sank knee-deep into the desert mud at every step. As he struggled ahead, weaving first to the right, then to the left, then to the right again, water rolled from his back and foamed in cataracts down his dragging tail. A river coursed down the crooked path he left behind him. He grew weak again after he had plowed through the mud for hours and the fever had left his blood. When the storm passed his strength left him and he sought rest on a high plateau.

There Paul Bunyan and the loggers found him, after a three weeks' search which had begun when the Big Swede brought the news of his disappearance. At first the loggers were sure he was dead, and groans of sorrow rose in dismal thunders from the vast host. But Johnny Inkslinger would not give up hope. He had repelled the lure of grand ideas at last, and he had his old medicine case with him now. In a moment he had emptied its store of alcohol and Epsom salts down Babe's throat. In a few minutes the blue ox opened his eyes. The loggers frantically cheered. Babe answered them with a bellow that threw even the loggers on the farthest hills to the ground. Though the blue ox was thin and feeble still, the vitality of health was in his voice again. "He is cured!" said Paul Bunyan.

"He is cured!" shouted the loggers, as they scrambled to their feet.

"Yah," said the Big Swede blissfully.

Johnny Inkslinger alone said nothing. He, too, was cured.

Say the old loggers:

Ever since he took his drunken course through the West Desert a stream has flowed down the crooked trail made by the blue ox. It is called Snake River in all the geographies. The great whale corral is known as Coos Bay. And Babe's unfinished grave has become the islands and waters of Puget Sound. The Cascade Mountains of Washington were made from the dirt thrown up by the loggers and Paul Bunyan when they began to dig the grave, and a bitter dispute still rages regarding the name for the loftiest peak. The loggers and the people of Seattle call it Mt. Bunyan, the people of Tacoma and the Indians cal lit Mt. Tacoma, and the geographers and tourists have named it Mt. Rainier, after the weather, which is rainier there than in any other part of the country.

So say the old loggers.

And loggers are truthful men.

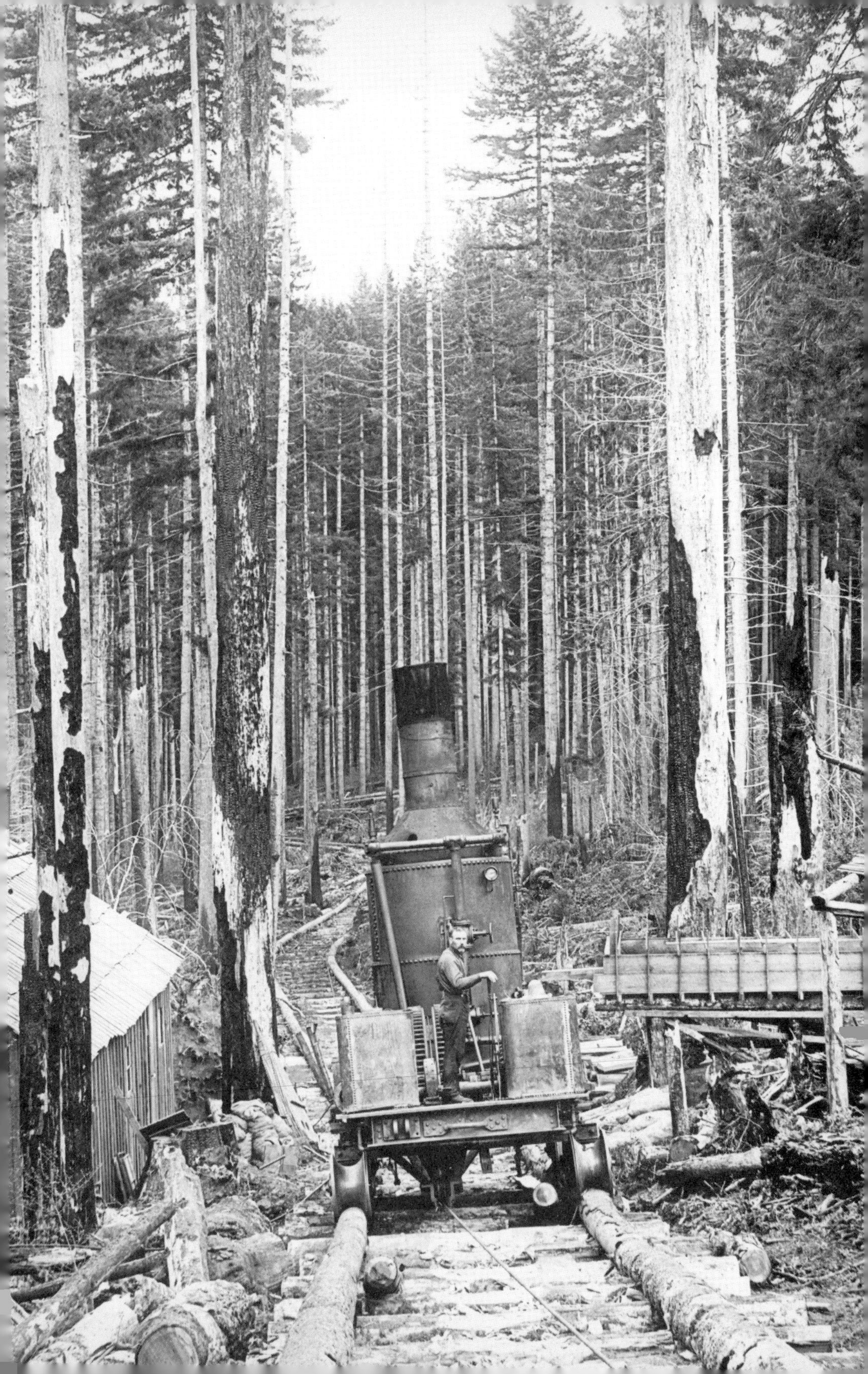

James Stevens and H. L. Davis, 1927.
(200 copies printed)

STATUS RERUM

I

The present condition of literature in the Northwest has been mentioned apologetically too long. Something is wrong with Northwestern literature. It is time people were bestirring themselves to find out what it is.

Other sections of the United States can mention their literature, as a body, with respect. New England, the Middle West, New Mexico and the Southwest, California—each of these has produced a body of writing of which it can be proud. The Northwest—Oregon, Washington, Idaho, Montana—has produced a vast quantity of bilge, so vast, indeed, that the few books which are entitled to respect are totally lost in the general and seemingly interminable avalanche of tripe.

It is time people were seeking the cause of this. Is there something about the climate, or the soil, which inspires people to write tripe? Is there some occult influence, which catches them young, and shapes them to be instruments out of which tripe, and nothing but tripe, may issue?

Influence there certainly is, and shape them it certainly does. Every written work, however contemptible and however trivial it may be, is conceived and wrought to court the approbation of some tribunal. If the tribunal be contemptible, then equally contemptible will be the work which courts it.

And the tribunals are contemptible.

From Salem, Oregon, from the editorial offices of one Col. Hofer, issues, in a monthly periodical somewhat inexplicably called "The Lariat", an agglomeration of doggerel which comprises the most colossal imbecility, the most preposterous bathos, the most superb sublimity of metrical ineptitude, which the patience and perverted taste of man has ever availed to bring between covers. And Col. Hofer encourages it. He battens upon it. Somewhere within the dark recesses of this creature's—we will not say soul, but nebulous sentience—is some monstrous chord which vibrates to these invertebrate twitterings.

In a healthy condition of society, this state of things would be merely funny. As things are, it is not funny. It is deeply tragic. Northwestern poetry, seeking, in the ingenuousness of its youth, some center about which to weave its fabric, has done no less than bind itself in thraldom to Col. Hofer and his astounding magazine, and the results are all too pathetically apparent. Read some of it!

Or contemplate the panorama of emotional indigestion, the incredible conglomeration of unleavened insipidity, spread before your eyes in the works of the Northwest Poetry Society, the begauded pastries of the Seattle "Muse and Mirror", which surfeit without satisfying. Regard the versicles emanating from the poetry classes of Prof. Glenn Hughes, of the University of Washington—a banquet of breath-tablets, persistently and impotently violet! Regard—but enough! "Palms," exotic *frijole* congealing among the firs of Aberdeen, you need not trouble to savor.

II

If this were all, it would be too much. Regrettably, we have still to contemplate a literary influence which has been, if possible, even more degrading. The Northwest has not escaped, any more than other sections of the United States, its share of "naturals," mental weaklings, numskulls, homosexuals, and other victims of mental and moral affliction. Unfortunately, our advanced civilization has neglected to provide an outlet for their feeble and bizarre energies. Yet, many of these unfortunate creatures are unfit even to teach school. What are they to do? In Chicago, the problem would be simple. There, such unfortunates can devote themselves to the services of some gang-leader, and gain a livelihood in the professions of bootlegging, blackmail and murder. In the South, they are privileged to lead active lives as members of the Ku Klux Klan, and appear prominently at nocturnal whipping-parties and Fundamentalist crusades. Such inoffensive and normal employments have, unfortunately, no place in our Northwestern civilization. What, then, are these unfortunates to do? Such puerile faculties as they may chance to possess demand some exercise. To deny it them would be inhumane.

The earliest white colonies of the Northwest, more merciful than we, found them normal employment. The lumber companies of that age availed themselves of the unfortunates of their time, for the purpose of filing upon timber-lands, then in the possession of a too suspicious Government. They were found useful instruments for murdering Chinese laundrymen and tracklaborers, thus establishing the supremacy of the Caucasian race. For hanging Basque and Mexican sheep-herders, and destroying sheep, by theft, poison, firearms, or dynamite, civilization has gained much from their exertions. We do not grudge them their meed of veneration.

But civilization, with impersonal cruelty, has used them and passed on. The agricultural commonwealth has given place to the industrial empire. What can we give our own numskulls, "naturals", homosexuals, and mentally afflicted to do? How can we even rid ourselves of the annoyance of their society? To our industrial leaders, the answer is simple. Put them where they will do no harm. Put them where their imbecility will be congenially occupied. Obviously, they could not be trusted to manufacture rocking-chairs, to pile lumber, to operate donkey-engines, or combined harvesters; to shear sheep, or castrate calves; in the operation of woolen, paper and flour mills, their employment would be a continual jeopardy, not only to themselves, but to the lives of men valuable in the industries which they serve. Fortunately, no doubt, for Northwestern industry, but calamitously for the welfare of Northwestern literature, an employment has been developed which offers the advantages of congeniality and inoffensiveness, without entailing the least risk to the continued prosperity of our factories, so much desired by all. That employment is, briefly, short-story writing.

III

From this cause, from the humane sentiments which desire to find harmless employment for these poor creatures, has come that pullulating institution, the short-story writing class. Teachers were, of course, easily recruited. As chiropractors, prohibition agents, saxophone players, radio announcers, and movie organists, have been seduced from more strenuous walks of life, such as pants-pressing, curve-greasing, track-walking, lumber-piling, tin-roofing, and cascara-barkstripping, by the superior usufructs of a life of authority without backache, so, and from these or similar walks, have been recruited our teachers of short-story writing.

Nor have they succumbed to this seduction without honor. On the head and shoulders of the most eminent apostle of short-story writing, Dean M. Lyle Spenser, have descended, suffocating, the cap and gown of the Presidency of the University of Washington. Candor compels us to add, that President Spencer's rise to eminence was due no less to his leadership of the youthful unfortunates of the State of Washington through the occult mysteries of short-story writing, than to his faithfully sustained administration of the office of Vice-President of the Seattle Chamber of Commerce. President Spencer's career has been aptly expressed in the slogans of the institutions with which he is allied, as follows: "Get the Seattle Spirit;" "Advertise Education;" "Produce Pecuniary Prose."

The University of Oregon can boast of no short-story instructor of the eminent attainments of President M. Lyle Spencer. If Professor W. F. G. Thacher's record includes a term of service as Vice-President of any Chamber of Commerce, we possess no knowledge of the fact. Professor Thacher has, nevertheless, certain individual claims to fame. He has been awarded honorable mention in the list of winners in a Chicago tire-naming contest, in which more than two and one-half million names were submitted. Professor Thacher has offered the fruits of his intellect in other national name and slogan contests, and has won distinction in practically all of them, for the winsomeness and *chic* of his titles. A movement is reported to be on foot among Professor Thacher's more devout disciples, to present him with a gift of 250 engraved calling-cards, bearing his name with the legend, neatly engraved in elegant script, "You Can't Go Wrong with a Thacher Title."

But these are the admirals, so to speak, of the service. To continue the figure, the lower decks offer a spectacle which, in charity, we do not encourage the reader to contemplate. What shall be said of Mme. Mable Holmes Parsons, the illuminatrix of the short-story writing department of the University of Oregon Extension Division? Not for her the Vice-Presidency of the Seattle Chamber of Commerce; not for her parched lips the fragrant moisture of Mention in a Chicago tire-naming contest. For her, only the enfeebled sighs, the emasculate twitterings, of the vapid ladies, trousered and untrousered, the mental unfortunates who inhabit the unstoried corridors in which her dictum runs as law. Hers only to feed her soul, between intervals pathetically wide, upon the empty honor of a kiddie poem in the Sunday Supplement of the Portland Journal. Let us not touch her further. There is enough, ay, more than enough, to engage us elsewhere. Scientists inform us, Nature is an excess. In the field of the short-story classes in the Northwest, surely she has outdone herself.

Shall we descend still further into the recesses? We shall encounter the vertiginous galley in which Pro. Borah, of the University of Washington, concocts his flashy and injurious messes, to dazzle the eyes and ossify the intestines of the hapless intellectual paralytics of his short-story classes. What lies further? The stokehold! Formless shapes there labor and conspire, yearning for greater power to lead victims into the path of error. There bend the leaders of the Y. M. C. A. short-story classes. There toil, in groaning discontent, the teachers of short-story writing in the high schools. What lies further? Shall we look further? Dare we look further? In common pity, no! There is a point at which curiosity ends, and perversion begins. We had almost crossed it. Let us turn our faces away.

IV

Until lately, it was difficult—it was impossible—to have formed the faintest conception of the abysmal degradation into which Northwestern letters had fallen. We had noticed that, when we announced ourselves as practitioners of literature, people regarded us suspiciously, and treated us with a wariness which impressed us as unnecessary. We could not imagine why. We had not seen the Parliament of Letters in Seattle. It included all the Writers' Clubs, all the Poetry Societies. Now, we have seen it. We have seen it all.

We have sat in the gallery of the Parliament of Letters in Seattle, and gazed with dreadful awe upon the tossing sea of puerile and monotonous imbecility raging beneath us. Sterile and barren wave after wave of frustrate insipidity swayed beneath the apostolic trident of their pitiable Neptune, the above-mentioned Col. E. Hofer. As the presiding deity, so were the votaries. What hope that a bright-hued phrase might leap glittering from that desert sea? What hope of any act of reverence for life, for character? What hope of any fruition, except that of selling a plot, conceived in avarice, written in slavish and feeble-witted devotion to the dictates of a porcine mind, squalidly inhabiting the skull of a professor of a short-story writing class? We faced the appalling truth. This, then, was the image upon which the public had formed its impression of Northwestern writers!

But worse than this had to be faced. How many times had some tired Eastern editor, chained to his desk by the necessity of earning his daily bread, cringed from the gruesome monument of driveling manuscript, overshadowing, like some monstrous fungus, the desk which, perhaps, has felt the glory of the writings of such men as Theodore Dreiser, Sinclair Lewis, James Branch Cabell, Robert Frost, Carl Sandburg—men of whom American literature may be proud? How could we, as Northwestern writers, ever again dare to commit our manuscripts to this devastating flood of imbecility? In our innocence, we had done that which the imagination rebelled to contemplate.

V

Our first impulse was to vow abstention from a pursuit which linked us with such posers, parasites, and pismires. Horror at contemplating a spectacle so blasphemous, so mortifying, so licentious, so extravagantly obscene, drove all sense of loyalty, duty and self-sacrifice from our minds. Our own thoughts were washed away in the black flood, and we could only repeat, with the Elizabethian, Webster:

> *"Thou has led me, like a heathen sacrifice,*
> *With music and with fatal yokes of flowers,*
> *To my eternal ruin."*

But it need not be eternal. It lies with us, and with the young and yet unformed spirits, to cleanse the Augean stables which are poisoning the stream of Northwestern literature at the source. Our Hercules has not yet appeared, but hope is surely not lacking. We have had a vision, and we have gained faith boldly to prophesy his coming. We can yet cry, even in this darkest and most hopeless hour, from the mountain tops of vision—

> *"Yet, Freedom, yet thy banner, torn, but flying,*
> *Streams like a thundercloud against the wind!"*

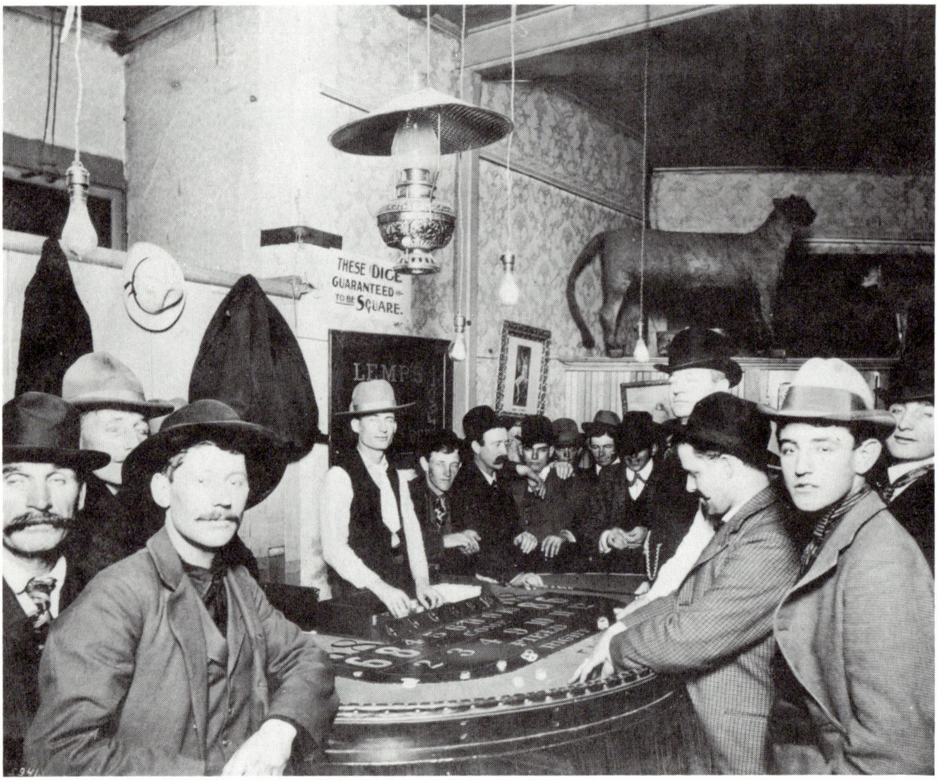
THESE DICE
GUARANTEED
TO BE SQUARE.
LEMP'S

James Stevens

From *HOMER IN THE SAGEBRUSH* (1928)

Three Bartenders

I

The German duke, the English lord and the Swedish professor were talking about poetry. What could be more beautiful than that! thought the tramp poet sadly. He was sad because he yearned to join the conversation and did not dare. For the duke, the lord and the professor were educated, refined and civilized men. They held mixed drinks gracefully in their hands and talked beautifully about poetry. Listening to their speech, the tramp poet felt like nothing but the commonest of hinds. So he was sad, though he had been reading and writing poetry for six months and knew a great deal about it. He was sad, also, because he was eighteen, in love, and going on a journey. The tramp poet did not object to this sadness in himself; he knew it was a necessity in the composition of poetry. He would still be sad, but he would be satisfied, nevertheless, if he could only join the talk of the German duke, the English lord and the Swedish professor. This was the first time the tramp poet had ever heard the speech of educated, refined and civilized men.

The tramp poet did appear a little out of place, dressed as he was in mackinaw and overalls. The scene was the smoking room of a steamship bound down the Coast for San Francisco. Shaded lights glowed softly among huge polished oak pillars, and over heavy oak tables, roomy leather chairs and a floor of black-and-white tile. The men playing cards, drinking and smoking at the tables all appeared excessively well-dressed to the tramp poet. Feeling conspicuous, he had pressed himself into the remotest depths of a great chair. Even when his interest was caught by the three men at the table next to him, he only gazed sidewise at them.

At first none of his face but the eyes showed above the bulge of his big mackinaw collar. As his interest increased in the duke, the lord and the professor, his head slowly emerged and pressed toward the group until he was resting his chin in the palm of his hand, which slanted out from the elbow resting on the thick arm of the leather chair.

The German duke was superb. He was wearing a blue serge coat so smooth yet unbinding on his shoulders it seemed to caress them. The duke's face was rosy and full. Under a round, pink chin was a wing collar. A diamond sparkled in a black necktie. Only a shadow of the duke's mouth was revealed under a mustache with spikes that turned up to flank a wide, stubby nose. Straw-colored hair bristled in a thick pompadour. He would have been a fierce-looking duke, had it not been for the tender glow of his pale-blue eyes as he talked about poetry.

The duke was the star of the group. The lord also talked ardently and at length, in unmistakable English. He was much younger than the duke, and quite handsome, with a devilish dancing light in his gray eyes and a mop of black, curly hair tumbling over them. The Swedish professor had little to say; he forked his hand, rested his chin in it, and hearkened.

Three educated, refined and civilized men, certainly! Sadly and yearningly the tramp poet in mackinaw and overalls drank in their talk. He learned that their names were Adolf, Alf and Carl. He knew, however, that they were a German duke, an English lord and a Swedish professor, because he had read a grand story just a week ago about a French count, an English lord and an Italian professor traveling incognito through America. The story had made him imagine meeting three such educated, refined and civilized aristocrats sometime. And here they were! The reality even more glorious than the imagining. For the tramp poet much preferred Germans and Swedes to French and Italians. If only he might join them! But the tramp poet knew too well that dukes, lords and professors did not talk to young working stiffs in mackinaws and overalls. He could only lean and long across the arm of his leather chair. He could never join that little group, the tramp poet reflected. . . . Ah, little did he think! When the English lord began to talk of Byron, when the John Collinses were brought forth in their tall glasses, when the liquor glowed, when the ice sparkled and the lemon peels smiled. . . .

II

The tramp poet had begun this journey, leaving his love and his land behind, to search for the formless image of his desire. Here, so soon, the light of it was shining on his eyes. The sparkle of a star, the glow of a match—whatever it was, here was glory for the young tramp poet. Regard him for awhile, as he sits there in his rough clothes, yearning toward the three aristocrats, while a little of his story is told. . . .

The tramp poet discovered his talent by accident. It occurred the night he met Effie Sparks at a public dance in Astoria. Effie's mother was a Finn. Her father was an American real-estate dealer. She worked in her father's office, as a stenographer and bookkeeper. The young strapper of a teamster was enchanted when Effie smiled on him at the dance. Never before had he received favors from a girl who was not only a beautiful blonde, but a stenographer, a bookkeeper and a real-estate-dealer's daughter as well. He was in a dazzling daze as he danced with her, as he walked home with her, the moonlight shining upon them through maple leaves, as he kissed her good night. Returning to his boarding house, he thought over and over that her hair was like gold, her eyes were like stars. He could think of nothing else about Effie Sparks. Then the words turned into a song, beating measures through his head—

> Her hair is like gold,
> Her eyes are like stars.

The rhythm roused an unfamiliar impulse in him. It dimmed his memories of Effie in a search for words, for rhymes. The search produced only sounds. He went to sleep that night with one lone verse sounding in his ears, in this form:

> Her hair is like gold,
> Her eyes are like stars.
> Te—tum—te—tum—told—
> Te—tum—te—tum—tars.

Thus the young hobo teamster became a tramp poet.

For weeks he wrestled with phrases and rhymes, attempting to put into poetry his ideas that Effie's cheeks were like roses, her hands like lilies, and her teeth like pearls. He was more successful with Effie than with the muse, but as his ardor for the former diminished his passion for the latter increased. He became a sad, tormented young man.

Then, one fine night he was soothing his soul with beer in the Combination Dancehall, and half-heartedly attempting to catch the eye of a Spanish girl in a green dress. A huge, boozy sailor staggered up to his table and announced that he was the original Wolf Larsen. The curiosity of the tramp poet was aroused. He asked who Wolf Larsen was. The big sailor sneered at the ignorance the query revealed, and swung into a lecture on the great writers of sea stories. The tramp poet was bored, and his looks and thoughts again followed the Spanish girl in the green dress. They continued after her until he heard a rhyme bawled across the table. The sailor had taken a bulky book from the pocket of his storm coat and he was reading rousing passages from its pages. The lines shone and rang for the tramp poet. He forgot the Spanish girl. Here was the kind of poetry, living in the sailor's booming voice, that he had been wanting to write. Suddenly the sailor closed the poetry book, sprang from his chair and stood swaying, resting stiff arms and clenched fists on the table, his eyes blazing through a tangled fringe of black hair. The tramp poet followed his look. Two fishermen were fighting over the Spanish girl in green. The sailor swore, and rolled toward them, bawling that he was the original Wolf Larsen, and threshing the air with his fists. In half a minute twenty men were fighting over the dance-hall floor, swinging fists and feet, smashing tables and chairs. The tramp poet kept his safe place at the corner table until the fight had surged out into the street. Then he noticed that some one was crouching behind him. He turned and looked into the face of the Spanish girl. Her eyes were wide with fright, lovely, dark. The tramp poet saw them still as he slipped out the back way. He hardly knew that he held the sailor's poetry book in his hand. But before he went to sleep that night he had read half of *Don Juan*. Now he was truly a poet. Byronic. Going to sleep to the singing of lines about Spanish love. Seeing the frightened, dark, lovely eyes of a Spanish girl.

This is not a love story. Little more needs to be said about either Effie Sparks or the Spanish girl. From them sprang a poet's first poetic visions and raptures. Let us leave them now and stand with the tramp poet on a steamship ready to leave the Astoria docks.

He was sad, for he was a poet leaving his love and his land. He remembered his boyhood in the sagebrush country of the Northwest, the roving and toil of his later years. A hard and bitter life, but he regarded it with a poetic melancholy now. His loves—the reproaches of Effie Sparks were still keen to his ears; the kisses of the Spanish girl warmed his lips, even now. All that must be regarded with a Byronic melancholy. Lines . . . Where once I roved, a happy child . . . roll on, thou desert hills of sagebrush, roll! . . . on yonder foam-striped strand . . . strange, dark-eyed and pale . . . on with the dance . . . and wilt thou e'er forget . . . ah, the star of my hope has declined.

. . . But a poet should not only lament the past. Here a quest for glory was begun; something rapturous and proud should be sung for the start of the journey. Romantic California was ahead, or,—who could tell?—a wreck, and a haydee discovered on some enchanted isle. . . .

The sunset red and gold turned dark over the sky, lights began to glow dimly in the town, and the timbered hills above the river appeared cool and black. The steamship's whistle roared. Departure was near. It was a poetic hour. The tramp poet thought hard, then he rallied his forces for the first stanza of a poem of farewell:

> I stand on the deck at sundown;
> > The captain rings a bell;
> The engines beat beneath my feet—
> > My love, my land, farewell!

The poet thrilled. So far, splendid! "Regret," he decided, was the word to make noble ending for the second stanza. Again he raised his sword and led a charge.

> A deckhand, he rolls up a rope,
> > While I roll a cigarette.

That attempt ended in a distinct repulse. The lines, after being repeated a few times, certainly sounded flat and dull. But the poet clung stubbornly to his position. "Regret" should be the last word. Surely there were more poetic words than "bet," "wet," "sweat," "debt," and "pet" to rhyme with it. He was wrestling with "forget" when the whistle sounded again and the steamship drifted away from the dock. The creative impulse was stifled by the emotion of departure. The tramp poet could only repeat his first stanza over and over as he stood by the rail and watched distance and the dark slowly blot out the lights of Astoria. . . . The ship started swaying, swung down and up, like a giant hammock. The tramp poet could see nothing but the white splashes of the great rollers of the Columbia River bar. Poetry entirely subsided. The life ahead lost its mask of romance. Its aspect was threatening and dark. The tramp poet remembered that he was a teamster in mackinaw and overalls. He had to live by hard labor. That wherever he might go. What would a great, strange city offer him? What could it want with him? He was leaving his home land, leaving a girl who looked at him with love in her large, dark eyes. Poetry had done this to him, made him dream and perform like a fool. He sighed for consolation. It occurred to him that he might feel better after a cigarette and a bottle of beer. He tramped down the deck toward the smoking room. There he discovered the actuality of poetry and romance, in talk around a table, in appreciative souls, in the glow of a lovely liquor, the sparkle of ice, and the smile of a lemon peel.

III

Let us return to the first picture. The tramp poet in mackinaw and overalls, unconsciously edging his chair toward the table of the German duke, the English lord and the Swedish professor. The three aristocrats pausing in their conversation on poetry to argue mildly concerning mixed drinks. They agreed that the steward did not know how to mix a John Collins. The duke then voiced a preference for Knickerbeins and offered to mix some himself for the next round. The professor spoke a few words in favor of the Morning Glory Fizz. The English lord insisted that a John Collins was the king of all drinks aboard ship; he would show the steward how to mix the next round and prove his point.

The tramp poet enjoyed this mild diversion from the main topic. The three were aristocratic even in their drinking. They lifted the tall John Collins glasses with sureness and grace, they sipped the pale, glowing liquor slowly, and the talk ran smoothly on.

The duke quoted a verse in German. His voice shook with feeling. Then he began to extol the name of Heine, one unfamiliar to the tramp poet. The duke's voice sank to the soft, low tone of sentiment. A girl named Freda had taught him to love Heine. That was in a Bavarian beer garden, long ago. *Ja*, Heine was the greatest of all the lyric poets, excepting Goethe, whose moral tone was so noble and grand. And one must not forget Schiller, whose "Ode to Joy" was by the godlike Beethoven used.

"*Ach*, Freda!" sighed the duke wiping his eyes.

The English lord had been listening, with his head leaned against the back of his chair, his eyes halfclosed, and a superior smile slightly curving his mouth. He spoke, remarking that he had little respect for the literary opinions of a man who allowed them to be influenced by the female company he kept. He had never permitted that himself. Once he had a girl who had a pure passion for the verses of Tennyson. She detested Byron because the noble lord didn't cherish the proper respect for women. Had he let his emotion for this girl influence his literary opinions? Rather not.

"I told her," said the English lord, "that Lord Byron was a flower of English genius matched only by the flaming rose of Shakespeare. She left me without a farewell. I have never seen her since." He drained his glass, gazed sadly into its depths for a moment, sighed, then looked scornfully at the duke. "As for Heine —poo! Too moony. Does a great poet snatch a mere kiss from a girl and then moon over her as a frightened bird? Regard Lord Byron. He thought, lived and died as a hero. He was one in spirit with Casanova and Cellini. Let the girls have their sentimental say over poets like Heine and Shelley. But a self-respecting man can't take seduction so seriously as to allow it to influence his literary opinions."

The tramp poet stared with pity at the duke. He would not have been surprised if the man had sunk to the floor in shame. But the duke was unperturbable. He said, gently, that he was happy to see that his friend had come to his senses at last and admitted that Goethe was greater than Shakespeare. The English lord indignantly retorted that he hadn't done any such damn' thing. The duke responded, gently still, that if one was to judge a poet's work by the number of women he had seduced, Goethe, according to history, surpassed Shakespeare by fifty to two. The lord looked hurt at that and said that everybody was always misunderstanding him. He was not arguing about the relative merits of poets, but on the influence of love on literary judgments. Shakespeare certainly hadn't been influenced in this respect; regard Cleopatra, the realest woman in literature; then regard Goethe's Marguerite, a sentimentalized innocent at the mercy of the devil and wicked men; and was it a passion for reality or sentiment for women that produced the moralizing about the eternal feminine leading us upward and on? Byron's diary, now—

"*Was für ein verdammtes Land ist das?*" growled the duke. "Who can poetry disguss with an Englishman?"

The professor announced that he had a few words to add to the general confusion. He had been thinking of Ibsen. When Ibsen was young and a master of himself among women he had portrayed women truly in *Brand* and *Peer Gynt*; but when he was older, and consequently more sentimental, he portrayed women as persecuted slaves.

The tramp poet was exalted and inspired by the realization that at last he was listening to three educated, refined, and civilized aristocrats conversing in a style that excelled his grandest dreams. They spoke about great books and famous authors as carelessly as a teamster would speak about his horses; they addressed themselves to affairs of art as familiarly as a cowboy would address his steers. They argued the fine points of what was literature with the off-hand assurance of loggers discussing the fine points of felling big trees. The tramp poet was exalted and inspired, but his sadness increased. He was outside the gates. Inside the portals and the walls were lights and banners, songs and wine, the laughter of girls, the twanging of musical strings, the seductive dance. The tramp poet stood alone, a figure in mackinaw and overalls, a figure with a lonely dream and a lonely desire. It was the most poignant hour of his life.

IV

The gates were to open for him, however. His memory was the key. Fortunately for the tramp poet, the English lord, in attempting to recall some Byronic lines, was stuck at the end of the first line of the first stanza. He paused, frowned, and there was silence around the table, a silence that was broken by the voice of the tramp poet. The lines gushed from his mouth as the spring gushed from the rock struck by the staff of Moses. His eyes flashed and his face shone like a rose. His moist hair tumbled over his forehead; in his exaltation he had the feeling that his locks draped a brow as noble as Byron's, and it seemed that his voice was sounding from a golden horn:

> "The isles of Greece, the isles of Greece,
>   Where burning Sapho lived and sung!"

They were listening, too, those three educated, refined and civilized aristocrats! All three leaned toward the tramp poet, their right hands half-closed around their glasses of John Collins. . . .

> "The mountains look on Marathon,
>   And Marathon looks on the sea. . . ."

On and on. Ah, the grand and lordly time! The tramp poet's voice was a thunder of music as he cried, "Dash down yon bowl of Samian wine!" It was heavy and dark with lamentation in the stanza on the Greek girls whose glorious black eyes shone, and this cry was uttered as Byron's own:

"To think such breasts should suckle slaves!"

"Beautiful, by God!" exclaimed the German duke, wiping his eyes.

"Byron!" It was a soft exclamation from the English lord. "There was never a better poet for a man who is young, drunk, in love, and going on a journey."

The Swedish professor nodded and smiled.

"But I am not drunk," said the tramp poet wistfully.

The English lord at once announced that he would immediately mix *four* John Collinses. In half an hour the tramp poet was calling the three aristocrats by their first names—Adolf, Alf and Carl.

V

Beautifully, angelically drunk. And the end was not yet. A glass was shoved into the tramp poet's hand. Pale liquor glowed under his eyes, ice sparkled, and a lemon peel smiled. A keen, cool smell wafted up his nose. He lifted his glass. A slow, cold stream spread over his tongue. It poured down his throat. There it all was again—the fine, fresh flavors inside his mouth, the pleasant cool prickling down his throat, the warm, comfortable glow in his stomach, the rosy haze over his eyes, the delicious swim of heat in his head. Poetry ideas bubbled anew and poetry words bloomed afresh.

But the tramp poet was not in a mood to speak them now. He was content with leaning back in his chair, watching how gloriously hazy-mellow the drift of light and smoke in the big room had become, gazing on the refined, intelligent faces of his three new friends, not trying to make much sense from their speech, simply reveling in it because it was so civilized. The tramp poet was happy to listen now, also, because the conversation had turned to life in San Francisco. It awakened delightful dreams.

All three aristocrats appeared to be familiar with every café, saloon, theater and dance hall in the city. They talked as though they had lived in San Francisco all their years. One minute Alf, the English lord, was telling about the meals he had eaten and the wines he had drunk in twenty different Italian and French restaurants, the next minute Carl, the Swedish professor, was speaking calmly about burlesque and vaudeville in the Barbary Coast dance halls, the singers and dancers in cafés such as the Black Cat, the theaters where one might drink, smoke, and make love to a girl as one watched the show, and the marvelous Market Street theaters where New York shows and society crowds were on view. Then Adolf, the German duke, held forth on the "lofely moosic" which San Francisco had for one's enchantment—the concerts where a man with a soul could listen with a Hedwig, a Clara, a Gertrude, or a Johanna and be lifted to sublimity by the music of Beethoven or Schubert or Haydn. Music, beer and love! *Ach*, San Francisco! Sometimes it was beautiful as Munich!

Ah, San Francisco! There in the steamship smoking room the drunken praises of three of her adorers wrought for the young tramp poet a vision of a rapturous, golden city he could never lose. A poet, young, drunk, in love, and going on a journey. Leaving his love and his land for an impulse, the impulse toward a vague desire. What an adventure now! So beautifully, angelically drunk! Such an hour is the generosity of life.

Every light in the smoking room was glowing then like a rose in the morning sunshine, the other people and tables around were dim in a melow, golden mist, and the tramp poet's chair was a sunny cloud. He could shut his eyes and imagine drowsily that he was floating over fields of flowers, with birds singing about him, and the bluest sky overhead. . . . But it was Lord Alfred singing . . . some sailor's song. The tramp poet blinked his eyes blissfully, smiled rosily, picked up a John Collins glass, winked at the smiling lemon peel, lapped his lips over the rim of the glass, let the cold liquor tingle and spread through his mouth and down his throat, sighed deeper into his chair as his stomach glowed and the beautiful feelings bubbled so sweetly and drowsily in his head. Pretty soon, he thought, he would sing a little song. . . .

The tramp poet knew now why he was going to San Francisco. The gay crowds. The bright pleasures. Theaters. Music. Life had been bitter and hard. A bitter life in the desert sagebrush hills. Hard, hard labor on the ranches, in the camps. He was leaving his land without regret. His love—well, he would always think kindly of his love, as he reveled among the poetic delights of San Francisco. As he reveled there, with his three new friends—his three new friends—a clear, sober thought hauled the tramp poet up. That San Francisco life was for them because they were educated, refined, civilized aristocrats. They tolerated him now, a laborer in mackinaw and overalls, because he could spout Byron, and, being drunk, they enjoyed hearing Byron. In the morning, when they were sober, they would freeze him out. To-morrow he would be a plain laborer again, and that he would be in San Francisco. There he would have to take a common teaming job, perform with other laborers around the beer and redeye joints and in the cribs—but to hell with that! Now was the golden time! Now life was kind, lavish even. As long as it gave, he would receive. . . .

The tramp poet gulped down the cool, flavorish fire of a John Collins and looked for a chance to join in the conversation. He was astonished to see that the duke's head was sagging over the table, the tall glass wabbling in his hand. Tears were dropping from his cheeks into the liquor. The tramp poet was touched. He laid his arm over the duke's shoulder.

"What's the matter, old-timer?" he said.

"*Ach*, mine life!" sobbed the duke, entirely wilting under sympathy. "It a waste, a desert iss—a roon!"

"Well, hell!" the tramp poet exclaimed. "How can that be, Adolf?"

"My life degraded iss," the duke insisted, his voice thick with tears. "When I trink and off moosic sbeak somedimes my sorrow overwhelmss."

The tramp poet attempted to console his friend with facts. When we were drunk, he said, we always imagined that things were either better or worse than they actually were, so we should think only of the good things of life when we were drinking.

"Always forget trouble when you lift the glass," advised the tramp poet.

"Nefer can I forget it!" cried the duke. "Nefer! Would you belief what it iss? Efer since I was a boy in Munich I haf wanted to play the flute in a big orchestra. You will laugh, you who are young and a boet. For you that iss well. You a talent haf. For me, I haf looked no higher than flute-playing—*ach!* what a beautiful life it would be—playing the moosic of Haydn and Handel, of Mozart and Beethoven, so many girls hafing! But now—" Again the duke's voice was choked with emotion—"to haf only the talent to mix Knickerbeins and Bismarcks, to be only a bartender—"

"A *bartender!*" The tramp poet yelled the word. "You don't mean to say that *you* are a bartender?"

The English lord answered him, growling across the table:

"Sure he's a bartender. We're all bartenders. Been taking a vacation up here in the woods. What's the matter with bartenders, I'd like to know?"

"Well, hell!"

The tramp poet could say no more.

VI

Two hours later a cabin door closed between the tramp poet and his three bartender friends. He stood on the deck outside for a minute, listening to Adolf and Carl as they tried to hush Alf's singing:

> "A RO-ving, a RO-ving! Since ro-ving's been my roo-in,
> I'll go no more a ro-ving with you, fair maid!"

The tramp poet yearned to join Alf in bawling out the chorus. But he did not dare. Bawling such songs was why the steward had chased the quartet out of the smoking room.

> "I'll go no more a ro-HO—"

A grunt and a struggle sounded from behind the cabin door. Then Adolf's voice, boozy and thick:

"Gimme towel, Carl. Gag'm towel shuttup."

The tramp poet staggered on along the deck. A confusion of thoughts and feelings were swimming slowly and heavily in his head.

. . . Well, hell. Had to find own cabin now. Here she was—27. Had to roll in. Sleepy. Like to ser'nade beautiful new bartender friends. But they might gag *me* with a towel. Poor li'l Lord Alf, gagged with a towel. They'd never gag this li'l poet with a towel. Nossir. Had to roll in. Sleepy. 27. . . .

Wish damn' ship'd stan' still. Wanna fin' keyhole. Wearin' 'self out tryin' fin' keyhole. Res' minute. Cool off. Wind slappin' off black water, slappin' down deck. Mus'n get sheashick. Goin' make poem. Lessee. Goin' have won'erful idea. Somethin' 'bout life. Life is won'erful. Tha's it. Yessir, life is won'erful. Why is life won'erful? 'Cause common teamster can meet up on Sa' Frisco steamer with ej'cated, refine' civ'liz' bartenders and have one hell of beautiful, angelic time. John Collinses make life won'erful. That was idea. Ev'body have plenty John Collinses ev'body be ej'cated, refine', civilize'. . . .

Good by, ol' Nor'west country, back over black, slappin' water. Farewell, love and land . . . good ol' country—wheat fields, sagebrush desert, canyons, rivers, cattle ranges, sheep trails, mountain roads, headframes, mine dumps, timberlands. . . . All won'erful people—ranchers, religious women, sheep-herders, cowboys, miners, gandy-dancers, longshoremen, loggers, fishermen, sawdust savages, saloon-keepers, gamblers, bartenders, sportin' women, old characters, stories, girls, yessir . . . Effie . . . a Spanish girl in green, with eyes so lovely, so dark . . . feel like cryin' . . . somehow so Go' damn' sad. . . .

Mus' acshuly be drunk. Got to say farewell to love and land now. Good-by, ol' Nor'west country, back over black water. Sleepy. Got to roll in. Here's to you, old-timer. . . . G'night. . . .

Main street, Plush, Oregon.

Ethel Romig Fuller

From *WHITE PEAKS AND GREEN (1928)*

WIND IS A CAT

Wind is a cat
That prowls at night,
Now in a valley,
Now on a height.

Pouncing on houses
Till folks in their beds
Draw all the covers
Over their heads.

It sings to the moon;
It scratches at doors;
It lashes its tail around chimneys
And roars.

It claws at the clouds
Till it fringes their silk;
It laps up the dawn
Like a saucer of milk.

Then chasing the stars
To the tops of the firs,
Curls down for a nap
And purrs, and purrs.

SLIPPERS

When I was young
And my slippers were red
I could kick higher
Than my own head.

When I grew up
And my slippers were white
I could dance the stars
Right out of the night.

Now I am old!
My slippers are black;
I walk to the corner
And I walk back.

WINTER ORCHARD

These apples lying on the ground
Are the wormy and unsound;
Their unblemished brothers hymn
Holiness from every limb.

Yet which is lovelier filigree—
The fallen, or those on the tree?
And where is choice in either lot?
The saints dry up; the sinners rot.

A SONG FOR CHURNING

Churning is music;
Come child, and learn
Old dance steps
From a rhythmic churn.

Come, child, and hear
What the dasher is saying
Of wind in clover,
Of grasses swaying.

Come, make your body
A slim green stem,
Make your arms flowers
With rain on them.

Make leaves of your fingers—
Young leaves a-flutter—
Come, child, and dance
To the splashing of butter.

Vardis Fisher

from *THE ANTELOPE SONNETS* (1927)

Susan Hemp

Her conscience was a cauldron of distrust
    In which she burned her scruples till their red
    Devouring shame had triumphed, and love was dead,
    And all the hunger of her soul was dust.
    With attitudes of scorn she would adjust
    Her days to pallid virtues and a bed
    Of ruins; and when longings rioted,
    To little pious orgies of disgust.
Today she lives alone. Nobody knows
    Of what her mind is thinking any more.
    When winter comes, she wanders forth at night,
    A solitary black in fields of white;
    When April burgeons all the hills, she goes
Into her dark house and she locks the door.

From *TOILERS OF THE HILLS* (1928)

    The place far up on the southern mountain-side belonged to Susan Hemp, the gaunt woman who lived alone and worked like a man, and a mile farther lay the ranch of Jon Weeg. Opal saw a tiny place framed among aspen groves, a small plowed ridge here and another golden with grain there; and rising from trees she saw a cloud of pale smoke. Susan was another of the mysteries here, a lonely being who had come out of a dark uncertain past to hide up there among the trees. Her provisions, Dock had heard, were bought at a mail-order house and delivered in her box by the roadside. She never threshed her grain, but gathered it in sheaves and fed it sheaf by sheaf to her chickens and hogs. Sometimes she raised turkeys, and from a small spring, he had been told, she had built a pond for ducks and geese.

'I've always wanted to see her,' said Opal.

'Well, mebbe some Sunday we'll run up and see her. But she don't like people, I've heared, and like as not she'd as live shoot a man as look at him.'

From *APRIL, A FABLE OF LOVE* (1937)

Susan she had known for years, but not intimately, for this gaunt old maid lived alone and looked at intruders with hate in her eyes. She was queer, most people said, and let it go at that. For June she was one of the strangest persons alive, regarding men, as she did, with the loathing of cats for dogs and keeping a gun above her door. This she threatened to turn on the first pair of overalls that came in sight. There was something very dark and buried in Susan's life, June reflected, taking her way down a long slope: a bitter unhappiness that had turned to gall. There was a wolf under any man's skin, Susan had declared. "The sons-of-bitches, don't talk to me about them!"

And Susan had a sardonic sense of humor. She gave to her animals, even to the males, the names of women. Her gelding was called Polly and her boar was called Bridget. Her roosters and her drake were Dora and Agnes and Blanche. Agnes, she had once explained to June, meant chaste, and she had laughed a bitter laugh. But stranger still, in June's mind, was Susan's behavior toward children: she called them dirty little snooping geeks and she jumped at them as if full of murder. And once of the photograph of a boy in a magazine she had said: "He'll be a flirt when he grows up. You'n see it in his eyes. I wouldn't trust him as far as you'n throw a bull by its horns. He'll be a Mormon bishop, likely as not. . . ." And strange, too, was her hatred of the clothes of men. Many girls in Antelope wore overalls and when Susan saw them dressed in such fashion she was terrible in her wrath. . . .

. . . Every old maid whom June had known was a little terrible to look at and think about.

And she wondered what kind she would be: fat or lean, stupid or mad. Susan's shack was in sight now, roofed with slabs and earth; and a little way south was a slab barn with a pile of manure at its door; and near it was a small pond where the ducks slept. Under some leafless aspens, killed long ago by smoke from the house, were a hand plow, an old harrow with wooden teeth, a shabby old drill. Everything here was very quiet, save the flow of wind in a white sheet that hung from a line. No smoke came from the house and there was no sign of life within but June knew that Susan was there, brooding in shuttered gloom. Inside the barn she saw Polly and his lean mate, standing in patient hunger before an empty manger. On the pond was Blanche with his harem, sitting with heads against their wings.

She knocked softly on the door. She waited and listened, and knocked again. A voice that seemed paralyzed with rage cried:

"Who are you?"

"It's June Weeg."

"Well, why don't you come in?"

June turned the broken knob and entered. She saw nothing at first, for the shades were drawn; and she smelled the odor of mice mixed with the fragrance of wild flowers. She saw the flowers in a jar on the table and went to them and Susan watched her with unfriendly eyes. June wanted to raise the shades but dared not: in summertime Susan kept the shades down, her shack darkened, but when autumn came and the loneliness of death was upon the earth, she kept the shades up and her door ajar much of the time.

"It is sure beautiful today," June said, looking at the flowers.

Susan grunted and went over and framed herself in the doorway. "Beautiful?" she said. "Flowers and trees and sky. Soon the flowers will be dead and the trees naked. Soon——"

"Oh, but it's lovely now. Millions of flowers, millions of trees. The sound of water and wind, the song of birds all over the hills ——"

"But what of it?" asked Susan. She shrugged. "Birds and their one silly little song. Flowers, lazy, soon dead. That sky."

"But it's lovely when fall comes too. Then the trees are red and yellow and the earth smells like a clean, faraway fire. And all the leaves under your feet. And in winter——"

"But you can't eat beauty, can you? Can a person live on beauty?"

"I could—almost."

"You're a fool," said Susan, turning to look at her. "I guess you'd need beans, too, and biscuits. I never could see why you make so much fuss about beauty."

"Maybe it's because I'm so homely myself."

"I guess," Susan admitted, and looked again at the world.

"Susan, tell me something. Will you?"

"As like as not I won't."

"Were you ever in love?"

"Beauty," said Susan, "is all right to look at. It sort of rests the eyes. But that sky, what use is it? Them there trees: they make good stovewood and that's about all."

"Susan, were you?"

"Were I what?" asked Susan impatiently.

"Ever in love?"

"Come out here," said Susan. "I want to show you a thing."

Susan crossed the yard and June followed, remembering that Susan's eyes were the color of granite, and just as cold. She went past the pond and down a little hill where she threw her old cans and other refuse; and there, in the pile of ugliness, were wild flowers, growing among the cans and out of the filth.

"If you think beauty is so much, then why does it grow in such places as that?"

"Well——" said June.

Susan laughed. "You can't answer that, can you? Nobody can."

"But that's just it, Susan. In spite of all we do to make things ugly——"

"Come here," said Susan. She went up the hill and stopped by an old galvanized tub that was bottom side up. She kicked the tub over; and there, under it, looking very fresh and green, was wild grass that had been growing without sunlight. "There's more of what you call beauty. You can't eat it. You can't wear it. And without you kick the tub over you can't even see it."

"You're funny. And besides, you haven't answered my question."

"Sure, I answered it. You're just too dumb to understand."

"Oh," said June, realizing now that this strange woman had been answering her with fables.

"And as for love," Susan went on, "what of it? You're as bad as Sol Incham. He's always talkun about love. The homely old fool. He thinks he loves the whole world."

"I think he does. He seems to."

"He pretends to. And I guess you'll marry him."

"Oh, I guess I won't."

"And I guess you will. Women marry the fools if they keep hanging around. And he's been hanging around you for years."

"No, Susan, I'm going to be an old maid like you."

"Oh, the hell you are. Listen, you little fool. There's old maids by choice and there's old maids by necessity. A woman who turned men down, she isn't an old maid. Don't ever think it."

"Well, I'll be a real old maid. I'll be the most real old maid on earth."

"But you could marry. Sol, I mean."

"Oh—Sol!"

"He's a man," said Susan. "They're all alike behind their beard."

"Susan, tell me: honest, weren't you ever in love?"

"No!"

"Not even once?"

"Never."

"I think you're a liar," June said. "I think you're a big monstrous liar."

"Oh, do you?" Susan smiled faintly. "You're the liar, June Weeg. You intend to marry that homely old fool. And you know it."

"I certainly will not."

"I say you will." And suddenly this strange woman did a strange thing. She swung and grasped June's shoulders in her large hands and looked searchingly into her eyes. Then, with a swift powerful blow, she slapped June's face. "You lie!" she cried. "You lie like a house afire!" And while June was still lost in amazement, Susan turned and entered her house and slammed the door.

June turned homeward up the mountain and sat in a grove blown off, but there was no movement, no sound. The whole shack was blind, with the door and the shades drawn against love and the sun.

* * * * * * *

And while telling herself that she would be a harlot as sure as fate, she came to Susan's door and knocked. She pushed the door open and went in.

"Hello, you old maid. Another old maid has come to visit you."

"Oh-ho!" cried Susan. "I guess Sol has jilted you."

"No, Miss Hemp. I came to tell you about William Wallace Argyll. Only an hour ago I was proposed to by Mr. Argyll, a college graduate and a poet."

"Do tell."

"And I spurned him."

"Oh, what a lie!"

"I said, sir, you presume."

"My God, I'n imagine that!"

"And he went down on his knees just like Reginald Montrose in *Lucretia's Strange Wedding*. He said, 'June, I love you! I adore you! You're the sun and moon and stars of my existence, my breath and life——' "

"What a liar you are!"

"He said, 'June, I can never live without you. Your beauty is tendrils around my heart and your name is song in all my thoughts. Darling,' he said, 'marry me and I'll devote my life to your happiness. I'll love you, love you, worlds without end. I adore your fingers and toes, your sweet mouth, your eyes, your hair, the ground you stand on, the bed you sleep in, the dish you eat out of!' And," said June, making a face at Susan, "I spurned him."

"You awful liar," said Susan, staring in amazement.

"I said, 'Mr Argyll, for a woman like me you're nobody at all. I have observed the growth of your infatuation and have been distressed.' I said, 'A woman does not like to refuse a man and send him to whiskey and ruin but I have discouraged your advances——' "

"June, you're the biggest liar in Antelope!"

"I said, 'I discouraged you and you persisted. You have bored me to death. And really,' I said, 'you look pretty silly, kneeling there in the leaves——' "

"In the leaves!" cried Susan, and choked with scornful laughter.

" 'Mr Argyll,' I said, 'get on your feet———' "

"Oh, didn't you! I say shut up!"

" 'Wipe the tears off your cheeks,' I said———"

"Oh, in God's name!"

" 'And next time,' I said, choose a woman of your own social rank. For I am Miss April of Idaho Drouth and Antelope Dust.' "

"Antelope dust, sure enough!"

"Miss Hemp, do you know I'm going to be an actress?"

"Oh, I'n imagine."

"I'll do the funny parts."

"You'll live right here. You'll marry Sol."

"Like hell and high water I will!"

"You'll marry Sol," said Susan, watching her shrewdly. "You'll have a lot of kids."

"Like this—and this—and this," said June, measuring their heights. "And a big one like this—and a little one like this."

"Sure, you'll have twelve like Maggie Oakley and you'll live on relief. Roosevelt will feed you and you'll all vote for him."

"Oh, how lovely!"

"And your old man will be a gin-toper like the other men on relief."

"Oh, sweet-sweet!"

"And then you'll start havun twins."

"Litters, darling."

"And they'll tax me to death to feed your brats."

"Listen, why don't you marry Sol yourself?"

"Me?" said Susan, rising in astonishment. "You fool!"

"Why don't you?"

"Listen, you can't come and insult me like that!"

"Insult you?"

"Get out now and be on your way!"

"But listen———"

"Go on, scat out of here! You damn snoop. . . ."

June backed away and Susan followed, her big hard face dark with fury. Then June fled. Upon looking back, she saw Susan in the yard, towering there like a threat and a curse. Why this strange woman always flew into a tantrum over Sol, June had never known until this moment and she was filled with compassion and pity. She went homeward, thinking of this strange woman and her unaccountable ways. Well, for herself, too, there must come a time when, like Susan, she would sit around and make faces at everything.

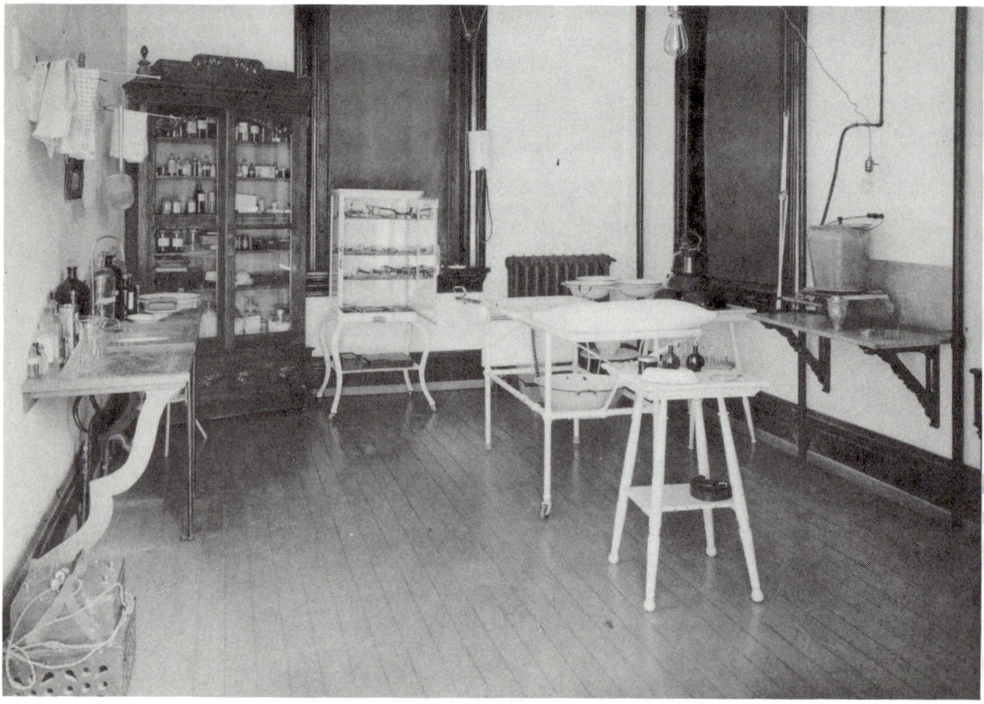

Ben Hur Lampman

from HOW COULD I BE FORGETTING (1933)

He Was a Country Doctor

For almost forty years Dr. Otis Dole Butler practiced medicine in the little city of Independence, Oregon—the town that was his birthplace. There he held the keys of life and death, in so far as any mortal may hold them, and in all ways was an honor to the privileged and important post that was his. For he was a country doctor. This would be the best of epitaphs to carve on his stone. That he died in harness, and through one of the hazards of his calling, lends a sort of humble splendor—if it were needed—to the passing of this unpretentious friend of man.

Dr. Butler was the son of an early and respected Oregon family, and his educational progress found its milestones in the public schools of Polk county, Christian college at Monmouth, and the old Willamette Medical college in Portland. He had practiced in Independence since 1887. Will those novelists who write of the futility of life in country towns, of the lost endeavor of men who serve in country towns, give a glance to the pages of this record? Not they. For how could they comprehend that one might love his neighbor so greatly as to spend the better part of a lifetime in a country town, ministering to mothers in childbirth, contending against cruel and insidious epidemics, soothing and smoothing the inevitable decline of age, sharing each joy and sorrow of that small community—and sharing sorrow in far greater proportion than joy? Main street—and here a friend that had been returned from the very borders of death, and there a smiling girl whose life, in infancy, had been given back to her by the country doctor. Thus, wherever he might look were those who had called to him for aid and comfort and healing when they had somehow lost a grip on life.

We are aware that the country doctor has been upbraided by his fellow practitioners of the city for an alleged failure to keep stride with medical, surgical and scientific advance. Though the indictment does not apply to the late Dr. Butler, his life is its most fitting answer. It may be doubted that any city doctor knows the gruelling toil of a country practice, or is quite so tired at times as country doctors are. It may be doubted that he knows what it is to make the best of adverse circumstances, over which he has no possible control; to pick up the challenge and to fight with terrible earnestness against defeat made probable by lack of those appliances and remedies for which the city doctor has but to beckon. Each is a friend to humanity, and in such friendship there can be no important gradations, yet one thinks that country doctors have ever the sterner battle in fields more barren.

This good man, Dr. Butler, practiced in Independence long before the time of highways and of automobiles. He knew the penetrating drift of the rain storm, the shrewd fingers of the sleet, the swollen stream, the all but impassable roads, the bridge that was down, the gale of snow—and the high and terrible urgency that drove him on even as he drove the floundering, weary team. He knew the night ride, the terrified pounding at the door, the lantern on the porch, the long miles ahead. One thinks that the country doctor was and is a hero of sorts, and that figures less noble than his have been cast in bronze and set up for the homage of the race. A casual, unconsidered, friendly, available and modest hero— quite literally the humanitarian who lived in a house by the side of the road and was a friend to man.

It would be a fine epitaph for Dr. Otis Dole Butler. "He was a country doctor." It compresses the code of a most exacting service, and there is a ring to the words like the tone of a trumpet.

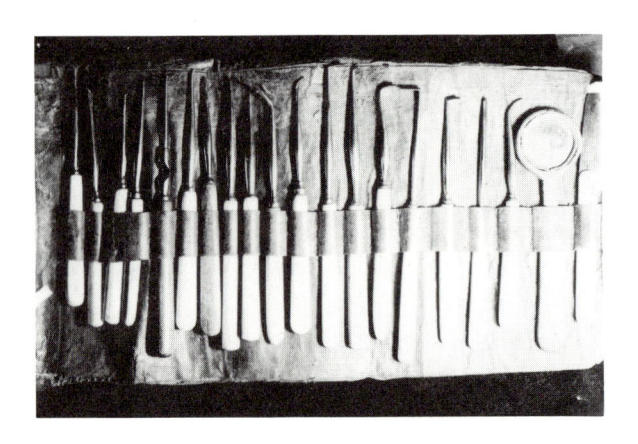

This is the introduction to, <u>Ten of Woody Guthrie's Songs</u>, Book One, dated April 3rd, 1945. We have included "Grand Coolee Dam" elsewhere.

In these ten songs you will hear a lot of music of a lot of races. Songs of every color. Every people loves and copies the songs and the music, the ideas, the customs, of all the other races.

Songs like these soak into every wall, hall, factory, every hull of every ship, every hammer coming down on every anvil, every seed falling down into every row, every hand moving with a dust rag, a wheel, a lever, a dial, a handle, a button pushed.

If you will listen to yourself while you do your work you will hear yourself hum and sing your own song about your own life. You are making up a folk song. You have really made up a whole ballad. If you take the time to write down all of these whirling words and tunes in your own mind about the folks that you know you would be famous as a composer.

I have never heard a nation of people sing an editorial out of a paper. A man sings about the little things that help him or hurt his people and he sings of what has got to be done to fix this world like it ought to be. These songs are singing history. History is being sung. I have sung them in several hundred Union Halls and not one single time have I seen them fail. People clap and yell, get hot and sweat, unloosen their collars, and sing on for hours.

Our ships are manned by men of all tongues and colors and I saw the whole world there before my eyes while I sang to the men a dozen spells a day, between working hours washing dishes. No matter who you are or where you're from, no matter what your color or your language, you will taste, hear, see and feel an old spark of your whole life somewhere in these songs. Cubans, Mexicans, Philipinos, Chinese, Scotch, Irish, Russian, French and German, all have told me, "This sounds exactly like it is in my country." These songs are a world mixture. The tunes and the words have been sung across all of the oceans by all of us, and up out of the past dark centuries.

I have walked and listened to these songs in the Tennesee Valley and heard versions on top of Pike's Peak and along the Columbia River. But I did not hear any of them on the radio. I did not hear any of them in the movie house. I did not hear a single ounce of our history being sung on the nickel juke box. The Big Boys don't want to hear our history of blood, sweat, work, and tears, of slums, bad housing, diseases, big blisters or big callouses, nor about our fight to have unions and free speech and a family of nations. But the people want to hear about all of these things in every possible way. The playboys and the playgals don't work to make our history plain to us nor to point out to us which road to travel next. They hire out to hide our history from us and to point toward every earthly stumbling block.

Hollywood songs don't last. Broadway songs are sprayed with hundreds of thousands of dollars to get them sprouted and going. They sprout, they burst, they bloom and they fade. Wagon loads of your good money are shoveled and scattered onto them, but they are not our true history and we don't take them deep into our heart.

The monopoly on music pays a few pet writers to go screwy trying to write and rewrite the same old notes under the same old formulas and the same old patterns. The songs have no guts. They sound sissified, timid, the spinning dreams of a bunch of neurotic screwballs. How can they be otherwise when they have no connection with the work and the fight of the whole human race? They are bad. They are hurtful, poisonous, complacent, distracting, full of jerky headaches and jangled nerves. I have seen soldiers and sailors on ships sail these insane records over into the water by the dozens. I have heard fighting men in war zones scream and demand that the gibbery radio be shut off or it would be smashed.

Several million skulls have been cracked while our human race has worked and fought its way up to be union. Do the big bands and the orgasm gals sing a single solitary thing about that? No. Not a croak. Our spirit of work and sacrifice they cannot sing about because their brain is bought and paid for by the big Money Boys who won and control them and who hate our world union. They hate our real songs, our fight songs, our work songs, our union songs, because these are the Light of Truth and the mind of the racketeer cannot face our Light. I woud not care so much how they choose to waste their own personal lives but it is your money that they are using to hide your own history from you and to make your future a worse one. Some day you will have a voice in how all of your money is spent and then your songs will have some meaning. The British Government and the Soviets were forced to take over all of these things and their songs, records, and programs are a thousand times better, they had to milk out all traces of complacency, sissiness, cowardliness, and tendencies to run and hide, or to turn into a nation of jerks. They took away all racial hatred, racial teasing, racial insults, racial jokes that were narrow and shallow, and it has been for the good of their people. They sing of the dignity of the work of the people and no racketeer cashes in on foney sexual fits. Workers smile and work and soldiers smile and fight, with no rattle brained mouth frothers to wreck your nerves.

THE BIGGEST THING

This is a Bible Story sort of brought up to streamline. It's told like a big tall tale but I'll stand for the truth of it. I'll meet any living person in a public debate at high noon on the green grass of Union Square to prove that it is nothing but pure unwatered goldplated facts. Never do I stretch the facts even a smillionth of an inch. I tell you how a man jumped up across the ocean and I guess you know him well, his name is Adolph Hitler, we'll burn his soul in hell. This world is digging Slavery's grave and when this work is done that will be the biggest thing that man has ever done.

GRAND COOLEE DAM If you ever want to build a house or light up a town, or bring the people power, the secret is this: Sing about your people, not about your millionaire play folks. The rich ones hired airplanes full of entertainers and stars to come up to Oregon, Washington, Montana and Wyoming and tell the people that they didn't need no Coolee Dam at all, that is, not for the next couple of centuries. Take too much work and materials and would make the wheels run entirely too nice and light up the country entirely too bright. The world didn't need no more houses with electricity in them, no more factory towns singing with light metals and aluminum, no more flying fortresses zipping through the clouds. Then I sung another little song to sort of put these airplane loads of fonies back in their place.

THIS LAND IS MADE FOR YOU AND ME
After we built the Coolee Dam we had to sell the people out there a lot of bonds to get the money to buy the copper wire and high lines and pay a whole big bunch of people at work and I don't know what all. We called them Public Utility Bonds, just about like a War Bond, same thing. (And a lot of politicians told the folks not to buy them but we sold them anyhow). The main idea about this song is, you think about these Eight words all the rest of your life and they'll come a bubbling up into Eighty Jillion all Union. Try it and see. THIS LAND IS MADE FOR YOU AND ME.

HARD TRAVELING
This is a song about the hard traveling of the working people, not the moonstruck mystic traveling of the professional vacationists. Song about a man that has rode the flat wheelers, kicked up cinders, dumped the red hot slag, hit the hard rock tunneling, hard harvesting, the hard rock jail, looking for a woman that's hard to find.

JACKHAMMER JOHN
I guess I went by a million names and nobody knows me yet. And I don't guess I even know my own self yet. Maybe I don't know my own country here yet. I danced my duck on the Whippachuck and skippered the blue canoe. I outworked old Paul Bunyan and six of his blue babe oxes. I can knock down more rock with my jackhammer in ten minutes than old Pecos Bill can by riding a cyclone to a dead stop. I hired out up here on this Saint Lawerence Seaway just lately and I ain't seen nobody around here that can turn out half as much work with both hands as I can with one. My name's Jackhammer John and I say we need more seaways, more shipways, more skyways, shiptrails and barge lines, more loading ports and more hands at work around here. My old jackhammer runs white hot to win this war and to kill fascism, but she runs a lot hotter to build this old world back up again. Gonna be a mighty nice old world to look at when we all get to working together on her.

BED ON YOUR FLOOR I sing this song mainly just to make you think that I had a little run in with a man and had to lay him dead down on the floor, that the sheriff's on my trail with his big forty-four, that the clock's striking midnight with daylight to go. But the mainest reason why I'm singing it is just to get to lay my head in a bed on your floor.

TALKING BLUES Me walking. Me a talking. Out of my way folks this is me. Just me just me. You don't have to tell me who I am, I already know it's me. I know you're liking it and it's tickling me smack smooth to death.

EAST TEXAS RED is a tale that I heard riding the freights and bumming around down along the Southeast Texas Gulf. Story of a man that thinks (or thought) like a fascist, I mean like a bully, or something super drooper. He thought he could push other folks around or sock them in jail if they sassed him back. He had the power to make a work slave out of you just for speaking your mind in front of him. He thought that no human brain was supposed to operate except his own. He caused hundreds and thousands of men, women, kids to worry, to wonder, to walk the long walk, to bow down their heads and cry. Red and men like him have been a part of an old wore out slave system in a lot of states, actually giving him the power of a Nazi Storm Trooper. This song will show you that East Texas Red didn't get his business fixed.

DON'T LIE TO ME Song about a family that worked on the railroad. Built the railroad. Killed by the railroad. Never did ride the nice big easy coach nor drive the big engine on account of a disease called Jim Crow. A disease as bad if not worse than the cancer. But now we're fighting a war to kill every trace of this plague called White (or any other color) Supremacy. Jim Crow and Fascism are one and the same vine. And this song will be sung by me and by you a thousand years after fascism is killed, this song we'll sing the first thing in the morning of our new union world. I know. I know because I just happen to be the daddy of all of this whole big family of nations. A song about a family by the big fast railroad that always whistled on past them. You will sing this story like this was your family because this song will go to show you that we are all in the same big family. I got some awful wise children. They'll build some awful fast railroads in the air.

> Woody Guthrie

FASCISM FOUGHT INDOORS AND OUT GOOD & BAD WEATHER

FACES AND PLACES AND PEOPLE

April 26, 1946

    I almost believe that I have seen as many faces and places as any of us
    Forty-six of these forty-eight, Mexico, Canada, towns, cities, farms and villages, Africa, Sicily, freight trains and ship convoys, and the British Isles
    And I walked and rode low enough and slow enough to see the people and even to hear them talk
    And even to stop and talk to them and to live and sing and work and eat with them
    And this was before I heard about the people as a word
    I had not heard any word that I could speak and bring all of you back into my mind again
    But everytime I met and talked and sung with a new stranger I did think back over most of the others and maybe all of them
    I just did not know that I was thinking about all of you
    But this hard and easy traveling does give me my right to guess at what the people are
    A right to try to say all of you
    A right to hear and to see and to sing all of you
    The same as every work hand earns the right to write his page
    I wish that you would write your page so I could read it and think about you even plainer than I can today here by my fifth ocean
    And my house here is the house already of my second wife and my fifth child
    But I feel other wives and other children
    The same as I feel other peoples and other skin colors everywhere
    I can look out across this eastern ocean and see my dried up farm blowed away
    And my dried sands here show me pictures of my green and growing farms and my going towns

And my window glass here is full of your faces and eyes of all of you that I owe a debt for helping me and teaching me as you met up with me down your road there

These are days and nights of memories and I'm not an old man yet only thirty four years old and worried medium

Worried to hear some of you sing songs and speak words that are too smooth and too peaceful when I see no smooth place and when I see no peace

The people have been hit

The people have been beat up and gassed and bombed and bruised and dragged away to your jail

The people have been falsely arrested and falser tried in your court

The people have been celled away and salted down and jailed apart from their helpers

The people have been framed up on and squeezed down on

The people have been cheated, held back, kept in ignorance and in the dark places

The people have been kept too idle and have been robbed with high prices and low wages and even by long hours

The people have given you padded seats and cars and rooms and the people have been kept in shacks and holes not clean enough for animals

The people have been treated worse than wild animals

The people have tried to love as they see love but their love is changed by their owners into an insane nightmare of hot fear

The people are better poets and singers than I am

The people know this

FACES AND PLACES AND PEOPLE
By Woody Guthrie
© Copyright 1979 by WOODY GUTHRIE PUBLICATIONS Inc.
All Rights Reserved   Used by Permission

Grades 3 and 4, Brownsville.

Builders of the Lowell Bridge.

Dad and Pearlie and Dad's Engine.

HIT THAT OREGON LINE

I been a grubbin' on a little farm
On them flat an' windy plains;
I been a listenin' to them hungry cattle bawl;
I'm gonna pack my sad belongin's
I'm a gonna strike that west'rd road;
I'm gonna hit that Oregon trail this comin' fall.

I'm a gonna hit that Oregon Trail this comin' fall;
I'm gonna hit that Oregon Trail this comin' fall;
Where th' good rains falls a plenty,
Where th' crops an' orch'rds grows
I'm a gonna hit that Oregon Trail this comin' fall.

Well, my land is dry an' cracklin',
An' my chickens they're a cacklin',
'Cause th' dirt an' dust is gettin' in their craws;
They been a layin' hard boil'd eggs;
I got to bust 'em with a sledge;
I'm a gonna hit that Oregon Trail this comin' fall.

Now, my good ole hoss is bony,
Yes, he's dry an' hungry, too;
You c'n see his ribs three quarters of a mile;
Throw my kids up on his back,
Both th' bay hoss an' th' black,
An' we'll hit that Oregon Trail this comin' fall.

Now, my wife gits sort of ailin'
When that mean ole dust gets sailin'
An' she wishes f'r th' days beyond recall;
If we work hard there's a future
In that North Pacific Land;
So, we'll hit that Oregon Trail this comin' fall.

HIT THAT OREGON LINE
By Woody Guthrie
© Copyright 1979 by WOODY GUTHRIE PUBLICATIONS Inc.
All Rights Reserved   Used by Permission

No196 HUG POINT CANNON BEACH ECOLA ORE.

Since worn away by waves, 1942.

THE SONG OF THE GRAND COULEE DAM

Way up that Northwest land of the Skies,
Columbia River's head waters rise;
    Mountain to Mountain all covered with snows,
    I'll follow that River wherever she goes.

Winter and summer, springtime and fall,
She makes her way down her high canyon wall;
    Bright rippling waters, sparkling so bright,
    Seldom you see such a beautiful sight.

It's ninety two miles north west of Spokane,
There you will see her Grand Coulee Dam;
    Woodwork and steel, and cement and sand,
    Biggest thing built by the hand of a Man.

Power that sings, boys, turbines that whine,
Waters back up to the Canadian Line;
    Four hundred miles of waters will stand
    400 miles of waters will stand
    Rich farms will come from hot desert sand.

Waters will flow with the greatest of ease
A hundred miles west, boys, and a hundred miles east;
    Factories that work for Old Uncle Sam
    Run on the Power from Grand Coulee Dam.

Ships on the ocean, ships in the skies,
Inch after inch her waters will rise,
    High Lines will top your mountains and hills,
    Driving your shops, and factories, and mills.

Niagra Falls sends mist to the sky,
But Grand Coulee Dam is just twice as high;
    She's 4300 crost her top,
    5 hundred and 50 down to her rock.

I'll settle this land, boys, and work like a Man,
I'll water my crops from Grand Coulee Dam;
    Grand Coulee Dam, Boys, Grand Coulee Dam,
    Biggest thing built by the hand of a man.

BIG GRAND COOLEE DAM

Recorded by ASCH Records
U.S. Dept. Interior
Bonneville Power Administration
Portland, Oregon

Well the world has seven wonders that the travelers always tell
Some gardens and some flowers I guess you know them well
But now the greatest wonder is in Uncle Sam's fair land
It's that king Columbia River and that Big Grand Coolee Dam!
    She heads up the Canadian Rockies where the rippling
        waters glide
    Comes rumbling down her canyon to meet that salty tide
Of that wide Pacific Ocean where the sun sets in the west
In that Big Grand Coolee country the land I love the best.
    She winds down her granite canyon and she bends
        across the lea
    Like a silver running stallion down her seaway
        to the sea
    Cast your eyes upon the greatest thing yet built by
        human hands
    On that king Columbia River it's that
        Big Grand Coolee Dam.
        In that misty crystal glitter of her wild and
            windward spray
        We carved a mighty history of the sacrifices made
        She ripped our boats to splinters but she gave us
            dreams dream
        Of the day the Coolee Dam would cross that wild
            and wasted stream
We all took up this challenge in the year of thirty-three
For the farmer and the factory and all of you and me
We said, roll along Columbia, you can ramble to your sea
But river while you're rambling you can do a little work for me!

Now in Washington and Oregon you hear the factories hum
Making chrome and making manganese and light aluminum
    And you see a flying fortress wing her way for
    freedom land
Spawned up on that king Columbia by that
    Big Grand Coolee Dam.

GONNA BRING WATER

Oh, my good Lord's gonna bring water;
    Yes, my good Lord's gonna bring water;
    Soak my ground down good an' deep;
    Wife an' kids can peaceful sleep;
    Work in that harvest when we reap;
'Cause my good Lord's gonna bring water after a while.

It's my travelin's gonna take me yonder;
    It's my travelin's gonna take me yonder;
    Take me 'crost these mineral sands;
    Take me 'round them mountain bends;
    Set my feet on a piece of land;
It's my travelin's gonna take me yonder after a while.

It's my hard work's gonna give my heart ease;
    It's my hard work's gonna give my soul ease;
        I just love to bend my back
        On my own little Forty Acre tract;
        Place I own, yes, that's a fact;
It's my hard work's gonna ease me after a while.

This TVA dam's a gonna give me power;
    This TVA dam's a gonna give me power;
        Big ice box with 'lectric light;
        Make my nights all pretty an' bright;
        Turn on my light in my barn all night;
TVA's a gonna give me power after a while.

GONNA BRING WATER
By Woody Guthrie
© Copyright 1979 by WOODY GUTHRIE PUBLICATIONS Inc.
All Rights Reserved   Used by Permission

WASHINGTON TALKING BLUES

Long about 1929
Owned a little farm, was a doin just fine;
Raised a little row crop, raised some wheat,
Sold it over at the county seat,
      Drawed the money. Raised a family.

But the Dust come along, and the price went down,
Didn't have the money when the bank come around;
Tumble weeds and the black dust blowed,
So we hit the trail to the land where the waters flowed.
      Way out across yonder somewheres.

Well, the hot old rocks and the desert sand
Made my mind run back to the dust bowl land,
But my hopes was high and we rolled along
To the Columbia River up in Washington.
      Lots of good rain. Little piece of land. Grow something.

We settled down on some cut over land
Pulled up brush and the stumps by hand
Hot sun burnt up my first crop of wheat
And the river down the canyon just 500 feet.
      Might as well to been 50 miles. Couldn't get no water.

We loaded our belongings and we lit out for town
Seen the old vacant houses and farms all around
And folks a leaving out, if you're asking me
That's as lonesome a sight as a feller can see.
      Good land. Grow anything you plant if you can get the
      moisture.

I struck a lumber town and heard the big saw sing,
And when business is good, why lumber's king;
I went to lookin' for a job but the man said no
So we hit the skids on the old Skid Row.
      Traipsing up and down. Chasing a bite to eat. Kids hungry.

Heard about a job, so we hit the wheat
Made about enough for the kids to eat,
Picked in the cherries, gathered in the fruit,
Hops, peaches, and the apples, too.
    Slept in just about everything except a bed.

Been to Arizona, been to California, too,
Found the people was plenty but the jobs was few;
Well maybe it's like the feller said,
When they ain't enough work, well, business is dead.
    Ailin'. No money a changin' hands. Folks wastin' gasoline
    a chasin around.

Now what we need is a great big dam
To throw a lot of water out acrost that land,
People could work and the stuff would grow
And you could wave goodbye to the old Skid Row.
    Work hard. Raise all kinds of stuff. Kids, too.
              Take it easy.

        WASHINGTON TALKING BLUES
              By Woody Guthrie
© Copyright 1979 by WOODY GUTHRIE PUBLICATIONS Inc.
All Rights Reserved   Used by Permission

I'M ALWAYS ON THE GO

> This and
> Pretty Polly
> 12-16-'40

I have rambled all around
In and out of every town
From east to west, from coast to coast,
I'm always on the go, boys,
I'm always on the go...
>   I rode the rails and limited mails
>   Sun and rain and wind and hail
>   I'm rough and tough and rowdy-oh,
>   I'm always on the go, boys,
>   I'm always on the go.

I been to Pocatella Idaho,
Chicago and Buffalo,
Down to the Gulf of Mexico,
And out to Californi-o,
>   I seen the Mississippi flow
>   The Hudson river and the Ohio
>   The silver Coloradio
>   And the Golden Sacramento.

From Monroe Louisianio—
To Burmingham Alabamio—
And Phoenix Arizonio—
And good old Hot Springs Arkansaw
I'm always on the go, boys,
I'm always on the go.
>   I love Atlanta Georgio
>   And good old Carolinio
>   The big high Rocky Mountains-oh,
>   And the hills of Pennsylvanio...

I'll fight and die to make my home
The U.S.A. of Americo—
But I want to look it over so
I'm always on the go, boys,
I'm always on the go . . .

Well I guess the main reason Pipe Smoking Time fired me was on account of I done just what they told me to do and it was no good. It didn't make me feel none too good because it sounded like too much war—so what I done wasn't good—so I'm broke again. I feel natural but just ain't satisfied.
  (Note in Woody Guthrie's handwriting on the song manuscript)

I'M ALWAYS ON THE GO
By Woody Guthrie
© Copyright 1979 by WOODY GUTHRIE PUBLICATIONS Inc.
All Rights Reserved   Used by Permission

PORTLAND TOWN

A standin' down in Portland Town one day;
I was a standin' down in Portland Town one day;
I was a standin' down in Portland Town one day;
And it's Hay, Hay, Hay, Hay!

I come from Louisiana where the Red Fish in the bay;
I come from Louisiana where the Red Fish in the bay;
Lord, I come from Louisiana where the Red Fish in the Bay;
And it was Hay, Hay, Hay, Hay!

I said, Which a way does Columbia River run?
I said, Which a way does Columbia River run?
I says, a Which a way does Columbia River run?
From the Canadian Rockies to the ocean of the Settin Sun.

I walk down th' road and I see your Bonneville Dam;
I walk down th' road and I see your Bonneville Dam;
Walk th' rocky road and I see your Bonneville Dam;
'Lectricity run th' fact'ry makin' airplanes for Uncle Sam.

Well how many rivers have you got in Portland Town?
I said, How many rivers have you got in Portland Town?
I said, How many rivers have you got in Portland Town?
They said, The Columbia river is the river that they all run down.

Oh, Columbia River, takes 'em all to the ocean blue;
That Columbia River takes 'em all to the ocean blue;
That Columbia River takes 'em all to the ocean blue;
Snake, Hood, Willamette, Yakima, and th' Klickitat, too.

I'm a ramblin' man, and I ramble all the time;
I'm a ramblin' man, and I ramble all the time;
I'm a ramblin' man, and I ramble all the time;
But every good man has got to ramble when it comes his time.

I'm out of work, ain't a workin, ain't got a dime;
I said, I'm out of work, ain't a workin, ain't got a dime;
Yes, I'm out of work, ain't a workin, ain't got a dime;
But a hard workin man gets it down and out some time.

Well when I seen that great big Bonneville Dam;
It was when I seen that great big Bonneville Dam;
Yes, when I seen that great big Bonneville Dam;
Well I wish't I's a workin' makin' somethin' like a natural man.

I had a job last year, but I ain't had a good job since,
I had a job last year, but I ain't had a good job since,
I had a job last year, but I ain't had a good job since,
I'll get a job along the River just for Uncle Sam's Defense.

I never took relief, but I need relief right now;
I never took relief, but I need relief right now;
I never took relief, but I need relief right now;
But me an' th' River's gonna roll along somehow.

PORTLAND TOWN
By Woody Guthrie
© Copyright 1979 by WOODY GUTHRIE PUBLICATIONS Inc.
All Rights Reserved   Used by Permission

STATE LINE TO SKID ROW

Woody Guthrie

This piece was first published in *Common Ground*, Autumn, 1942. It is part of the novel, *Boomchasers*.

There's a whole big army of us rambling workers—call us migrants. Hundreds of thousands of people fighting against all kinds of odds to keep their little families sticking together; trickling along the highways and railroad tracks; living in dirty little shack towns, hunkered down along the malaria creeks, squatting in the wind of the dust-blown plains, and stranded like wild herds of cattle out across the blistered deserts.

A whole army of us. It's a big country. But we can take it. We can sing you songs so full of hard traveling and hard sweating and hard fighting you'll get big clear blisters in the palms of both your hands just listening to us....

From Kingman, Arizona, to Barstow, California, is a long hot stretch. But it's not what you'd call empty. If you ease across over it in an airplane or a smooth-running V-8, you're apt to look out across this old rocky crackled country and not see very much. A little handful of people kneeling in the shade of a high, square road sign, maybe; another scattered bunch sticking around in the slick-off brown rocks or in the little snatch of shade under a desert cactus of some kind. And, if you're not pretty careful when you look, the people, the rocks, and hot weather will just sort of blur past your eye and all you'll see is a sign with a picture of a right pretty girl, grinning like an ape, with her head leaning back against a green cushion, and words painted up beside her saying: Next Time Try the Train.

I'd been walking the shoulder of this highway for four or five miles with my guitar slung across my back, and come up to a place where two families was setting around this sign. Quick as I got within earshot, one of the men, just about as dusty as I was, hollered out, "Hey, boy! Come over here and play that thing!" He was a sandy-headed man, with light skin and freckles popping out on him about the color of little pancakes. I got up in the shade of the sign board, and a lady with her back turned to me said, "Don't rush the boy. Maybe he's too hot and tired to play."

"Sing?" somebody asked me.

"Oh, make a racket," I said back to them.

"Yer jest a tellin' a big 'un," said another lady with an old gray, sweat-soaked, Western hat pulled down over her head. "I don't know, but I bet my last bottom dollar you can sing. I don't know how good—but you're from sommers down in my country, an' just about ever'body down in there can sing er play er do both. Most all of 'em had to sell their music boxes sommers along the road fer gas, fer eats, fer medicine; but since you hung onto your'n so far, all this ways, 'y granny, you ain'ta tellin' me you cain't sing... no, siree!"

I was sort of curious looking around. You could see all their bed clothes was faded and whipped pretty thin, patched a dozen times, and the old cloth rotting away from the new patch. They had a string of old skinned-up pots and pans, smeary black with soot. Their dresses was homemade, out of cotton, with hot skin shining through. One or two was on their knees to fix up a bite to eat; the others sat around on beer cases and got shooed off when the cooks needed to get something in them.

I set down cross-legged and run my thumb across my guitar strings.

"G string's a shade loose," the sandy-headed man told me.

"Beat the guitar, do you?" I looked over at him.

"Naw," he told me, "not no more." And he held up his left, hand—three fingers gone, only a thumb and a front finger left, and the rest just a slick whitelooking scar. "But I was a ear player to start with. An' I still yet got ears; still yet like to listen."

His wife or some lady goosed him in the ribs and told him, "If you're such a good listener, then you just rear back on that beer case an' listen. Go on, young man, sing." He quited down.

I got in D, played the tune, then dropped into chording and singing:

> *She's my curly-headed baby;*
> *Use to set on daddy's knee;*
> *She's my curly-headed baby,*
> *More than all this world to me.*

*I'm gonna tell you 'bout these women;
Yes I'm gonna tell you 'bout what they'll do;
Hang their head upon your shoulder,
Flirt around with another, too.*

*I'd ruther to be in some dark holler,
Where the sun refused to shine,
Than to see you with another
When you promised you'd be mine.*

"Well, well," a lady said, "outside of runnin' us women folks down, that's a awful nice piece."

"Mighty pretty. You'd ought to sing another'n now to run the women up. Here, eat this sow bosom and cold biscuit: it'll make you big an' fat."

I laid the sandwich down handy and said, "Okay, here's one that's about real—what I mean real—women":

*Well, John Henry hammered in the mountain;
Handle of his hammer strikin' fire;
He worked so hard that he broke his poor back,
And he laid down his hammer and he died, Lord God,
Yes, he laid down his hammer and he died.*

*Now John Henry had a little woman;
And her name was little Polly Ann.
When John Henry took sick and he had to go to bed,
Polly Ann drove steel like a man, Lord God,
Polly Ann drove steel like a man.*

Everybody scraped around a little and said, "Man, take a woman like that an' you got a woman!" "Yep sir, 'y gad, git some work done if ever'body was that a way." "You mean, if you can find the work."

After another hunk of salty pork, dry bread, hot onion, and a few more songs, I decided to be easing on down the road. I thanked them and stood looking at their old seedy car. Two of the men folks walked over and asked, "Think she'll take us to where we're a goin'?"

I said back, "'Cordin' to where you're headed."

The oldest man sort of looked, first at me and then at the car, then down the bending road and said, "California's about all we know."

"Hear she's a hell of a hell of a big place," I said.

"Yeah got them there mean dep'ties."

"Well, you might make it, 'cause that's it you can see right in through yonder."

"Yeah, but that's the burnt-up part," he told me, "an we's sort of hopin' to git to the green part."

I guess there was looks on all of our faces that asked questions.

As I started to mosey off, I thought about something I'd forgot to tell them, and I turned around and hollered, "Hey, folks, if you wanta keep your dishes an' skillets an' stuff clean, just use this here hot sand like it was hot dish water. Family told me about it yesterday. Works pretty good. . . . Hope to run onto you again, somewhere in California."

"If you ever get hungry out around Stockton, just drop in on my cousin, Lem Hawks. He'll put you up, long's you knock him off plenty of them kind of songs—just mention my name!" one man yelled after me.

"Okay," I told him back over my shoulder. "I been hungry so long I'm used to it." . . .

I walked out onto the highway. I knew how their faces looked out of their eyes, knew without looking back anymore. I just kept plugging ahead.

It was hot, with a kind of heat you can't argue with—you feel so little out there on the face of that rambling desert you just walk along trying to invent something to think of to make you feel tough —like no matter how hot it gets, you can walk it; other folks have walked it, drug it in covered wagons, and are dragging out acrost it now, in jalopies, wrecked cars, and afoot, and they're not dying out there; they're laughing, talking, and singing songs out there; they're finding out how tough they are, how much heat, cold, how much starving they can stand and still fight back. There ain't no kind of an ism that can kill the people, or even hold them down, as long as they know this.

I remember I picked up a last year's license tag and hitched it onto my belt where it would hang down behind and show all the drivers I had some kind of a right to be walking down that highway. Carloads of people drove by, slowed up a little and tooted their horns, laughed and cracked jokes, waved their hand at me. I sauntered along picking out little tunes on my guitar, dirty and hot, but having just a hell of a lot more fun than most of the folks that passed me up.

I'd sing to myself:

> *Won't you roll on, buddy;*
> *Don't you roll so slow.*
> *Tell me, how can I roll,*
> *When my wheel won't go?*

After walking three or four miles, I set myself down on a concrete culvert and watched the fast ones whiz by. The sun was so hot it made me sleepy. I got up and followed a little sandy creek bed about a half a mile, winding out into the desert.

Here's where I run onto a big, brandnew highway, crowded full of traffic, thick as it could stick, and nobody getting run over, nobody driving drunk and killing anybody. It was an ant highway, and from the looks of the crowds on the road, I figured there must be some sort of a big ant job, ant land rush, ant building boom, or new ant crop busted loose somewhere. So many ants trying to run the road they had to have traffic cops, road gangs fixing it up every few feet, foremen, straw bosses, and some ants around just to give out road maps and information as to where the work was. It was a 6 or 8 lane highway, and a lot safer than old 91.

Going out, every single ant stayed over onto his right-hand side, and every ant headed back toward the den was loaded down with a big fuzzy seed of some kind, his clinchers socked into the sides of that seed, holding ten or fifteen times his own weight way up in the air above his head, wiggling his feelers out in front, and running about 50 or 60 ant miles an hour. I wondered how long a haul they was making; so I tracked the road about a city block, wishing the people along the real highways could just get going and think up this much work to do together. The ant road was about as wide as your hand, and it ducked around under the hard sticker weeds and back into the shady spots close to the roots of the sticker bushes. No wrecks that I seen, but it made me hold my breath several times when a big fast one, redder than the rest, darker colored and huskier, would hit a clear stretch, throw her into overdrive and come wheeling down the road, catching a little traffic lull, throw out his feelers, tap his cushion air brakes a little, and ease his speed down to a slow idling gait, then catch his chance again and dart around the slow ones, in and out, just like a bad driver on a two-lane highway where careless drivers kill so many people.

I wondered where they was hauling all the groceries in from, and found the road ended at the foot of a desert shrub about as high as your head and ten foot around. I shook the limbs, and it was dry and brittle enough for the seeds to fall down all over everywhere; and you'd ought to seen the cops along the road signal one another to tell the main den to send out more haulers because there was more seeds on the ground.

I trailed the road back from the bush to the den. It was one of the busiest boom towns I'd ever hit: every single worker had a job; and it was a rare sight for several reasons—one to see cops that showed you where work was, but funnier to see bosses and politicians working. Maybe it was for ant defense—everything was wheeling and dealing; it was like a schoolhouse education. They'd dug five or six more extra holes around the main gate or city square, and—well, I got sleepy and rolled out on some hot sand, hanging my clothes up on the limbs of a old tree. Thought I'd soak up a couple or three inches of good, fresh Arizona sun. I drifted off to sleep thinking, maybe there's a Hitler ant den around here somewheres, hijacking other ants, making them work for low wages—

When I woke up, the sun was just barely out of sight over the west ridge. It was cold, and a chilly wind was drifting down the draw. When I moved my muscles, I had the sunburn all right, and ten years from now will still have traces of it. I walked over to the big ant highway, and it was empty, not a single ant on it, just as blank as the desert. The early night wind was whipping the loose sand and rotten twigs and leaves across it. The seeds under the bush were all gone, not a one left wasted. It was a lonesome feeling, almost made you think about the rambling crop hands; they'd worked, and moved on, and before morning their tracks would be whipped out by the wind and all covered over with rotten leaves and twigs. Everybody gone to chase down some more work....

This was the longest stretch I ever walked. The clear nights are the cold nights on the desert; there's no fog or low clouds to hold the heat down onto the earth. The moon was pale as a scared girl; and choppy hills, rims of the badland canyons, looked all sorts of funny shapes and colors. Cars passed, but not many, and nobody seemed to see my thumb in the dark. I didn't care much. Big trucks wobbled past, and I could see sleepy drivers, coffee heads, nodding under the steering wheels. Signs stuck on the windshield said: No Riders. I thought it might as well be: No Driver. I walked eight miles, glad to be there by myself, all by my lonesome, but sometimes a little shivery thinking about the hungry cougars, mama mountain lions, wild dogs, mad dogs, bob cats, rattlesnakes, gila monsters, and other deadly varmints trying to make a honest living on the face of this bald spot. But then, the ants had showed me the desert's not crazy.

I was tired out, sore and blistered from sleeping in the sun, and crawled off to lay down at the side of the road and grab a little shuteye. But the ground was too cold and I was too hot; and snakes, tarantulas, lizards, children of the earth, are always out looking for a good warm bedfeller to roll up with if the price is right; and I just couldn't go off to sleep. So I got up and walked nine more miles, making seventeen for this stretch. Then I looked down the road and seen a little splash of neon light and figured I'd make it in the next ten or fifteen minutes. I walked a couple of more hours, and then I remembered: the law of distance, time, space, and gravity ain't been voted in as law on the desert yet.

A big truck plowed up behind me, slowed down to a snail crawl, and the pusher yelled, "Run! C'mon! Cain't stop! Pile in!" I wrastled my guitar up onto the high fender, clumb over a spare tire as big as a Ferris wheel, and fell into the cab with my feet slung out across a tool box that was more than a load for most trucks. There in the dark the little lights on the dashboard looked like gauges on a defense factory; the gear shift levers and brake controls like young clumps of trees jumping up. The driver had on an all-leather helmet, and wool-lined, fur-trimmed goggles like a bomber pilot, and a heavy oily coat, and clumsy driving gloves. He pulled gears with three hands, and got me to help him for the first three miles.

I could see his mouth fly open and talk, but I couldn't make out what he said, so I just wiggled my mouth back at him, and he started smiling and looking satisfiied. When a truck driver like this looks sideways at you and frowns his face all up, that means pull out your guitar and sing him a song. You can yell your guts out, but all you'll hear will be the groan of that big Diesel engine. He let the clutch in and started coasting down a little flat slope, and it got quieter, and he said, "Gotta let you out about a mile this side of them lights yonder! 'Fraid of spotters! Company snitches! Keep on singing!" Then, when he let me out, he said, "Well, here you are. Ain't but a step down to that java joint. Thanks for the singing. Couldn't hear a damn word of it, but you looked like you was trying. Just wanted to see you try! I like to keep fellers at work!"

I stopped in at the feedmill, and the heat felt so good I decided to hang out there all night. People dropped in all along, and I started to play and sing to pick up a few nickels to eat on, but the boss lady with a tough brown skin hushed me up every time: "No noise tonight. Got a man that's gotta work; gotta get his sleep in." Five or six sets of local people, miners, ranchers, little farmers, young cowboys with their girls, dropped in and drank lots of hot coffee, pushed down apple pie, burgers, and cold beer; and two or three started to hand me a nickel or a dime to sing for them. But the lady with the tough brown skin would sort of look over at us just such a way as to keep me from making the nickel, without hurting the customer's feelings.

But just after sun-up, the lady and me heard a husky alarm clock ringing in the back room of the place, and she slid a big stack of wheats, two thick hunks of homemade sausage, and a cup of coffee down the counter, and says, "Man's up. You'll need this under your hide to do much walking today. . . . When you get it down, you can play and sing me your best song."

I sung her one of my best:

Well, I'll pawn you my wagon,
And I'll pawn you my team;
I'll pawn you my big diamond ring.
  If that train runs right,
  See my woman Saturday night;
  'Cause I'm 900 miles from my home!
  . . . . and I hate to hear that lonesome whistle blow!

Oh, that train that I ride on,
She's a hundred coaches long;
And her engine is like a cannon ball!
  If that train's on time,
  I'll see that little woman of mine;
  'Cause I'm 900 miles from my home!
  . . . . you can hear that whistle blow a hundred miles!

Yes, I'm walking down this track,
I got tears in my eyes,
Trying to read a letter from my home;
  I'm a stranger where I roam;
  Not a soul knows my name;
  And I'm tired of living this a way!
  . . . . there's that long, lonesome train whistlin' down!

The lady listened with her elbow resting on the counter and her hand on her cheek. We both nodded, said some little something about thank you, so long; and when I got out along the edge of the road, I heard her man saying, "Singin' ain't bad at all to get up on of a morning."

The sun got warmer, and I was a couple of miles around the bend, walking along looking at the wild canyons, and sort of wondering how many families of folks was caught and stranded in this place. I soaked in the morning air, as there was an oversupply of it, and the sun was hitting me warm across the back. I kicked at loose rocks, thumped chords on my rattle box; and all at once an old model touring car, 19 Zero model, big and ugly, with an old flapping canvas top, three men in the front seat, picked me up. When they said they was headed across as far as Barstow, I slunk down into the back seat and felt good all over. Told jokes. Stories. Tall tales.

They was from somewhere, going somewhere else. So was I. That was enough to know about each other.

From Barstow to San Bernardino to Los Angeles to everyhere, I set my hat on the back of my head and strolled from town to town with my guitar slung over my shoulder. I sung along a lot of boweries, back streets, and Skid Rows. I sung on Reno Avenue in Oklahoma City, and Community Camp and Hooversville, on the flea-bit rim of the City's garbage dump; in the city jail in Denver, in Raton and Dodge City; the jury table in Santa Fe, lower Pike Street in Seattle and Superior Street in Duluth; the saloons in Tia Juana, Juarez, Ensenada, and Baja California, where there are just about two musicians for every tourist and each Mexican plays a whole tree-full of instruments. I played, too, in the little camps called "Little Mexicos" on the dirty edge of California's pretty green places, where the Mexicans treated me like I was a member of the family.

I sung long tales and ballads for the railroad gangs on the Texas plains, the road workers along the border, the truck patchers in Colorado, New Mexico, and across Arizona; in the orchards of hungry people and rotten, wasted crops in California. In Portland I sung for a lot of ship scalers, inland boatmen, and timber workers; and in Reno for some playfolks and fading romances, and made better tips but landed in the city can for vagrancy. I hit Chicago on a wild cattle train from Minneapolis and sung in a dozen saloons along the Skid across the street from the big packing-houses, with the Swedes, the Slavs, Russians, Norwegians, Irish, Negroes. It looked like everybody leaned on everybody's shoulder, and the songs and tunes didn't have any race or color much, because what's right for a man anywhere is right for you wherever you are. Buffalo, Erie, around the edge of the Great Lakes, across over to Milwaukee, I found the same thing. Factory workers in New York and munition makers in Hartford, Connecticut, said, "Songs that say what's wrong say what's right; and songs that tell you how to fix what's wrong, that's what we all say."

Around the East Coast, I sung on the gravel barges, tug boats, anchor bars, and hotel lobbies, and along the New York Bowery, watching cops chase the bay-rum drinkers. I curved along the Gulf of Mexico and sung with the tars, oilers, tanker men in Port Arthur; grease men and oil workers in Texas City; and the marijuana smokers in the floptown in Houston. I sung in the coal towns in Virginia and in Kentucky's tobacco patches, the iron towns in Pennsylvania, including the crowbar hotel in Mifflintown; from the freight yards in Chicago to the blackrust wheat fields in North and South Dakota. In the pool halls and clip joints in Phoenix, Siloam Springs and Gravette, Arkansaw; in the Street of the Walking Death, the silicosis death that blows off the high piles of shale and slag from the lead and zinc mines in the tri-state country— the corner of Oklahoma, Arkansaw, and Missouri. . . .

Yes, there's a whole big army of us rambling workers, call us migrants, out milling around, doing a lot of nothing much. But farmers everywhere are crying for work hands, and we got the hands and are crying to do the work. We'll go anywhere. We been everywhere. You'll see us tonight, and we'll be 300 miles before the morning gets bright. Show us the work; we'll show you how to get it done.

Show us your wasted cherry crops in Washington; show us your peaches falling on the ground in California; just trot us out an oil field that needs overhauling, a string of 200-pound boilers to make fire; lope a railroad out across here anywhere and we'll drive ten jillion iron spikes in it running sixty miles an hour. Show us where you got your work hid out; bring your jobs out in the open: it's legal, you don't have to bootleg work. Where's them big bridges you want slung across your mean rivers? That TVA and Grand Coulee Dam and the Boulder are pretty fair starters, but now you just throw this rock across the river here to show us where you want some bigger dams built.

Take us down into your deep lead, zinc, coal, copper mines, aluminum deposits; give us the general idea of where you want a tunnel drove; point out across the forty-eight states where the roads are too little and the cars are too big and folks go too fast and get killed; mark a line here in the mud and give us a handful of dredges, mud shovels, and just plain old hand shovels, and get out of the way for us to build a canal. Throw us your red hot rivets; we was the champ workers where we come from. Who wants me to sling an airplane together? How about a whole flock of bombers to fly around over your ships on the ocean?

I come to work. I'm a hard man from a hard place, and I come down a hard road. I know all of the words there is, cuss words to work with, all kinds of words to sing with, and words to talk to my wife in the dark with.

Yes, guess I'm what you'd call a migrant worker. Guess you had to think up some kind of a name for me. I travel, yes, if that's what you mean in your redtape and your scary offices; but you can just call me any old word you want to. You just set and call off a whole book full of names, but let me be out on my job while you're doing the calling. That a way, we can save time and money and get more work turned out.

I ain't nothing much but a guy walking along. You can't hardly pick me out in a big crowd, I look so much like everybody else. Streets. Parks. Big places. I travel. Hell, yes, I travel. Ain't you glad I travel and work? If I was to stop, you'd have to up and leave your job and start traveling, because there's a hell of a lot of traveling that's got to be done. Oil booms, timber booms, land booms, housing booms, gold booms, coal, lead, zinc, steel, iron, canal booms; big dam jobs; and damn big jobs; fruit, vegetables, cotton, cattle, logs, hogs, bulls, bears, buffaloes, tanker ships, whalers, frieghters to ride herd on.

I ain't got nothing against you for living in your pretty house, just so long as you don't hire your cops or thugs to come along and beat me up. You and me can get along. We got to get along. You'd like me if I knew you better. You just ain't got no plan fixed up to keep me at work, and you can't figure out what makes me a tramp.

Tramp, that's a good name. Sorta come to like it. Means you travel and go places. Hell, don't a railroad engineer travel? Don't 10 million folks float around in them boats and travel? Don't the sun, moon, and seeds travel? Ain't traveling good? Ain't traveling honest? I seen salesmen and drummers travel; soldiers, sailors, street cars travel; when you work in your office you travel. If you do your own work around your house, you travel; birds, snakes, lizards, geese, and fish travel. Coffee travels, and tea. Rubber bounces across the ocean and rolls all over the roads. Tanks travel. Bombers and bombs travel. Hand grenades don't do much sleeping. Bullets don't mope along. Poison gas goes a long ways to kill people you're saving pictures of. MacArthur is traveling. The *Normandie* traveled, and she'll travel again.

> *I been havin' some hard travelin',*
> *I thought you knowed.*
> *I been havin' some hard travelin'*
> *Way down the road.*
> *I been havin' some hard gravellin',*
> *Hard ramblin', hard gamblin',*
> *I been havin' some hard travelin', Lord.*
>
> *I been ridin' them fast rattlers,*
> *I thought you knowed.*
> *I been a ridin' them flat wheelers*

Way down the road.
I been ridin' them blind passengers,
Dead enders, kickin' up cinders,
I been havin' some hard travelin', Lord.

I been a layin' in a hard rock jail,
I thought you knowed.
I been a layin' out ninety days,
Way down the road.
Mean old judge he says to me,
Ninety days for vagrancy,
I been havin' some hard travelin', Lord.

I been hittin' some hard rock minin',
I thought you knowed.
I been leanin' on a pressure drill
Way down the road.
Hammer flyin', air hose suckin'
Six foot of mud an' I sure been a muckin',
I been havin' some hard travelin', Lord.

I been hittin' some hard harvestin',
I thought you knowed.
North Dakota to the Rio Grande,
Way down the road.
Pickin' them crops, stackin' that hay,
Tryin' to make about a dollar a day.
I been havin' some hard travelin', Lord.

I been a workin' your Pittsburgh steel,
I thought you knowed.
I been dumpin' your red-hot slag
Way down the road.
I been a blastin', I been a firin',
I been a pourin' red hot iron,
I been havin' some hard travelin', Lord. . . .

I'm what you call not a shade-tree tester, not a mattress presser. I'm a feller made out of something pretty damn rough and tough, and Hitler's a shade sorry I am so tough. I'm a migratory worker, and I been all around these forty-eight states. I saw you work, saw you eat the stuff I harvested. Did you see me in your crops? I saw you, saw your house there, saw your mail box the way you got it fixed up.

We're gonna win out. We talk the same lingo.

Richard L. Neuberger

from OUR PROMISED LAND (1938)

Across the plains and over the Rockies they come—the Americans whose farms in the Dust Bowl are no more.

It is the most significant westward migration since the covered wagons of the old pioneers creaked on the Oregon Trail. Practically two hundred thousand people, their rural homes ruined by the fiery blasts of 100 degrees of searing heat, have crossed the continental divide and driven down into the uplands and valleys of the Pacific seaboard. More thousands are still coming. Other thousands are yet to come. So many nomads have not paraded consecutively into the Far West since the line of rail locked the country from coast to coast.

"Drive out on any of the main highways of our State," Senator Borah of Idaho said one sunny afternoon, "and you will see cars, sometimes almost caravans, fleeing from the devastations of the drought."

The venerable Senator predicted that soon the hegira of the wandering Dust Bowl refugees would attain amazing proportions, involving millions of people. He got out of his big armchair and walked to the window of his Boise hotel suite. He pointed to the gaunt hills in the distance. "The importance of the present migration cannot be overestimated," he said. "The Americans now coming West seek to colonize and develop this vast region of ours."

It is no romantic fiction that Middle Westerners dispossessed by the drought are invading the sundown seaboard. Felix Belair, covering the dust storms and heat spells for the New York *Times*, wrote, "Farmers with their possessions and families loaded into trucks that normally would be carrying a second crop of hay were headed West to Oregon, Washington, and Idaho."

The Resettlement Administration dipped into a limited budget and printed *Suggestions to Prospective Settlers in Idaho, Washington, and Oregon*. Thousands of families have read this information. They have been families seeking a new start in life—families fifteen hundred miles from their abandoned homes and still on the search for a place to live. Over every highway between the plains and the coast, drive people who do not know how long it will be before they sleep again with their own roof over their heads. From rusty rods hang the dust-splattered license plates of Oklahoma, Arkansas, Kansas, Colorado, Iowa, and the Dakotas.

There have been sporadic westward treks before. Intermittently, large groups of people from the Central States have set out for the coast. The present pilgrimage is different. It is sustained and continuous. Real and tangible reasons justify it. Thousands of farmers have been scorched off their acres in the Dust Bowl. Other thousands watched their farms blows away in great billows of topsoil that shrouded the land for days. What more natural and logical than for these people to head toward the nation's last frontier?

The Far West is thoroughly conscious and aware of what is happening. Placards in wayside emporiums announce, "We cater to drought refugees." Everywhere along the route the wanderers stop to ask questions, particularly about the water. Concern over weather conditions and water is practically a mania with them. "Is there plenty of rain?" they ask intently. People on the main highways hear that question from sunrise to sundown. A grocer in a little town in Idaho finally hung a sign in the window of his store:

NOT ENOUGH RAIN HERE. IRRIGATION O.K. THOUGH!

In a village a hundred miles west of Spokane, a druggist tacked a neatly lettered sign to his wall beside a picture of the President:

SURE YOU'RE WELCOME? F. D. R. SAYS SO HIMSELF.

Beneath this was a newspaper clipping of a speech by Mr. Roosevelt, urging that people crowded in the slums of the East and sweltering in the Dust Bowl of the Middle West look for new home on the far side of the Rockies. "The President Sees a Promised Land,' " the banner headline read.

That is what these nomads are seeking as they pilot their dilapidated automobiles over the tortuous roads that cross the mountains—a Promised Land. They want fertile acres where there is ample rainfall. And if there is not enough moisture from the air, they seek plenty of it in the ground. They hesitate to stop at any place that lacks either a whopping precipitation record or a network of bubbling irrigation canals. The drought refugees have been burned off their farms once. They could not stand it a second time. They ask about water with almost fanatical anxiety. Localities that are hopelessly arid, they shun like a wasteland.

Some of the Dust Bowl pilgrims are glum and despondent. Others can laugh at misfortune like the bearded farmer—at least he had the ruddy cheeks of a farmer—I saw driving along U.S. Highway 30 in the Idaho hills. At the wheel of an antiquated green roadster with a Kansas license, he jolted past the crossroads where I had stopped. Suitcases, jugs, and sacks were strapped to both running boards. I wondered if he had to unload each time he opened the door, or if he was still spry enough to vault over the top. He resembled a rustic version of Chief Justice Hughes. On the sloping back of the ancient pilgrim's car was a piece of white cardboard with a message in black paint:

> Thirty miles from water,
> Forty miles to wood,
> Life is hell in the Dust Bowl
> And I'm leaving for good.

Whether the nomads thus can smile in the grip of disaster or whether they are crushed by their homeless plight, their experiences have been mainly uniform and similar: years of struggle on practically submarginal farms, then heat and dust, and now the long trek west. Most of these wanderers tell the same story of how they happened to start to the coast. I met a lean and rangy fellow with a family and an old touring car who was particularly vivid and literate in his description of the catastrophe that had turned him out of his South Dakota ranch and sent him in quest of the will-o'-the wisp of a Promised Land beyond the Rockies. He said his name was Emmett.

— 2 —

The weather was scorching; it had long ceased to be merely hot. Drops of sweat as big as green peas trickled off Jim Emmett's forehead and splattered on his denim shirt. He did not bother to wipe them away. He had stopped doing that two weeks before, when the thermometer in the shade of the back porch hit 102 degrees for the first time. He just leaned against the wobbly fence, as motionless as the windmill that towered above the water hole in his pasture. There was not enough breeze to make the windmill even creak. And what was the use of wind, he thought. The water hole was dry—as dry as the dust of what had once been his cornfield.

He finally summoned enough energy to move his tall, overall-clad frame across the barnyard. The heat was so heavy it was almost like walking through the dust storms that frequently followed the hot spells. He remembered how during the first dust storms they had sat on the steps of Duncan's general store and joked about which counties of Wyoming or Montana were being blown past then.

They didn't joke any more—not since their own South Dakota topsoil had been added to the huge swirls of dust hurtling toward the Atlantic Ocean, two thousand miles away. Jim looked down at the ruins of his fields. The corn still standing was dry and brown. Most of the stalks were broken in the middle and bent over to the earth. What the searing heat had not withered the grasshoppers had chewed. Half of his cattle had died. The ones that survived stood at the arid water hole and lowed mournfully.

Jim trudged slowly up the steps of the gaunt, weatherbeaten farmhouse. Inside, a layer of dust coated everything. They kept the windows closed continually, but still it seeped through. Jim's wife, Martha, had stopped trying to fight it. Even their food tasted of dust. Whether they ate lima beans or canned peaches, the bite and grit of dust was the predominant taste. A fuzz of dust covered the gilt-framed picture of Jim's grandfather on the mantel. Old Wilson Emmett had started for the Far West on the Oregon Trail, but the rich loamy soil of the Great Plains had induced him to unload his prairie schooner in the Dakotas.

Jim wondered what Grandfather Emmett would say if he could see that soil either blown away by the wind or caked into crumbly lumps by the scorching sun. Upstairs one of the children coughed. Jim thought he recognized Marjorie. The cough came again and again. Jim moved nervously. He had not forgotten the death of the little Brooks boy down the road from dust pneumonia. Jim looked at his grandfather's picture again. Maybe the old argonaut's journey to the Pacific coast would be finished yet. Jim had heard there was plenty of water in Oregon; too much water, someone had told him. Too much water! Jim didn't believe it.

He went outside and began tinkering with the motor of the six-year-old touring car parked near the gate.

Three days later the Emmett family took a last look at their dried-up farm, entrusted the keys and deed to Clyde Duncan at the general store with instructions to sell for what he could get, and Jim headed the radiator cap of the automobile into the West. A thin roll of ten-dollar bills was tucked in his pinch-clasp purse: the proceeds of the sale of the remnant of his livestock. Martha sat at Jim's side in the front seat, holding the youngest child on her lap. The other three children shared the dilapidated but spacious tonneau with pillows, books, pots, dishes, jars of preserves and pickles, andirons, baskets, and sundry other indispensible articles of household equipment. From a cartlike trailer, jolting rockily along behind, protruded bedsprings, chairs, tables, lamps, and the spinning-wheel that had belong to Martha's Aunt Ruth.

The trek which Grandfather Emmett had started to the Oregon Country in a covered wagon in 1849 was about to be completed almost a century later by his grandson in a battered touring car.

— 3 —

There have been a lot of Jim Emmetts in the past two years. Exactly how many, not even the government knows. No accurate census of the drought refugees is available. It is not easy to catalogue impoverished Middle Westerners huddled in third-class tourist camps in Oregon, begging for seasonal employment in Idaho, or scrambling desperately to get on crowded relief rolls in California. That there have been at least fifty thousand families in this plight is a conservative calculation. Most statements place the number of Dust Bowl emigrants at a minimum of two hundred thousand. Some estimates are as high as three times that number. In the San Joaquin valley of California thousands of ragged families from the heat-stricken plains are starving to death or dying of disease. The trek from the Dust Bowl to the West is of such proportions that President Roosevelt has told Congress it ranks with the rise in unemployment as the most important unforeseen factor to intrude into the complicated Federal relief situation.

As they head into the sundown, these modern pilgrims are following the Oregon Trail, the course blazed years ago by their predecessors of wagon train and long rifle. Up through the lofty passes of the Rockies in Montana and Wyoming, and down into the Sawtooth Range of Idaho, the drought refugees rattle in their heavily laden automobiles. Some of them stop in Senator Borah's home State, but others motor on toward the upland plateau of eastern Washington, and then swing down the Columbia River canyon where it cuts through the Cascade Mountains and merges with the fertile lowlands of the Pacific seaboard. An historical map will show that this was the route Lewis and Clark traveled in 1804, when they carried the flag from ocean to ocean. The drought sufferers who rest their sputtering engines at the Bonneville Dam picnic grounds in Oregon eat their ham sandwiches and drink their coffee within a few rods of where once gleamed the campfire of the first white men to travel westward across the American continent.

There is ample evidence of the extensiveness of the present trek. A glance through the nonresident automobile registration lists of the State of Oregon showed me numerous cars from such places as Huron, South Dakota; Palisade, Nebraska; Coldwater, Kansas; Garrison, North Dakota, and Keokuk, Iowa. Not all information must be gathered in such colorless fashion. One need only park alongside a through highway on the coast to see for oneself the caravans of these modern pioneers. They roll westward almost like a parade. In a single hour from a grassy meadow near an Idaho hoad I counted thirty-four automobiles with the license plates of States between Chicago and the mountains. Conversation with the occupants of these cars is the best way to understand the problems and complexities of a migration that may some day parallel in historic significance the journey of the prairie schooners that first rumbled on the Oregon Trail.

I talked to seven bronzed young men, grouped around an aged Oldsmobile truck parked above a clear creek which the highway bridged. The license was from Oklahoma. "Had to let the old crate cool," the tall driver said, and pointed to the radiator from which steam and water were escaping in a miniature geyser.

All seven lads, I learned, were from different families. The drought had put their fathers on WPA rolls, and the boys had driven West to see what opportunities there were on the coast. They intended to stay a few months, hiring out as farm hands to get their information about soil and crop conditions direct. Then they would meet at Seattle or Boise or Portland, or some other prearranged point, and drive back to Oklahoma to report to their folks. If their verdict of the farming possibilities in the Pacific Northwest was favorable, their families would join the westward procession.

The boys told me they were camping along the way and they were getting harvest work in wayside fields and orchards to pay for their food. "We take our time slips out in grub," one of the youths confided. "We get 'bout twice as much that way." He showed me three or four sacks of fruits and vegetables on the floor of the truck. The oldest lad boiled some turnips and fried a big slab of bacon and a pan of potatoes. He and his friends ate like hungry lumberjacks.

"The drought fried out farms just like that," remarked the tall driver, nodding at the skillet of sizzling potatoes.

Another lad chimed in: "I sure hope we get a chance to get new farms here or in Oregon. Farming's all our folks have ever done." The driver told me that the fathers of several of his companions were anticipating bumper fruit or wheat crops before the drought struck. "The sun nearly baked their apples right on the trees," he explained. "My golly! We've just got to find somewhere our folks can start over again." For a moment his good humor vanished, and his calm gray eyes were worried and anxious as he gazed into the West.

I remember thinking that perhaps some pioneer boy of almost a century earlier had looked with the same troubled expression— possibly from the very meadow where we were standing—for signal smoke on the horizon. The specter of poverty, I thought, was no less real than the peril of painted savages on the warpath.

The last I saw of the lads from the Dust Bowl, they were sitting in the rear of the truck as it swayed around a bend in the road. Their truck once had carted wheat and other produce to market from the ranch of the tall boy's father. Now the ranch was arid and withered, and the truck was the covered wagon for a modern reconnoitering expedition into the Far Northwest. Probably it was such peregrination as that of the Oklahoma lads which prompted President Roosevelt on one of his trips across the country, to declare that a wholesale population drift westward was under way.

The speeches of the President have been an astonishingly important factor in deciding people to turn toward the coast in quest of new lands. Farm families, uncertain whether to struggle along in the Dust Bowl or to pile their goods in a trailer and go west, have been swayed by the rich, cultured voice that comes over the radio sounding a modern "Westward ho!"

High on the uplands of the State of Washington I met a rangy, taciturn farmer who acquainted me directly with the tremendous influence of Mr. Roosevelt has had in spurring on this trek over the Rockies. The farmer was from South Dakota. Out of a worn wallet he pulled a frayed newspaper clipping. He handed it to me and gestured at the dozen dilapidated automobiles parked at a crossroads on U.S. Highway 97. All the cars were either heaped high with household goods or coupled to heavily loaded trailers.

"We been followin' that newspaper piece there ever since we left the Dakotas," the farmer said.

I looked at the clipping. It was the story of an address delivered several hours' drive from where we stood by the President in the summer of 1934. The occasion of the speech had been the start of actual construction on the great Bonneville and Grand Coulee dams.

"The piece was in the newspaper 'bout the time the first drought hit us," my friend from South Dakota said. "I cut it out and tacked it in the kitchen. We used to read it whenever the dust trickled in at the windows and the sun and heat gave our wheat another scorching."

I looked again to see what the President had said in the rugged fastnesses of the Columbia River region that held such significance for people caught in the furnace of the Dust Bowl, almost two rays' travel eastward on a limited train. Here is what I read:

In this Northwestern section of the land, we still have an opportunity for a vastly increased population. There are many sections of the country, as you know, where conditions are crowded. There are many sections of the country where land has run out or been put to the wrong kind of use. America is growing. There are many people who want to go to a section of the country where they will have a better chance for themselves and their children—and there are a great many people who have children and need room for growing families.

Out here you have not just space, you have space that can be used by human beings—a wonderful land—a land of opportunity.

I returned the clipping to the farmer who had abandoned his parched acres in South Dakota to search for a new home in the vast basin of the Columbia River. He trudged back to his old touring car, stepped on a starter that whined protestingly and finally worked, and then drove off up the road. The other automobiles followed him, until they were rolling like a caravan over the sagebrush plateau of eastern Washington. I noticed that the majority of the cars had North or South Dakota license plates, although one or two were from Oklahoma and Kansas. To the running boards and fenders of all of them were strapped lamps, kettles, quilts, pictures, and other domestic articles. In most of the back seats could be seen the chubby faces and waving arms of little children. It was evident that the cars belong to families who had pulled up the roots they had sunk in the scorched soil of the Middle West drought areas and headed into the sunset seeking another start in life. These people were not traveling west to see Mount Rainier or Yellowstone National Park. They were not on a camping trip. They had come to stay.

The automobiles of the wandering farmers from the Dust Bowl dwindled in the distance. I watched them becoming specks against the grim lava cliffs towering above the highway. Probably the wagons of the forty-niners had looked exactly like that against the same cliffs.

— 4 —

"A land of opportunity"—that was what the President had said. Opportunity? For some, but not for everyone.

A field secretary of the Gospel Army has reported that the most shocking conditions of squalor and filth he has ever observed exist among poverty-harassed drought refugees in California. School districts in Oregon have faced bankruptcy because of the increased strain placed on their budgets by the additional teachers and facilities needed for the children of the Dust Bowl emigrants. A considerable portion of the drought families in Washington and Idaho are destitute and would starve were it not for the subsistence doles they receive from Federal and State relief.

The plight of these pilgrims takes many forms. A taxi dancer in a shanty town near a big construction project asked me if I wanted to go to her cabin. It would only cost a dollar, she promised. She had tawny hair and a slender figure. She had not camouflaged her face beneath as much lipstick and rouge as the other girls, nor was she as hardboiled as her contemporaries. Over a glass of beer—for which she earned a few pennies' commission from the dance-hall management for persuading me to drink—I asked how she happened to be at her present occupation.

Her family had driven west from Nebraska when their farm dried up and the wind blew away what the sun had not shriveled. At Oregon City they had tried to find a farm in the Promised Land. But the $130 they had left from the sale of their Nebraska tract to the government at $4 an acre was not enough for even a down payment. Her father, she explained, had been unable to get work at either the pulp or the woolen mill which stood on the outskirts of town. "Plenty of our local people out of jobs, as it is," the foremen had said. When the $130 was gone and she had lost her part-time job in a novelty shop, they had been forced to go on relief.

The investigators and relief officials had been tough. There were enough Oregon citizens unemployed without these jobless invaders, the WPA office said. "Alien paupers," was what the Governor of the State called them. After a few weeks the relief headquarters had given them enough money to get back to Nebraska, and warned them that was all they would get. They used this money to live on for a short time, and then found the relief people had been in earnest. No more assistance; even the pittance on which they had been existing was gone.

They drove south along the coast, through the lush Willamette Valley. To buy gasoline and get food they picked hops. The wages were terrible, the food filthy. She remembered that a lot of the pickers had what a doctor in a near-by town called *Ascaris lumbricoides*, which was a long name for worms. She had stood that as long as she could, then had borrowed dimes and nickels from a lot of the other workers and taken a bus to Portland. Her family stayed on in the hop-pickers' camp. Her story of what had occurred in Portland was pretty melodramatic. She had needed money badly and found only temporary employment. Finally she had lived with a man for a while, and later had made good money dancing naked at stag parties. She had drifted around a lot, writing letters to her family now and then. They found work only at seasonal agricultural employment and nearly starved between jobs. They did not know what she was doing, however.

The girl looked around the ramshackle dance hall built from laths and tar paper and discarded lumber. "So here I am," she said. The men paid her ten cents a dance; she kept five, and the management took the other nickel. She also earned a commission on any beer and sandwiches she could induce her acquaintances to buy. These pickings were slim, indeed; occasionally she augmented them when she shared the bed in her cabin with some man she had meet on the dusty street or in the smoke-filled dance hall. She wore neither a brassière nor stockings, and learned that this commercial foresight helped all phases of her business. Her greatest fear was venereal disease. The town was full of it, and only a few of the men used the prophylactic stations in the construction camp.

Whether her highly theatrical tale was true, I cannot say. I only know she was one of the wanderers who traveled the Oregon Trail in 1937—and whatever opportunity she found was of a strange and dubious sort.

Other drought refugees have failed to find the Promised Land. This advertisement appeared in a number of Middle Western newspapers:

WANTED, 40 men to work in wood-cutting camp in Oregon.

No experience necessary. Cabins and bedding provided, wood and water free. Tools and groceries obtainable at local prices on credit. Earn from $3 to $4 a day. Five years work available.

The end of this rainbow turned out to be a squalid lumber camp, where men toiled in the rain and sleet, and slept in leaky shacks. Three boys from Kansas worked there two months, and had a profit of exactly $3.80 to show for their combined efforts. They said they were fortunate. Most of their fellow workers were in debt to the company, which charged outrageous prices for third-class accommodations.

"Cutters from the drought area are very satisfactory workers," the owner of the camp sanctimoniously wrote the Federal employment service in Kansas. He asked that a whole caravan of families be sent him, adding, "Have them bring camping equipment only, as the winters are so open people can live in tents all winter."

The camp was on the Oregon coast, which has the heaviest precipitation record of any place in continental United States!

Unscrupulous land agents and real-estate salesmen wait for the Dust Bowl nomads as grimly as the Sioux and Cheyennes once lay in ambush for their bygone predecessors. Any farm in the Far West looks desirable to the people from the drought region. Generally, fuel and water are plentiful. Both were costly items back on the plains. The wanderers part with the four or five hundred dollars they may have left. They erect buildings, clear away stumps and trees, and till the land for crops. Then they harvest—weeds and sagebrush. When they have found they are on nonproductive soil, it is too late. Their money is gone, and so is their hard work. There is nothing they can do now except seek relief. The "farm" reverts to the mortgage company or real-estate firm, which can sell it in its improved form to another inexperienced and gullible family of wayfarers at a higher price per acre.

Tragic frauds of this sort occur frequently. The drought refugees want desperately to return to farming. It is all most of them have ever done. It is all they can do. When they see what appears to be a desirable chance to farm again, they grab at it. They are unfamiliar with local conditions and investigate only superficially. Not until afterwards—when their work and money are gone—do they consult the reports on soil and crops and weather. Unlike Davy Crockett, they do not make sure they are right before going ahead.

Yet not all the drought refugees have encountered failure and disappointment. Many of them have prospered in the great land beyond the mountains. Those fleeced by real-estate sharks or stricken in filthy camps are only part of the story. The rest of it is the account of families who have found better farms and a new chance. The Pacific Northwest is seven times as large as Illinois; at the same time it has fewer people than Chicago. In this sparsely settled region of fertile lowlands and green hills, thousands of people from the Dust Bowl are getting an opportunity to start over again. The families who have been rehabilitated provide a happy contrast to those who are still homeless wanderers.

Red Light Row.

Ernest G. Moll

From *CAMPUS SONNETS* (1934)

PRONOUNS AND SPRING

Spring on the Campus; azaleas bloomed again
And rhododendrons and the white May flower!
But in the class I spoke with learned power
Of pronouns till Spring died in every brain.
Then suddenly against the window pane
Two robins fluttered in a passion-shower,
And all along the ledges of the tower
I heard the ivy shaken as with rain.

> Sadly I mused, "desolating is man's law,
> That chills the native impulse at its spring,
> Till freedom's only in a robin's wing."
> And then along the second row I saw
> A girl's eyes seek a boy's; they met, and I,
> Reached for my bag of pronouns hurriedly.

EXAMINATION IN ROMANTIC POETS

She knew the names of all of Byron's guesses
And had the dates on Wordsworth and Annette;
Talked Fanny Brawne until her eyes were wet
And her voice shook with phantoms of caresses.
She fixed poor S. T. C. his proper jesses,
How he and Sarah never could forget
Till all his days were dark and his feet set
In bogs and vast Satanic wildernesses.

> Then looked at me with clear and steady eyes
> Void of all evil; and I never knew

Till then what life and thirst of life could do.
I grabbed my hat and muttered on the rise:
"You're fair and twenty and you may recover—
Go, shut your book and get yourself a lover!"

ON ASKING A CLASS TO READ JEFFERS

There'll be no quiz: Who looks upon the seed
Of his own soul in the primeval slime
Sees that which locks his lips for after-time
With silence deeper than a miser's greed.
There'll be no quiz: I give you to the need
Your souls must feel to know the way they climb
Up the earth darkness, stern and white with rime,
Fierce eyed, proud mouthed, with hands that grasp and bleed.

    But having read, come back again to me
    That we might sit a little while together
    Quietly dreaming in the quiet weather
    After the storm that struck us from the sea;
    Quietly dreaming to the drone of bees
    And drift of voices speaking words like these.

ROBINSON JEFFERS

I.

Poet in Stone

I watch you write stone poems, build stone towers,
Gathering that mind into one point of light
That lay dispersed for aeons in the night
Before earth knew the gentleness of flowers.
Out of the rock a hawk. In him a soul
Too clean for passion. Out of the hawk a man
Whom thought defiles with vision and a plan
Futile in all save its own stern control.

> The cold thin agony of stone bites deep
> In flesh of those that feel it. The proud dream
> Of stone stabs bitter music through the mind.
> For you I fear not—even in that wild leap
> Of seeing that lays bare the eagle's scream
> And shows the gray stone anguish that's behind.

II.

Builder of Tor House

I think I'd know the marks upon your hands
That have grown firm with the cool touch of stone
And the slow surge of strength along the bone
What time you built a tower in empty lands.
I think I'd know the light in your still eyes
That, when the work was done and quiet came
About you, and the wonder of a name,
Looked from that height with something of surprise.

> I knew you in the granite long ago
> On hills you'll never see; but you were proud
> Beyond my strength—a spirit darkly met
> In the faint glimmerings far beneath the snow.
> And you'll go back, but round you like a cloud
> Will be the memory of the tower you set.

Ben Hur Lampman

from *AT THE END OF THE CAR LINE* (1942)

My Traveled Uncle Jim

I gave him my tobacco and thereafter said to him:
"You've been in many distant lands, they tell me, Uncle Jim;
In Finland and in Java, and in Egypt and Peru,
To Madrid and to Shanghai town, and twice to Timbuctoo.
You've seen the camels laden in the musky eastern marts,
You've known the curious customs of the oddest foreign parts!
As for me, I have not wandered, although I've yearned to roam—
Ah, tame and tasteless is the bread that one must eat at home!
I would I might this very hour muse by the northern sea
Where of old the golden seahawks set their dragon galleys free!"

My Uncle Jim considered, and a smile was in his eye;
He looked upon a tumbled cloud and slowly made reply:
"Why, I mind a lass named Hilda, whose laugh was light as mead,
And she was cleaning herrings while the gulls stood round to feed.

> Those northern girls are very fair,
> And they have April in their hair,
> And once I spent an April there—
> A-working for a Swede."

He sighed, I thought, quite cheerfully—for one as old as he;
But I was clamorous for facts, who had not been to sea.
"Quite so," I said, "yet I am sure that Java, to my mind,
Is as queer a pagan country as ever man might find,
Thence comes great store of rubber, and a wealth of wry quinine,
And timber, hides and kapok, and much rice and spices fine;
And frequently, I speculate—you'll tell me, won't you please?—
On the native arts and culture of the genial Javanese.
Or if your memory chooses, I should like to stroll with you
Down the gay, gray bund at Shanghai with a thousand junks in
    view."

So Uncle Jim reflected, and I cocked an eager ear,
Yet that which glimmered in his eye seemed strangely like a tear.
"Ah, well," said he, "in Shanghai there is nothing much to do,
But I recollect that Sunday when the Captain paid the crew.

> Those eastern girls are gold and brown,
> And they've a trick of looking down,
> And once I was in Shanghai town—
> When I was twenty-two."

My exasperation kindled, for he seemed, indeed, obtuse;
And I asked myself this question: It is really any use?
Yet I must pursue the topic for—and here we find the rub—
I had in mind a paper I had promised for the club.
"Precisely, Uncle Jim," I said, "but tell me, is it true
That the flower of Inca splendor bloomed its fairest in Peru?
Ah, the feather-crowns and jewels, and the llamas one by one
Golden freighted for the temples, and the virgins of the sun!"
Anxiously I scanned his visage, craggy brow and grizzled beard,
And I'm sure I need not tell you what I very greatly feared.

Then Uncle Jim remembered, while his look was far away,
And I rose and left him rudely, for he had but this to say:
"There's a little shop in Rio that I'll never see no more,
Nor her a-smiling at me from the shadows of the door.

> Those southern girls are dusk and flame,
> And they are never wholly tame—
> And there was music in her name,
> The night I swam ashore."

This article was originally published by Encore Publishing, *Encore* magazine, Feb.-March, 1978, in a slightly different form.

THE ODYSSEYS OF MARY BARNARD

by Anita Helle

Mary Barnard is an important poet, not only because of the quality of her verse, but because of her associations with some of this century's most prominent American writers. If she was among the first Northwest poets to gain a national reputation it is, as she has put it, because "I have a lot of resolution." In one way, she is part of this place: most of her life has been spent and much of her writing has been done in Vancouver, Washington. But she has also been apart from it. Her friends were leaders of the modernist movement in poetry, and her early poems were published in vanguard "little magazines" such as *Furioso* and *New Westminster*, now collectors' items. National honors came early; at twenty-six she won *Poetry* magazine's Levinson Prize, and at thirty her first book, *Cool Country*, was published in a volume which included first books by John Berryman and Randall Jarrell. Since then her artistic scope has broadened: the 1958 translation of Sappho's poems (*Sappho: A New Translation*) and *The Mythmakers*, a systematic inquiry into the nature and origin of myths, earned her a scholarly reputation. Other poems and short stories have appeared in publications such as *The New Yorker, Saturday Review*, the *Kenyon Review* and the *Hudson Review*. A California composer, David Ward-Steinman has based a musical suite on her fragments from Sappho; Tibor Serly's "The Pleides," a choral composition (1978) uses lyrics from one of her poems about the constellation of star-women who legendarily dance across the sky.

Images of exile and return, isolation and reintegration link Barnard's life and work. Born in Vancouver, Washington in 1909, she got acquainted with Oregon backroads as a child, when she traveled to lumber mills with her father, a timber wholesaler. She began writing poems in grade school, but her first contact with the avant-garde of the 1920s came at Reed College. A classics major, she had taken creative writing from Lloyd Reynolds, now best-known as a calligrapher. One day Reynolds wrote some lines from Ezra Pound's poem, "Homage to Sextus Propertius" on the blackboard. "The man who could do that could do anything," she remembers Reynolds saying.

When she tells this story Barnard likes to emphasize that she originally regarded the platitude with a healthy skepticism ("Harumph, I thought, that's a pretty tall statement!"). But after studying Pound on her own she became an admirer. Soon after graduation she surprised her father by announcing that she'd send a packet of poems to Pound in Rapallo, Italy—maybe he'd tell her what he thought of her work. Pound's side of this exchange with the "unknown Mary Barnard" (sic) is recorded in his *Selected Letters* (New Directions, 1950):

> "Age? Intentions? Intention? How MUCH intention? I mean how hard and how long are you willing to work at it? . . . Nice gal, likely to marry and give up writing or what Oh?"
>
> (sic)

"I wrote back to Pound, 'Nice girl, not likely to marry, and as for giving up writing, the only thing that would discourage me would be advice from you, but even that wouldn't stop me,'" Barnard recalls in a recent interview at her apartment in Vancouver, Washington. At sixty-nine, her tall stature is still one of her most imposing features; her way of choosing words as if there is only one right one, even for speech, is another. She has picked a straightbacked chair nearest the window; afternoon light softens the purposefully grouped bookcases, chairs and objets d'art.

Barnard describes her relationship with Pound, which lasted until his death, as one in which "he was the master and I was the apprentice." She also confesses that she didn't always follow his advice concerning her work. Nevertheless, Pound was her pipeline to the people and ideas who were shaping the future direction of poetry. When she visited New York for the first time in 1936, Pound's introductions led to meetings with the leading personages: Marianne Moore ("A dizzying talker—but rather abstract!"); *Poetry* magazine editor Harriet Monroe ("A chipper little lady"); e.e. cummings ("He laughed from his boots") and William Carlos Williams ("As far as criticism of my work, his was along one line—condense!").

After several months at Yaddo writers' colony, Barnard returned to Vancouver and took a job as a social worker, but not happily. One letter from Williams to Barnard in Vancouver during that period (part of Barnard's gift of five Williams' first editions to the Reed College Library) suggests second-hand her discontented feeling of cultural isolation. "It must be lonesome out there," Williams' letter begins, "Fight it if you can."

By 1938 Barnard was back in New York hunting for odd jobs to support her writing. She became a research assistant for Carl Van Doren, eventually taking a position as curator of the Poetry Collection at the Lockwood Memorial Library in Buffalo. About her decision to move East, Barnard says, "I left Vancouver in desperation. I wanted to be a regional poet . . . but I realized that the regions weren't going to have any culture, or I couldn't contribute to it in isolation. I had particularly the tendency to overvalue my work—I was the only one who was doing what I was doing. I didn't have anyone to compare my work with here, so I swung between feeling I was better than I was, to feeling that I wasn't worth anything. When I came back again [in the 1950s and 60s] the region had changed, and my position in it had changed. When Marianne Moore and W.H. Auden came to Portland I was seated next to them. But when I was growing up in Vancouver, I knew two people who had gone to Europe. While I was at Reed, we heard one Englishman read his poetry one night, but nobody had ever heard his name."

Barnard's first book, *Cool Country* (New Directions, 1940), contains poems written before and after she was apprenticed to Pound. In addition to demonstrating a sensitive ear and precise powers of observation, the poems form a sort of novel of initiations, looking forward and backward in time for their influences. The prosody follows the Imagist principles set down by Pound. There are no excess adjectives, concrete words take the place of abstract ones, and lines sound more like musical phrases than metronomic beats. The titles, however, are mostly native—"Logging Trestle," "Shoreline," "Highway Bridge," "Rapids." In "Provincial II," the theme of the would-be regional poet's dilemma is confronted directly. A "European" makes his appearance, and he shows the persona in the poem that the silk she thinks she wears is "merely paper," her buckskin "out of date by nearly one hundred years." Collecting her wits, the poet finds an unconvincing consolation in the "large/Plums of the provinces." The book ends on a winsome note, as the poet writes of Miranda, Shakespeare's stranded daughter in *The Tempest*: "There is a green place in my mind/That paces my mind's conceptions."

Illness sent Barnard home to Vancouver in 1951, but her poetic odyssey continued in new directions. "I had been led from one endeavor to another," she explains. "Pound had recommended that I translate, and when I said I hated translation, I said I would try working on metrics, especially Sappho's metric. It was when somebody sent me a volume of Quasimodo's Italian translation of Sappho [in the 1950s] that I began to translate the fragments. I tried one, then another. When I got to twelve, I began to think I would finish."

"Then Sappho led me to *The Mythmakers*. I was working on what became a footnote, and I was trying to say something about Sappho's religion. Scholars were writing about her as the priestess of a religious cult that carried on its ritual in sacred groves. The more I read that the potion was merely ritual, the more I became obsessed with working it out. I felt that something was mixed in the drink, and I felt I wanted to justify my theory. I also felt that Aphrodite was a moon goddess in Sappho's poetry, and I kept finding scholars saying that Aphrodite was *not* a moon goddess, and I was trying to justify that theory, too."

Classicism and modernism are closely linked in Barnard's *Sappho: A New Translation* of 100 poems and fragments by the ancient Lesbian poet. In his foreword, scholar Dudley Fitts praises the "direct purity of diction" of "the new" version, especially as it contrasts with nineteenth-century corruptions by Swinburne and Symonds, who made Sappho over into an image of "Yellow Book neodiabolism." Barnard's Sappho is more elegant and wise: her expressions have economy. The unstintingly clear, precise diction which Barnard had restored in Sappho was exactly what Pound and other early modernist poets were after in their own verse, and the Greek poets had been among their most-admired models.

The most important innovation of Barnard's "new translation," however, is its meter. Wanting to come as close as possible to the sound of the speaking voice, Barnard considered the convention of the Japanese haiku, as well as strictly quantitative metrics—which some scholars felt were impossible to convey in English. Her solution was a looser adaptation, balancing the number of weighted syllables from line to line. Consequently, Sappho's colloquies with friends, as well as her wedding songs and passionate soliloquies read as though they have form, but one which resembles conversational stresses instead of humdrum repetition:

> You may forget but
>
> Let me tell you
> this: someone in
> some future time
> will think of us.

The Mythmakers (1966) takes Barnard's many-sided interest in literature to a practical conclusion. It addresses a number of questions. By what process does a "faraway twinkling point of light become a mythical personality?" What is the origin of myths associated with plants? Were tribal shamans also poets? Reading the book is like being on an exotic safari, led by a cheerful guide in sensible shoes who's convinced that a little common sense and clear thinking is all that's needed to penetrate the wooly underbrush. The clarity of style and logic convinces us that many myths had their origin in useful, pleasurable and imaginative facts, not, as Jungian theory suggests, "as emanations of a pre-conscious psyche." Summing up from the text, Barnard says "Gods grew up through impersonations—that is, in the case of the Northwest Indians, the mask preceded the god."

More than her poetry, Barnard's prose style in *The Mythmakers* reveals the common-sensical wit, intellectual curiosity, tenacity and toughmindedness which have been her resources. These are old-fashioned words to apply to a modern poet, but not to one whose craftsmanship has kept pace with fifty years of change. When she tells me that her latest project is a metric adaptation of Homer's *Iliad* into modern English I'm not surprised. I didn't say it, but I thought it fitting that her first translation of an epic poem should feature another wanderer, whose cunning labors took him far from home, and brought him back again.

Anita Helle is a free-lance writer who teaches at Clackamas Community College and at the Writing Skills Center of Lewis and Clark College.

Chronology of Published Works by Mary Barnard
Cool Country in Five Young American Poets (New York: New Directions), 1940

A Few Poems (Portland, Oregon: Reed College Graphic Arts Workshop), 1952

Sappho: A New Translation (Berkeley, California: University of California Press), 1958

The Mythmakers (Athens, Ohio: Ohio University Press), 1966

Later: Four Poems (Portland, Oregon: Prescott Street Press), 1975

Mary Barnard

From COOL COUNTRY IN FIVE YOUNG AMERICAN POETS (1940)

A Note on Poetry

Any artist is to me a person who takes nothing for granted; one who, while perceiving the thing's traditional wrappings, sees the thing itself with freshness, as though never encountered before; sees the article as itself, the package as something else, and neither as a reproduction of the picture in the ubiquitous advertisement.

If I have made myself clear, it must also be clear that I could ask nothing more important of poetry just now. Poets, in their particular field, work with words—not only the meaning of words, but the sounds of words, and this to me is extremely important. Beyond these two things, poetry may do different things and be good in different ways; but without freshness of vision, and craftsmanship in the building of metrical and melodic patterns, the poetry might as well be journalism.

What I am trying to do in my own work must be apparent in whatever I have accomplished. My approach to almost any experience is, by an accident of life, through a little-known landscape which proves a barrier to some readers. I think of that accident as the luckiest chance of my life, and cannot be sorry for it. Very few of the poems collected here have been written during the past two years, when I have had little opportunity for writing; but I feel that my aims have been sharpened rather than changed, as the world changed.

Logging Trestle

Neither cloud nor rain casts
A chill into the valley
Like that of a trestle fallen into disuse.

The rails move out from the hillside,
Across the piling lengthening its stroke
Where ground slopes riverward.

Abruptly, the rails terminate.
Sky opens between the cross-ties lifted
Each upon five upright timbers. The gray wood

Leads the eye to nothing further.
The broken column stands against cloud
As though an abandoned wharf extended into wind.

Cool Country

This green is the pod,
The enveloping color of our triangular valleys
Where rivers still young spring
From the coast range into salt estuaries.

Mist blown between promontories
Saturates the earth's every crevice,
Making the grass deep and sweet in all seasons
And the forest heavy.

From these come the red cheeses,
The apricot-colored lumber, deckloads
Moving into the green like lanterns.
The pod is broken for vermilion steaks of the salmon,
The chill wave itself opened
For the red-ripeness of harvest.

Storm

A vessel is breaking in half under the headland.
The ocean is swollen with storm and the lives
Of drowned men. Foam drawn over them.

Above my left eye a pain burrows.
Conspirator, awaiting dangerous weather,
If I were there, you would be suffocation,
Pain and the ocean obliterating each other.

The radio brings Bach from Philadelphia.
Closer within than sickness and outside death,
The well-plumed music drives beyond the lighthouses
Toward the extreme coastland—

$$\mathrm{ἀκτὰν\ πρὸς\ ἑσπέρου\ θεου}$$

                                          On our beaches
Dead sea birds under yellow curds of foam.

Wine Ship

A mast askew in the surf.
Wood of another climate
Bedded forever in half-liquid sand.

The sharp-eared foreigner
Struggling out of the sea wrack
Felt his flesh wither in the cold winds of this coast.

Here were no myrtle groves,
No familiar shrines,
Only the splintered casks and the sweet wines
Spilt in the sea.

Here were no grapes,
But bitter berries grew in the marsh.

Here was no moss,
But sea worn logs and the harsh
Grass on the dune top.

In this forlorn meeting of sea and land
Mirth is lost over the stormy water
And the sand
Lies suddenly cold under the hand.

From this shore an exile learns
To keep where a fire burns,
But there is no disguise
In small hand or white throat
When still by night a disturbing rhythm returns
From groves forgotten.

When the long eyelids are lifted
Suddenly, outlandish lights appear
In the woman's eyes: we think we hear
The tap of hidden hooves
Somewhere in our closed corridors.

Lai

Nothing availed then in the starless darkness with the sea
    giving a gray light.
Nothing availed then either by sea or by land
For the boats were filled with a shallow and unlit water, their
    sails riven.
But her hands spread upon the bolt of the door refused to
    believe
And the waves spoke for her since she had no voice.

I said, striving with her, "He is long since dead.
I have seen the queens who ride fast along dark roads
Bearing death upon their lips and love upon the palms of
    their hands.

I know they now have left the mired ways and the channelled
  meadows.
Where blue roads echo under the stripped high-singing trees,
  tower-ward they bear him.
In the yellow tideland shallow water laps unheard."

But she shook her head and the waves spoke for her as they
  do still,
Sighing a furtive song in the spread foam
While the troubled stones of the beach turn in my heart.

The Orchard Spring

Not in the forest with its air of childhood—
The secret fern, the tree tops
Run through with wind—
But in an orchard planted and grown
In the traditions of men,
I heard for the first time
An ancient sequence of words, a rhyme
That like the fragrance of warm grass
Tempted an illusive appetite
But seemed meaningless.

A doorsill was buried in the dew
Of a steep orchard: from what quarter
Did the difference come
to unsettle that room?
A twelfth-century nightengale
Half-heard, still, in the western coast range
Of the continent, troubles
The dreams of little green children.

Doves, gold rings, words
Out of the English island.
Fresh delight of rain on our hillsides
And the earth answering with springs.

Provincial II

The European made his appearance
Wearing velvet and the jewels
Of his inheritance
Gravely, without unbecoming pride.

He courteously made it plain to her
The silk she wore was paper.
Dismayed, caught in the shower
Of his disapproval, she bragged
In buckskin, which (he remarked)
Was outdated fully one hundred years.
At last, cowering in a few rags
Of homespun, she dried her tears with grass
And consoled herself with the large
Plums of the provinces.

Mary Barnard

From A FEW POEMS (1952)

The Fitting

She is imprisoned among mirrors
While a trio of hags with the cold hands
Of elderly dressmakers entangle,
Bind and define her body with tape-measures.
They compress withered lips upon pins.

Again and again she will re-enact
This fitting. Censure will be a knuckle
Shocking the flushed skin; all women
These women, their muttered words
Breathing distortion upon the mirror's reflection.

The knocking of hammers comes
From beyond the still window curtain
But her hands will make nothing:
Her life is confined here, in this depth,
In the well of the mirrors: on the carpet
The pulled threads, at her heel the scissors
Making a soft snipping sound.

The Whisperer

Where the sea runs a cobalt wedge under the coast bridges
And rhododendrons burn cool above concrete piers, an eddy of air
At the bridgehead will be I, as much I as
Walks alone here between watered lawns at moonrise.

The eyes lie in daytime, that say these chairs, fields,
Faces, are I, who am a strand of air raveling in the sound of leaves.
If the winds of the soul be unconsumed, I am lost,
Left clinging at a bridgehead over sea water.

There is no reprieve in the touch of flowering trees.
Finger is sister to bark, both mute and solid, both
Independent in death. Pity the poor soul, the public wind
Imaged in language, proud to whirl papers down a littered street,
A draft at the door whining for the bellows under your ribs.

Anadyomene

This is confusion of sea mist,
A white clot of it, bred of uncertain weather.

A cloud, that has no skeleton,
Skin, lips, or any defined
Outline, could not
Moving feel more wonder,
Moving without volition
Towards the bare mountain.

See where the sunlit headland
Changes! Light-dazzle on rock fades
And shadow softens. Cliffs, rising,
Widen in encircling vapor—
Cloudself, a nothingness which
Touching the warm stone
Distils radiance.

Far down, the sea,
Loud on the rocks.

Inheritance

I have no inheritance in
The only sense you know—one teaspoon
Out of a Virginian dozen
That twinkled after Boone's
Bold star into Kentucky.
Spoon-clink fell to axe-chink
Falling along the Ohio. Those women
Made their beds, God bless them,
In the wandering, dreamed, hoped-for
Hesperides, their graves
In permanent places.

And, dying, left no inheritance?
I call to witness those women,
(Mary Marshall, Mary Noel—
Did they leave me only their names?—
Polly Connor, Susan Carroll)
Whose daughters had a woman's value.
My own pride is theirs
Descended through that willful girl,
Proudest of all, who turned
Twenty on her death-bed—
And, dying, left me neither pride
Of place, nor pride of blood,
But memory of the pride of
Her love, and a night ride.
A thing easy to carry, the right
Thing to be found dead in:
Armor stronger than silver
Against time and men and women.

Midnight

Now the dead lend us
Peace for the dark hours.

At midnight the never-to-awaken
Sleep lightly; yet those who lay
In love at death-fall have quiet to lend.

Only the murdered must walk.
The murderer clutches at sleep
As at scant covers; wakes chilled.

Come now,
Comes now death-lent oblivion. I love
Her who died unknown to me.
I adjust my bones to the composure
Of hers.
Peace fall on my exile
From hers.

Monica Sone

From *NISEI DAUGHTER* (1953)

Chapter VIII

Pearl Harbor Echoes in Seattle

On a peaceful Sunday morning, December 7, 1941, Henry Sumi and I were at choir rehearsal singing ourselves hoarse in preparation for the annual Christmas recital of Handel's "Messiah." Suddenly Chuck Mizuno, a young University of Washington student, burst into the chapel, gasping as if he had sprinted all the way up the stairs.

"Listen, everybody!" he shouted. "Japan just bombed Pearl Harbor . . . in Hawaii! It's war!"

The terrible words hit like a blockbuster, paralyzing us. Then we smiled feebly at each other, hoping this was one of Chuck's practical jokes. Miss Hara, our music director, rapped her baton impatiently on the music stand and chided him, "Now Chuck, fun's fun, but we have work to do. Please take your place. You're already half an hour late."

But Chuck strode vehemently back to the door, "I mean it, folks, honest! I just heard the news over my car radio. Reporters are talking a blue streak. Come on down and hear it for yourselves."

With that, Chuck swept out of the room, a swirl of young men following in his wake. Henry was one of them. The rest of us stayed, rooted to our places like a row of marionettes. I felt as if a fist had smashed my pleasant little existence, breaking it into jigsaw puzzle pieces. An old wound opened up again, and I found myself shrinking inwardly from my Japanese blood, the blood of an enemy. I knew instinctively that the fact that I was an American by birthright was not going to help me escape the consequences of this unhappy war.

One girl mumbled over and over again, "It can't be, God, it

can't be!" Somebody else was saying, "What a spot to be in! Do you think we'll be considered Japanese or Americans?"

A boy replied quietly, "We'll be Japs, same as always. But our parents are enemy aliens now, you know."

A shocked silence followed. Henry came for Sumi and me. "Come on, let's go home," he said.

We ran trembling to our car. Usually Henry was a careful driver, but that morning he bore down savagely on the accelerator. Boiling angry, he shot us up Twelfth Avenue, rammed through the busy Jackson Street intersection, and rocketed up the Beacon Hill bridge. We swung violently around to the left of the Marine Hospital and swooped to the top of the hill. Then Henry slammed on the brakes and we rushed helter-skelter up to the house to get to the radio. Asthma [the cat] skidded away from under our trampling feet.

Mother was sitting limp in the huge armchair as if she had collapsed there, listening dazedly to the turbulent radio. Her face was frozen still, and the only words she could utter were, "*Komatta neh, komatta neh.* How dreadful, how dreadful."

Henry put his arms around her. She told him she first heard about the attack on Pearl Harbor when one of her friends phoned her and told her to turn on the radio.

We pressed close against the radio, listening stiffly to the staccato outbursts of an excited reporter: "The early morning sky of Honolulu was filled with the furious buzzing of Jap Zero planes for nearly three hours, raining death and destruction on the airfields below. . . . A warship anchored beyond the Harbor was sunk. . . ."

We were switched to the White House. The fierce clack of teletype machines and the babble of voices surging in and out from the background almost drowned out the speaker's terse announcements.

With every fiber of my being I resented this war. I felt as if I were on fire. "Mama, they should never have done it," I cried. "Why did they do it? Why? Why?"

Mother's face turned paper white. "What do you know about it? Right or wrong, the Japanese have been chafing with resentment for years. It was bound to happen, one time or another. You're young, Ka-chan, you know very little about the ways of nations. It's not as simple as you think, but this is hardly the time to be quarreling about it, is it?"

"No, it's too late, too late!" and I let the tears pour down my face.

Father rushed home from the hotel. He was deceptively calm as he joined us in the living room. Father was a born skeptic, and he believed nothing unless he could see, feel and smell it. He regarded all newspapers and radio news with deep suspicion. He shook his head doubtfully, "It must be propaganda. With the way things are going now between America and Japan, we should expect the most fantastic rumors, and this is one of the wildest I've heard yet." But we noticed that he was firmly glued to the radio. It seemed as if the regular Sunday programs, sounding off relentlessly hour after hour on schedule, were trying to blunt the catastrophe of the morning.

The telephone pealed nervously all day as people searched for comfort from each other. Chris called, and I told her how miserable and confused I felt about the war. Understanding as always, Chris said, "You know how I feel about you and your family, Kaz. Don't for heaven's sake, feel the war is going to make any difference in our relationship. It's not your fault, nor mine! I wish to God it could have been prevented." Minnie called off her Sunday date with Henry. Her family was upset and they thought she should stay close to home instead of wandering downtown.

Late that night Father got a shortwave broadcast from Japan. Static sputtered, then we caught a faint voice, speaking rapidly in Japanese. Father sat unmoving as a rock, his head cocked. The man was talking about the war between Japan and America. Father bit his lips and Mother whispered to him anxiously, "It's true then, isn't it, Papa? It's true?"

Father was muttering to himself, "So they really did it!" Now having heard the news in their native tongue, the war had become a reality to Father and Mother.

"I suppose from now on, we'll hear about nothing but the humiliating defeats of Japan in the papers here," Mother said, resignedly.

Henry and I glared indignantly at Mother, then Henry shrugged his shoulders and decided to say nothing. Discussion of politics, especially Japan versus America, had become taboo in our family for it sent tempers skyrocketing. Henry and I used to criticize Japan's aggressions in China and Manchuria while Father and Mother condemned Great Britain and America's superior attitude toward Asiatics and their interference with Japan's economic growth. During these arguments, we had eyed each other like strangers, parents against children. They left us with a hollow feeling at the pit of the stomach.

Just then the shrill peel of the telephone cut off the possibility of a family argument. When I answered, a young girl's voice fluttered through breathily, "Hello, this is Taeko Tanabe. Is my mother there?"

"No, she isn't, Taeko."

"Thank you," and Taeko hung up before I could say another word. Her voice sounded strange. Mrs. Tanabe was one of Mother's poet friends. Taeko called three more times, and each time before I could ask her if anything was wrong, she quickly hung up. The next day we learned that Taeko was trying desperately to locate her mother because FBI agents had swept into their home and arrested Mr. Tanabe, a newspaper editor. The FBI had permitted Taeko to try to locate her mother before they took Mr. Tanabe away while they searched the house for contraband and subversive material, but she was not to let anyone else know what was happening.

Next morning the newspapers fairly exploded in our faces with stories about the Japanese raids on the chain of Pacific islands. We were shocked to read Attorney General Biddle's announcement that 736 Japanese had been picked up in the United States and Hawaii. Then Mrs. Tanabe called Mother about her husband's arrest, and she said at least a hundred others had been taken from our community. Messrs. Okayama, Higashi, Sughira, Mori, Okada—we knew them all.

"But why were they arrested, Papa? They weren't spies, were they?"

Father replied almost curtly, "Of course not! They were probably taken for questioning."

The pressure of war moved in on our little community. The Chinese consul announced that all the Chinese would carry identification cards and wear "China" badges to distinguish them from the Japanese. Then I really felt left standing out in the cold. The government ordered the bank funds of all Japanese nationals frozen. Father could no longer handle financial transactions through his bank accounts, but Henry, fortunately, was of legal age so that business could be negotiated in his name.

In the afternoon President Roosevelt's formal declaration of war against Japan was broadcast throughout the nation. In grave, measured words, he described the attack on Pearl Harbor as shameful, infamous. I writhed involuntarily. I could no more have escaped the stab of self-consciousness than I could have changed my Oriental features.

Monday night a complete blackout was ordered against a possible Japanese air raid on the Puget Sound area. Mother assembled black cloths to cover the windows and set up candles in every room. All radio stations were silenced from seven in the evening till morning, but we gathered around the dead radio anyway, out of sheer habit. We whiled away the evening reading instructions in the newspapers on how to put out incendiary bombs and learning about the best hiding places during bombardments. When the city pulled its switches at blackout hour and plunged us into an ominous dark silence, we went to bed shivering and wondering what tomorrow would bring. All of a sudden there was a wild screech of brakes, followed by the resounding crash of metal slamming into metal. We rushed out on the balcony. In the street below we saw dim shapes of cars piled grotesquely on top of each other, their soft blue headlights staring helplessly up into the sky. Angry men's voices floated up to the house. The men were wearing uniforms and their metal buttons gleamed in the blue lights. Apparently two police cars had collided in the blackout.

Clutching at our bathrobes we lingered there. The damp winter night hung heavy and inert like a wet black veil, and at the bottom of Beacon Hill, we could barely make out the undulating length of Rainier Valley, lying quietly in the somber, brooding silence like a hunted python. A few pinpoints of lights pricked the darkness here and there like winking bits of diamonds, betraying the uneasy vigil of a tense city.

It made me positively hivey the way the FBI agents continued their raids into Japanese homes and business places and marched the Issei men away into the old red brick immigration building, systematically and efficiently, as if they were stocking a cellarful of choice bottles of wine. At first we noted that the men arrested were those who had been prominent in community affairs, like Mr. Kato, many times president of the Seattle Japanese Chamber of Commerce, and Mr. Ohashi, the principal of our Japanese language school, or individuals whose business was directly connected with firms in Japan; but as time went on, it became less and less apparent why the others were included in these raids.

We wondered when Father's time would come. We expected momentarily to hear strange footsteps on the porch and the sudden demanding ring of the front doorbell. Our ears became attuned like the sensitive antennas of moths, translating every soft swish of passing cars into the arrival of the FBI squad.

Once when our doorbell rang after curfew hour, I completely lost my Oriental stoicism which I had believed would serve me well under the most trying circumstances. No friend of ours paid visits at night anymore, and I was sure that Father's hour had come. As if hypnotized, I walked woodenly to the door. A mass of black figures stood before me, filling the doorway. I let out a magnificent shriek. Then pandemonium broke loose. The solid rank fell apart into a dozen separate figures which stumbled and leaped pell-mell away from the porch. Watching the mad scramble, I thought I had routed the FBI agents with my cry of distress. Father, Mother, Henry and Sumi rushed out to support my wilting body. When Henry snapped on the porch light, one lone figure crept out from behind the front hedge. It was a newsboy who, standing at a safe distance, called in a quavering voice, "I . . . I came to collect for . . . for the *Times*."

Shaking with laughter, Henry paid him and gave him an extra large tip for the terrible fright he and his bodyguards had suffered at the hands of the Japanese. As he hurried down the walk, boys of all shapes and sizes crawled out from behind trees and bushes and scurried after him.

We heard all kinds of stories about the FBI, most of them from Mr. Yorita, the grocer, who now took twice as long to make his deliveries. The war seemed to have brought out his personality. At least he talked more, and he glowed, in a sinister way. Before the war Mr. Yorita had been uncommunicative. He used to stagger silently through the back door with a huge sack of rice over his shoulders, dump it on the kitchen floor and silently flow out of the door as if he were bored and disgusted with food and the people who ate it. But now Mr. Yorita swaggered in, sent a gallon jug of soy sauce spinning into a corner, and launched into a comprehensive report of the latest rumors he had picked up on his route, all in chronological order. Mr. Yorita looked like an Oriental Dracula, with his triangular eyes and yellow-fanged teeth. He had a mournfully long sallow face and in his excitement his gold-rimmed glasses constantly slipped to the tip of his long nose. He would describe in detail how some man had been awakened in the dead of night, swiftly handcuffed, and dragged from out of his bed by a squad of brutal, tight-lipped men. Mr. Yorita bared his teenth menacingly in his most dramatic moments and we shrank from him instinctively. As he backed out of the kitchen door, he would shake his bony finger at us with a warning of dire things to come. When Mother said, "Yorita-san, you must worry about getting a call from the FBI, too," Mr. Yorita laughed modestly, pushing his glasses back up into place. "They wouldn't be interested in anyone as insignificant as myself!" he assured her.

But he was wrong. The following week a new delivery boy appeared at the back door with an airy explanation, "Yep, they got the old man, too, and don't ask me why! The way I see it, it's subversive to sell soy sauce now."

The Matsuis were visited, too. Shortly after Dick had gone to Japan, Mr. Matsui had died and Mrs. Matsui had sold her house. Now she and her daughter and youngest son lived in the back of their little dry goods store on Jackson Street. One day when Mrs. Matsui was busy with the family laundry, three men entered the shop, nearly ripping off the tiny bell hanging over the door. She hurried out, wiping sudsy, reddened hands on her apron. At best Mrs. Matsui's English was rudimentary, and when she became excited, it deteriorated into Japanese. She hovered on her toes, delighted to see new customers in her humble shop. "Yes, yes, something you want?"

"Where's Mr. Matsui?" a steely-eyed man snapped at her.

Startled, Mrs. Matsui jerked her thumb toward the rear of the store and said, "He not home."

"What? Oh, in there, eh? Come on!" The men tore the faded print curtain aside and rushed into the back room. "Don't see him. Must be hiding."

They jerked open bedroom doors, leaped into the tiny bathroom, flung windows open and peered down into the alley. Tiny birdlike Mrs. Matsui rushed around after them. "No, no! Whatsamalla, whatsamalla!"

"Where's your husband! Where is he?" one man demanded angrily, flinging clothes out of the closet.

"Why you mix 'em all up? He not home, not home." She clawed at the back of the burly men like an angry little sparrow, trying to stop the holocaust in her little home. One man brought his face down close to hers, shouting slowly and clearly, "WHERE IS YOUR HUSBAND? YOU SAID HE WAS IN HERE A MINUTE AGO!"

"Yes, yes, not here. *Mah, wakara nai hito da neh.* Such stupid men."

Mrs. Matsui dove under a table, dragged out a huge album and pointed at a large photograph. She jabbed her gnarled finger up toward the ceiling, saying, "Heben! Heben!"

The men gathered around and looked at a picture of Mr. Matsui's funeral. Mrs. Matsui and her two children were standing by a coffin, their eyes cast down, surrounded by all their friends, all of whom were looking down. The three men's lips formed an "Oh." One of them said, "We're sorry to have disturbed you. Thank you, Mrs. Matsui, and good-by." They departed quickly and quietly.

Having passed through this baptism, Mrs. Matsui became an expert on the FBI, and she stood by us, rallying and coaching us on how to deal with them. She said to Mother, "You must destroy everything and anything Japanese which may incriminate your husband. It doesn't matter what it is, if it's printed or made in Japan, destroy it because the FBI always carries off those items for evidence."

In fact all the women whose husbands had been spirited away said the same thing. Gradually we became uncomfortable with our Japanese books, magazines, wall scrolls and knickknacks. When Father's hotel friends, Messrs. Sakaguchi, Horiuchi, Nishibue and a few others vanished, and their wives called Mother weeping and warning her again about having too many Japanese objects around the house, we finally decided to get rid of some of ours. We knew it was impossible to destroy everything. The FBI would certainly think it strange if they found us sitting in a bare house, totally purged of things Japanese. But it was as if we could no longer stand the tension of waiting, and we just had to do something against the black day. We worked all night, feverishly combing through bookshelves, closets, drawers, and furtively creeping down to the basement furnace for the burning. I gathered together my well-worn Japanese language schoolbooks which I had been saving over a period of ten years with the thought that they might come in handy when I wanted to teach Japanese to my own children. I threw them into the fire and watched them flame and shrivel into black ashes. But when I came face to face with my Japanese doll which Grandmother Nagashima had sent me from Japan, I rebelled. It was a gorgeously costumed Miyazukai figure, typical of the lady in waiting who lived in the royal palace during the feudal era. The doll was gowned in an elegant purple silk kimona with the long, sweeping hemline of its period and sashed with rich-embroidered gold and silver brocade. With its black, shining coiffed head bent a little to one side, its delicate pink-tipped ivory hand holding a red lacquer message box, the doll had an appealing, almost human charm. I decided to ask Chris if she would keep it for me. Chris loved and appreciated beauty in every form and shape, and I knew that in her hands, the doll would be safe and enjoyed.

Henry pulled down from his bedroom wall the toy samurai sword he had brought from Japan and tossed it into the flames. Sumi's contributions to the furnace were books of fairy tales and magazines sent to her by her young cousins in Japan. We sorted out Japanese classic and popular music from a stack of records, shattered them over our knees and fed the pieces to the furnace. Father piled up his translated Japanese volumes of philosophy and religion and carted them reluctantly to the basement. Mother had the most to eliminate, with her scrapbooks of poems cut out from newspapers and magazines, and her private collection of old Japanese classic literature.

It was past midnight when we finally climbed upstairs to bed. Wearily we closed our eyes, filled with an indescribable sense of guilt for having destroyed the things we loved. This night of ravage was to haunt us for years. As I lay struggling to fall asleep, I realized that we hadn't freed ourselves at all from fear. We still lay stiff in our beds, waiting.

Mrs. Matsui kept assuring us that the FBI would get around to us yet. It was just a matter of time and the least Mother could do for Father was to pack a suitcase for him. She said that the men captured who hadn't been prepared had grown long beards, lived and slept in the same clothes for days before they were permitted visits from their families. So Mother dutifully packed a suitcase for Father with toilet articles, warm flannel pajamas, and extra clothes, and placed it in the front hall by the door. It was a personal affront, the way it stood there so frank and unabashedly. Henry and I said that it was practically a confession that Papa was a spy, "So please help yourself to him, Mr. FBI, and God speed you."

Mother was equally loud and firm, "No, don't anyone move it! No one thought that Mr. Kato or the others would be taken, but they're gone now. Why should we think Papa's going to be an exception."

Henry threw his hands up in the air and muttered about the odd ways of the Japanese.

Every day Mrs. Matsui called Mother to check Father in; then we caught the habit and started calling him at the hotel every hour on the hour until he finally exploded, "Stop this nonsense! I don't know which is more nerve-wracking, being watched by the FBI or by my family!"

When Father returned home from work, a solicitous family eased him into his favorite armchair, arranged pillows behind his back, and brought the evening paper and slippers to him. Mother cooked Father's favorite dishes frenziedly, night after night. It all made Father very uneasy.

We had a family conference to discuss the possibility of Father and Mother's internment. Henry was in graduate school and I was beginning my second year at the university. We agreed to drop out should they be taken and we would manage the hotel during our parents' absence. Every week end Henry and I accompanied Father to the hotel and learned how to keep the hotel books, how to open the office safe, and what kind of linen, paper towels, and soap to order.

Then a new menace appeared on the scene. Cries began to sound up and down the coast that everyone of Japanese ancestry should be taken into custody. For years the professional guardians of the Golden West had wanted to rid their land of the Yellow Peril, and the war provided an opportunity for them to push their program through. As the chain of Pacific islands fell to the Japanese, patriots shrieked for protection from us. A Californian sounded the alarm: "The Japanese are dangerous and they must leave. Remember the destruction and the sabotage perpetrated at Pearl Harbor. Notice how they have infiltrated into the harbor towns and taken our best land."

He and his kind refused to be comforted by Edgar Hoover's special report to the War Department stating that there had not been a single case of sabotage committed by a Japanese living in Hawaii or on the Mainland during the Pearl Harbor attack or after. I began to feel acutely uncomfortable for living on Beacon Hill. The Marine Hospital rose tall and handsome on our hill, and if I stood on the west shoulder of the Hill, I could not help but get an easily photographed view of the Puget Sound Harbor with its ships snuggled against the docks. And Boeing airfield, a few miles south of us, which had never bothered me before, suddenly seemed to have moved right up into my back yard, daring me to take just one spying glance at it.

In February, Executive Order No. 9066 came out, authorizing the War Department to remove the Japanese from such military areas as it saw fit, aliens and citizens alike. Even if a person had a fraction of Japanese blood in him, he must leave on demand.

A pall of gloom settled upon our home. We couldn't believe that the government meant that the Japanese-Americans must go, too. We had heard the clamoring of superpatriots who insisted loudly, "Throw the whole kaboodle out. A Jap's a Jap, no matter how you slice him. You can't make an American out of little Jap Junior just by handing him an American birth certificate." But we had dismissed these remarks as just hot blasts of air from an overheated patriot. We were quite sure that our rights as American citizens would not be violated, and we would not be marched out of our homes on the same basis as enemy aliens.

In anger, Henry and I read and reread the Executive Order. Henry crumpled the newspaper in his hand and threw it against the wall. "Doesn't my citizenship mean a single blessed thing to anyone? Why doesn't somebody make up my mind for me. First they want me in the army. Now they're going to slap an alien 4-C on me because of my ancestry. What the hell!"

Once more I felt like a despised, pathetic two-headed freak, a Japanese and an American, neither of which seemed to be doing me any good. The Nisei leaders in the community rose above their personal feelings and stated that they would co-operate and comply with the decision of the government as their sacrifice in keeping with the country's war effort, thus proving themselves loyal American citizens. I was too jealous of my recently acquired voting privilege to be gracious about giving in, and I felt most unco-operative. I noticed wryly that the feelings about the Japanese on the Hawaiian Islands were quite different from those on the West Coast. In Hawaii, a strategic military outpost, the Japanese were regarded as essential to the economy of the island and powerful economic forces fought against their removal. General Delos Emmons, in command of Hawaii at the time, lent his authoritative voice to calm the fears of the people on the island and to prevent chaos and upheaval. General Emmons established martial law, but he did not consider evacuation essential for the security of the island.

On the West Coast, General J. L. DeWitt of the Western Defense Command did not think martial law necessary, but he favored mass evacuation of the Japanese and Nisei. We suspected that pressures from economic and political interests who would profit from such a wholesale evacuation influenced this decision.

Events moved rapidly. General DeWitt marked off Western Washington, Oregon, and all of California, and the southern half of Arizona as Military Area No. 1, hallowed ground from which we must remove ourselves as rapidly as possible. Unfortunately we could not simply vanish into thin air, and we had no place to go. We had no relatives in the east we could move in on. All our relatives were sitting with us in the forbidden area, themselves wondering where to do. The neighboring states in the line of exit for the Japanese protested violently at the prospect of any mass invasion. They said, very sensibly, that if the Coast didn't want the Japanese hanging around, they didn't either.

A few hardy families in the community liquidated their property, tied suitcases all around their cars, and sallied eastward. They were greeted by signs in front of store windows, "Open season for Japs!" and "We kill rats and Japs here." On state lines, highway troopers swarmed around the objectionable migrants and turned them back under governor's orders.

General DeWitt must have finally realized that if he insisted on voluntary mass evacuation, hundreds and thousands of us would have wandered back and forth, clogging the highways and pitching tents along the roadside, eating and sleeping in colossal disorder. He suddenly called a halt to voluntary movement, although most of the Japanese were not budging an inch. He issued a new order, stating that no Japanese could leave the city, under penalty of arrest. The command had hatched another plan, a better one. The army would move us out as only the army could do it, and march us in neat, orderly fashion into assembly centers. We would stay in these centers only until permanent camps were set up inland to isolate us.

The orders were simple:

> Dispose of your homes and property. Wind up your business. Register the family. One seabag of bedding, two suitcases of clothing allowed per person. People in District #1 must report at 8th and Lane Street, 8 p.m. on April 28.

I wanted no part of this new order. I had read in the papers that the Japanese from the state of Washington would be taken to a camp in Puyallup, on the state fairgrounds. The article apologetically assured the public that the camp would be temporary and that the Japanese would be removed from the fairgrounds and parking lots in time for the opening of the annual State Fair. It neglected to say where we might be at the time when those fine breeds of Holstein cattle and Yorkshire hogs would be proudly wearing their blue satin ribbons.

We were advised to pack warm, durable clothes. In my mind, I saw our permanent camp sprawled out somewhere deep in a snow-bound forest, an American Siberia. I saw myself plunging chest deep in the snow, hunting for small game to keep us alive. I decided that one of my suitcases was going to hold nothing but vitamins from A to Z. I thought of sewing fur-lined hoods and parkas for the family. I was certain this was going to be a case of sheer animal survival.

One evening Father told us that he would lose the management of the hotel unless he could find someone to operate it for the duration, someone intelligent and efficient enough to impress Bentley Agent and Company. Father said, "Sam, Joe, Peter, they all promised to stay on their jobs, but none of them can read or write well enough to manage the business. I've got to find a responsible party with experience in hotel management, but where?"

Sumi asked, "What happens if we can't find anyone?"

"I lose my business and my livelihood. I'll be saying good-by to a lifetime of labor and all the hopes and plans I had for the family."

We sagged. Father looked at us thoughtfully, "I've never talked much about the hotel business to you children, mainly because so much of it has been an uphill climb of work and waiting for better times. Only recently I was able to clear up the loans I took out years ago to expand the business. I was sure that in the next five or ten years I would be getting returns on my long-range investments, and I would have been able to do a lot of things eventually. . . . Send you through medical school," Father nodded to Henry, "and let Kazu and Sumi study anything they liked." Father laughed a bit self-consciously as he looked at Mother, "And when all the children had gone off on their own, I had planned to take Mama on her first real vacation, to Europe as well as Japan."

We listened to Father wide-eyed and wistful. It had been a wonderful, wonderful dream.

Mother suddenly hit upon a brilliant idea. She said maybe the Olsens, our old friends who had once managed the Camden Apartments might be willing to run a hotel. The Olsens had sold the apartment and moved to Aberdeen. Mother thought that perhaps Marta's oldest brother, the bachelor of the family, might be available. If he refused, perhaps Marta and her husband might consider the offer. We rushed excitedly to the telephone to make a long-distance call to the Olsens. After four wrong Olsens' we finally reached Marta.

"Marta? Is this Marta?"

"Yes, this is Marta."

I nearly dove into the mouthpiece, I was so glad to hear her voice. Marta remembered us well and we exchanged news about our families. Marta and her husband had bought a small chicken farm and were doing well. Marta said, "I come from the farm ven I vas young and I like it fine. I feel more like home here. How's everybody over there?"

I told her that we and all the rest of the Japanese were leaving Seattle soon under government order on account of the war. Marta gasped, "Everybody? You mean the Saitos, the Fujinos, Watanabes, and all the rest who were living at the Camden Apartments, too?"

"Yes, they and everyone else on the West Coast."

Bewildered, Marta asked where we were going, what we were going to do, would we ever return to Seattle, and what about Father's hotel. I told her about our business situation and that Father needed a hotel manager for the duration. Would she or any of her brothers be willing to accept such a job? There was a silence at the other end of the line and I said hastily, "This is a very sudden call, Marta. I'm sorry I had to surprise you like this, but we felt this was an emergency and . . ."

Marta was full of regrets. "Oh, I vish we could do someting to help you folks, but my husband and I can't leave the farm at all. We don't have anyone here to help. We do all the work ourselves. Magnus went to Alaska last year. He has a goot job up there, some kind of war work. My other two brothers have business in town and they have children so they can't help you much."

My heart sank like a broken elevator. When I said, "Oh . . ." I felt the family sitting behind me sink into a gloomy silence. Our last hope was gone. We finally said good-by, Marta distressed at not being able to help, and I apologizing for trying to hoist our problem on them.

The next week end Marta and Karl paid us a surprise visit. We had not seen them for nearly two years. Marta explained shyly, "It was such a nice day and we don't go novair for a long time, so I tole Karl, 'Let's take a bus into Seattle and visit the Itois.' "

We spent a delightful Sunday afternoon talking about old times. Mother served our guests her best green tea and, as we relaxed, the irritating presence of war vanished. When it was time for them to return home, Marta's sparkling blue eyes suddenly filled, "Karl and I, we feel so bad about the whole ting, the war and everyting, we joost had to come out to see you and say 'good-by.' God bless you. Maybe we vill see you again back home here. Anyvay, we pray for it."

Marta and Karl's warmth and sincerity restored a sense of peace into our home, an atmosphere which had disappeared ever since Pearl Harbor. They served to remind us that in spite of the bitterness war had brought into our lives, we were still bound to our home town. Bit by bit, I remembered our happy past, the fun we had growing up along the colorful brash waterfront, swimming through the white-laced waves of Puget Sound, and lolling luxuriously on the tender green carpet of grass around Lake Washington from where we could see the slick, blue-frosted shoulders of Mount Rainier. There was too much beauty surrounding us. Above all, we must keep friends like Marta and Karl, Christine, Sam, Peter and Joe, all sterling products of many years of associations. We could never turn our faces away and remain aloof forever from Seattle.

Stewart Holbrook

Bulkeley the P.T. Boat Man

from *NONE MORE COURAGEOUS* (1942)

Tropic night hung heavy and quiet over the sea and the Island of Luzon as the crews climbed silently aboard two mosquito boats. Tide lapped at their hulls and flapped at the dock while Lieutenant John D. Bulkeley, commander of the squadron, explained the mission ahead of them.

The order was clear enough, and simple. It merely directed Lieutenant Bulkeley to take his two boats into Binanga Bay and to see what could be done about an enemy ship, class unknown, that had just arrived there under cover of darkness.

To realize the importance of these two small boats and the conditions facing them at this time, which was in late January of 1942, one should know that they were virtually all that was left of the American Navy in Manila Bay. The rest of the Asiatic Fleet had gone to Java and other parts, destroying the supplies left behind when the Yard at Cavite was evacuated. The mosquito boats, which Navy men call PT's—or patrol-torpedo boats—were as yet to prove their full worth. Many Navy men thought they didn't amount to very much.

Lieutenant Bulkeley had faith in his boats, in his little navy. Designed to run from 70 to 80 miles an hour, their engines already had done too many miles to be in top trim, what with no spares to replace worn parts. Today, or tonight rather, they might do 40 miles, or maybe only 35 miles an hour. Yet Bulkeley had faith. His tin-pot navy carried two torpedo tubes to a ship. The torp tubes were aft; to fire a tin fish the PT's must run in against the enemy, turn quickly, then let go while running away from their target.

Bulkeley commanded the squadron. His flagship was the PT-41, in turn commanded by Ensign George E. Cox of Watertown, New York. The other boat, the PT-34, was in charge of Lieutenant Robert Kelley of New York City.

Tonight, the mosquito boats' engines were tuned as well as their condition allowed. The covers of the machine guns were removed, leaving the small steel mouths ready to start their grim stuttering in a dialect that is readily understood by all nations. The tubes were packed with smooth, blackcoated death. Hawsers were cast off, engines turned, and the two boats streaked away to turn from shadows into nothing in the ocean dark.

But Binanga Bay was dark only in spots and for brief periods that night, what happened to be the 19th of January. Searchlights on shore gleamed from Jap positions and swept the water in nervous eccentric arcs.

The foaming wake boiled past the bows of the speeding boats, leaving the telltale phosphorescent glow that might mark their voyage for the watching Japs, if the big lights didn't find them first. Twice the searching fingers swept over the leading boat but did not come low enough. Then they swept aft—still too high to catch Kelly's boat.

For twenty minutes the PT's kept their course without interference. Then the accusing eye from shore rested briefly on Bulkeley's boat, and passed on. All hands breathed easier, but too soon. The eye was returning uneasily for another look. On it came, sweeping the choppy sea, and now it caught the PT-41 and held it fair in the beam.

"It won't be long now," commented Chief Machinist's Mate C. C. Richardson. A moment later Jap shore batteries opened up with all they had. Fore and aft, on port and starboard, plume after plume of the sea erupted and rose high above the speeding boat. Shells screamed overhead. Even machine guns were spraying leaden hail, but in the PT's wake—so far. Meanwhile Lieutenant Kelly's boat was disabled. She made her limping way back whence she had come.

Bulkeley was sending his ship in speedy zigzags, keeping her nose in the general direction of where his quarry was said to be. In and out of the brilliant flashing light it sped, with shellfire following close but never hitting her. But where was the quarry?

"Enemy boat on starboard bow." The lookout called the news, and Lieutenant Bulkeley raised his night glasses. It was a Jap patrol boat, and before it could begin firing, the PT's 50-caliber deck guns were shooting. Bulkeley had no trouble leaving the patrol far behind.

On they went, with eyes straining through the dark to find what they had come for. They ought to be about there now. Another five minutes, perhaps ten minutes, and the sharp eyes of Benny Licodo saw something. Benny, the Filipino steward, had cat's eyes. "Ship ahead, sir," he called to the lookout, and the lookout, who had but ordinarily good eyes, had full trust in Benny's. "Ship ahead, sir," he repeated.

Bulkeley put the glasses on her. The PT pounded on, and presently the watching American could see something ahead that was looming up as big as a house, as big as a barn, no, as big as Madison Square Garden. Then he knew he was running right at a Jap cruiser. He gave his orders:

"Ten degrees left rudder. Full head on the engines. Torpedo crew stand by."

The Jap warship loomed terribly large as the mosquito bore down on her, but Bulkeley knew that one of his fish could whittle her down to size. He gave a quick order. The PT boat swung in a sharp, sudden arc that stood everything aboard her almost on end.

"Fire one," said Bulkeley.

A long shape of sleek destruction leaped clear of the tube with a hiss of compressed air and splashed into the sea, then hurried on its robot way toward the hulking apparition.

The mosquito boat sped away, and the seconds passed with the PT's crew waiting, waiting, for the big noise. It didn't come off. The fish had missed. The sharp eyes, the almost miraculous eyes of Benny Licodo saw it miss.

Lieutenant Bulkeley wasn't going to leave things that way. He pulled his boat around and again he started for the apparition. But the hulking monster was an apparition no longer. Its deck guns were shooting, blazing away, sending big shells screaming too high over the mosquito. The PT roared ahead through big splashes as the Japs attempted to bracket her with their fire.

Bulkeley was now calling the figures he wanted set on the torpedo's dials and gadgets.

"Ready, sir," came the word from his torps men.

"Full left rudder," said Bulkeley. The PT went over on her beam ends in a spray that shut out for a second the blazing guns on the Jap.

"Fire one," ordered Bulkeley. The torpedo hissed, then splashed, and spun away. This time the tin fish went spinning with fury in its mechanism and destruction in its warhead. A few seconds after the hiss, the crew of PT-41 saw a great blinding flash at the big Jap's bow. Then over the water came a mighty roar as tremendous flame leaped high to light the bay for a mile or more around.

The great roar, the mighty roar, died only to be followed in quick succession by other explosions. Now the big ship was silhouetted black against her own flames. She wasn't firing at the mosquito any more. Men were dropping down over her side. She was a goner, right now.

Lighter by tons now, with her tubes empty, the PT-41 sped away home in the light of a blazing warship.

Sending down the cruiser was not the first or the last of the deadly forays the PT squadron made against the Japs. On December 10 when scores of Jap planes were bombing the Cavite Navy Yard, two of the squadron's boats placed themselves in the raiders' path. As the bombers came down in their headlong rush, the turrets on the mosquitoes went into action, eight guns spouting a stream of lead into the planes. All three attacking bombers fell smoking and blazing into the sea.

Five days later, as the SS *Corregidor* was making her tortuous way across Manila Bay, she struck a mine near the fort and began to sink. Two PT's immediately put out into the Bay, threaded their way through the mine field, picked up 282 persons from the sinking ship and the water, and again made their way through the mine field to safety.

Sinking the Jap cruiser, though, had been the PT's great moment until the night of January 24. This one was even better than getting the cruiser.

With Ensign Cox again at the helm, Lieutenant Bulkeley took a mosquito out to Sampalac Point, at the entrance to Subic Bay, where a Jap aircraft tender had been anchored—incautiously, when John Bulkeley's gang was on the prowl. They had no trouble finding the Jap. They went in with their usual rush, made the turn-on-a-dime, and sent a torpedo crashing into the tender's midships.

The one fish doubtless was enough, but John Bulkeley is a man who likes to make certain of a job. He ran his PT to 500-yard range, then let go another torpedo. The crash and explosion was magnificent, and the PT's crew got a good view from their foaming stern.

Now a searchlight found the PT and played on her, and from shore came 3-inch shells, howling overhead. It was beginning to be time to get out of there, but Bulkeley didn't want any Japs from the sinking tender to drown. He ran in again, this time to within a hundred yards and then turned his machine guns on the Jap. The sinking tender's decks were alive with men, but only for a few minutes. Twice the PT swept past, her 50-calibers rattling, sweeping the tender's sides, her decks, and the water around her.

It was, as the lieutenant later admitted, a most satisfactory evening. "As I understand war," he said, "you've got to kill the enemy, a lot of him."

The various raids of the PT fleet had by now roused the Japs to furious action. Their patrol boats scouted day and night. Planes came looking for them. But the Americans hid out by day in one or other of the countless bays and inlets. On the night of February 1, one of the skeets rushed to the west coast of Bataan where a Jap light cruiser was landing troops. Two torpedoes struck the Jap. She didn't sink, but she must have been badly damaged. She raised anchor and went away.

For the next two weeks the mosquito squadron cruised by night and hid by day, seeing no action. The crews were letting their beards grow. Lieutenant Bulkeley's stiff black whiskers did famously well. They burgeoned daily and foliated until the boys said he looked more like a prophet than a Navy man with four years of Annapolis behind him. In truth, all but one of the skeet squadron's men appeared very much like the sailors one sees in old prints of Civil War days. The exception was young Ensign Cox whose fuzz remained fuzz and who had to take a lot of horsing regarding his naked condition.

It was during this comparatively inactive period that C. C. Richardson, chief machinist's mate, kept the boys' spirits up by his elaborate wagers on the outcome of the war. Not the outcome, really, but *when* the Americans would win. His odds shifted almost daily, and seemed to be predicated on all sorts of unrelated subjects, such as the daily health and disposition of Boat 41's mascot, a monkey christened Admiral Tojo.

Things started picking up again on the night of February 18. Learning that a Jap tanker was moored at Olongapo dock, a PT went out with one torpedo and set the tanker afire. At almost the same hour in another mosquito, the beardless Ensign Cox sighted a Jap encampment. He cruised past once to take in the lay of the land. It looked like a pretty good opportunity.

Running his boat close in shore, and holding his fire until the figures of Jap soldiers could be plainly seen, Cox's boat opened up with its four machine guns, strafing the camp unmercifully for two hundred yards.

Three-inch guns on shore set up a clatter. Machine guns in the camp started spewing. And the quiet bivouac of the Japs turned into bedlam.

When he got to the end of the camp, Cox turned his boat on her heels and started back the same way. His four guns were blazing to the unheard but fervent profanities of joy of the American gunners. How sweetly they rattled! Enemy fire raked the PT, but she never faltered. Her engines pounded and roared as if they were never in need of new gaskets.

At the end of the encampment again, Cox shouted for a quick turn. "Let's do it again!" he cried, and sure enough they went right over the old route and shot away every bullet they had except a string for possible emergencies on the way home. But they got home without incident.

For three weeks the squadron lived in another comparative lull. Machinist's Mate Richardson, never at his best in such periods, allowed that he'd have to lengthen his odds if the Americans didn't get busy and do something. "This laying around will never get us anywhere," he said.

An opportunity for doing something arrived on the night of March 11. Lieutenant Bulkeley and his tiny flagship were ordered to a hidden landing on Corregidor. That night, which was mercifully dark, the boat waited to execute a very special mission, a mission then known only to Lieutenant Bulkeley. Just before midnight a group of Army officers, one woman, and a boy, came quietly to the dock and began boarding. Members of the mosquito boat's crew were both amazed and thrilled to see a tall, straight man with four stars on his shoulders.

"It's the General!" Benny Licodo, he of the sharp eyes, whispered. It was MacArthur with his staff, his wife, and son.

So, the PT navy was to carry the commander in chief on the first lap of his journey to the new front in Australia.

Hearts beat fast at the thought, even faster at the thought of the

Jap shore batteries around Manila Bay. With all lights out the PT and its precious cargo pulled away from the dock.

"Full speed ahead," said Bulkeley, the boss admiral of the American fleet in Manila Bay, now engaged in ferrying the boss general of the American army in the Pacific.

Full speed was pretty fast. The PT had had some overhauling. Tonight she shook the full length of her seventy-seven feet from the pound of the engines.

One may ponder if any of the PT's crew thought of the voyage in relation to another time and another night, when "the fate of a nation was riding." Probably not. But fate was riding that night. Here was a small craft speeding through the night, speeding past the shore batteries of an alert enemy, carrying aboard the commander in chief of the South Pacific. It was a weighty load, no matter how you look at it.

On and on past the quiet batteries went the mosquito. Every moment the tightened minds of those aboard, especially the men of the boat's crew, expected to see a flash in the dark and to hear a shell on its way.

But not a flash was seen, either of cannon or searchlight; and two days later, on the mainland of the United States, millions of Americans felt better to know that their Number One man of the Pacific was safe in Australia. The mosquito boat didn't do it all, for a big plane took over at a secret rendezvous to finish the voyage. But the mosquito had the first lap and did it to America's taste.

By the time America knew of MacArthur's safe arrival Down Under, Lieutenant Bulkeley and his boys were planning another voyage. Back at Corregidor again, they stood by while President Manuel Quezon, his wife, two daughters, and his staff boarded the PT. It was to be the same thing all over again—that is, if the gods were with them still.

Choosing the same time of night and using the same cruising tactics, the boat set out to run the shore batteries. They did it again, and without seeing or hearing artillery. But a ghastly danger appeared much nearer than the shores of Manila Bay.

The sea was running high. The little boat was being slapped this way and that, like a mere chip. One of the boat's crew ran to Lieutenant Bulkeley to speak in a low voice:

"Sir, two of our torpedoes are loose. The retaining pins have broken."

Now John Bulkeley was a man inured to danger. He and his men had faced death from the sky, from the sea, from the land. He had seen several of his men killed. He had taken all these things in stride.

Here, however, was a new kind of danger, a horrible sort of danger, the kind a man couldn't stand up and fight against. Two deadly missiles, each twenty-two feet long—enough to blow not only a PT boat but a big battleship into pieces—were loose, alive, on one small boat. Bulkeley hurried aft to the tubes. He saw that the retaining pins, sure enough, were broken. The lethal cylinders were halfway out of their tubes, their grim mechanism set for action. A simple tap, a mere jar, in the right place . . .

Bulkeley later told a man that if he had had time to think even for an instant, he might have frozen with fear. But the sea was slapping the boat, it was slapping the two torpedoes. The boat and its cargo faced death in one mighty explosion that would have left nothing recognizable. If anything were to be done, it was now. And before Bulkeley could move further, it was being done.

Torpedo-man John L. Houlihan had run to the tubes, hammer in hand, and had started in. In a moment Bulkeley and two other men were at his side.

The four men went to work with an unhurried swiftness of motion that comes only from knowledge of the thing to be done and how to do it. Deluged by every wave that struck the boat aft, these four men went to work with hammers and gadgets. Each blow might be the blow to send them all to kingdom come, but the firing mechanism must be motivated. Hanging to the rail and the tubes for dear life, they struck between waves when they could see what they were striking at. Suddenly there came a great big whissh! and the two fish plunged into the sea and sped away . . .

One can wonder today, long afterward, if on some forgotten reef or shore are the two cylinders that might well have called for a new election of the Philippine Commonwealth-in-Exile and at the same time reduced Lieutenant John D. Bulkeley to a rank less than an ensign's.

The men besides Bulkeley who handled the "hot-run" torpedoes were John Houlihan, of Chicopee Falls, Massachusetts, already mentioned; James D Light, Chief torpedoman, of Vallejo, California, and none other than the brave and able if beardless Ensign Cox.

With MacArthur and Quezon moved to safety, most of the mosquito fleet's men thought their part in the Philippines was over. Mate Richardson again took to complaining about lack of action. Again his odds on the war shifted erratically. Even "Admiral Tojo," the monkey mascot of PT-41, seemed morose. Then came the night of April 8.

The two mosquitoes were operating in the Mandano Sea near the Island of Cebu. Lieutenant Bulkeley still commanded his well-worn Number 41, and Ensign Cox was still at the helm. The other boat, the 34, still had Robert Kelly in command. Without any warning at all a flotilla of Jap warships appeared.

Bulkeley looked them over as well as he could. He found his two-skeet navy face to face with one heavy Jap cruiser and four destroyers. He blinked his aft lights at Kelly to say that he was going to attack and for Kelly to follow at the right distance. Then the two boats raced past the nearest destroyer and closed in on the big ship. Just then the cruiser's lights swept by and paused on Kelly's boat, paused and held it in the beam while the warship's secondary guns began blasting. It looked to be all over for Kelly.

Bulkeley ran his boat close to the cruiser, heeled, and let go. Right on his tail Kelly came tearing in, to turn quickly, and fire another torpedo. Both found their mark on the big Jap, which began smoking.

The Jap's guns were still firing, and Kelly's boat seemed to be in the middle of it. Barking out some fast orders, Bulkeley raced his boat around the warship, hoping to draw some of its fire and thus permit Kelly to get in closer to loose another fish. Bulkeley got around the cruiser and in the face of gunfire from destroyers and the cruiser, too, he started sweeping the cruiser's decks with his machine guns. Just as expected and hoped for, the cruiser turned more of its guns on Bulkeley's boat.

While this maneuver was going on, Lieutenant Kelly saw his opening—and used it beautifully. Rushing in almost under the muzzles of the big ship's blazing guns, he let go a torpedo, dashed back on the return run, then loosed another. The two missiles struck the Jap with an explosion that rocked Kelley's boat like a cork. A moment later debris and Japs were falling back into the sea.

On the other side, one of the Jap destroyers was advancing on Bulkeley's boat, firing its machine guns and 3-inchers. The mosquito returned the fire, then ran away into the night, to hide near shore.

It wasn't quite all over yet. When daylight came, four Jap planes found Bulkeley's hide-out. They attacked at once, using both machine guns and bombs. Bulkeley maneuvered his boat very well and escaped, shooting down one of the enemy planes.

Kelly's boat had been badly shot up. He managed to get it to safety without help, then removed the dead and wounded. Bulkeley's boat was in little better shape, and all of its guns had been knocked out. Just before Corregidor fell to the enemy, the remnants of the mosquito fleet were destroyed to prevent their capture. Both Bulkeley and Kelly and their crews hated to treat their old boats that way.

Cox, Bulkeley, and Kelly were flown off The Rock just before it fell and were brought to the United States.

Lieutenant Bulkeley was pleased that the Navy gave him a Navy Cross and later the highest award of the nation—the Congressional Medal of Honor. He was more pleased that the destructive ability of his PT squadron was recognized and praised by the Navy. He doesn't believe for a moment that PT's alone will win the Navy's war, but he thinks they are pretty darned good. Doubtless the Japs think so too.

John Bulkeley is a stocky, well-built man, with a good fighting face. His black hair is thinning. His blue-gray eyes are steady. Born in New York City in 1911, he was appointed to the Naval Academy from Texas in 1929, graduated with the class of 1933, and was honorably discharged. He got his commission in 1934. After serving on various ships he was put in command of a submarine chaser division in 1941. He used to live in San Antonio, but his wife, daughter, and son—the son born when father was sinking a cruiser—make their home in Long Island City.

Shortly after Bulkeley arrived in Washington after his exploits in the Philippines, Manuel Quezon came to town. Hearing that the hero of Subic Bay was back from the Islands, the Philippine president asked to see him, to thank him for taking the Quezons to safety. The smooth-shaven, boyish lieutenant was presented. Quezon was puzzled. He recalled a bushy black beard. "But I mean the senior Bulkeley," he said. "Doubtless the father of this young man."

"But," the Filipino was told, "this is the man who took you from Corregidor."

Quezon was amazed. "Had I known," he said to Bulkeley, "had I known you were but a boy, I should not have dared to trust my family with you that night."

Quezon's surprise made John Bulkeley very proud of that set of battle whiskers he had grown in the Islands.

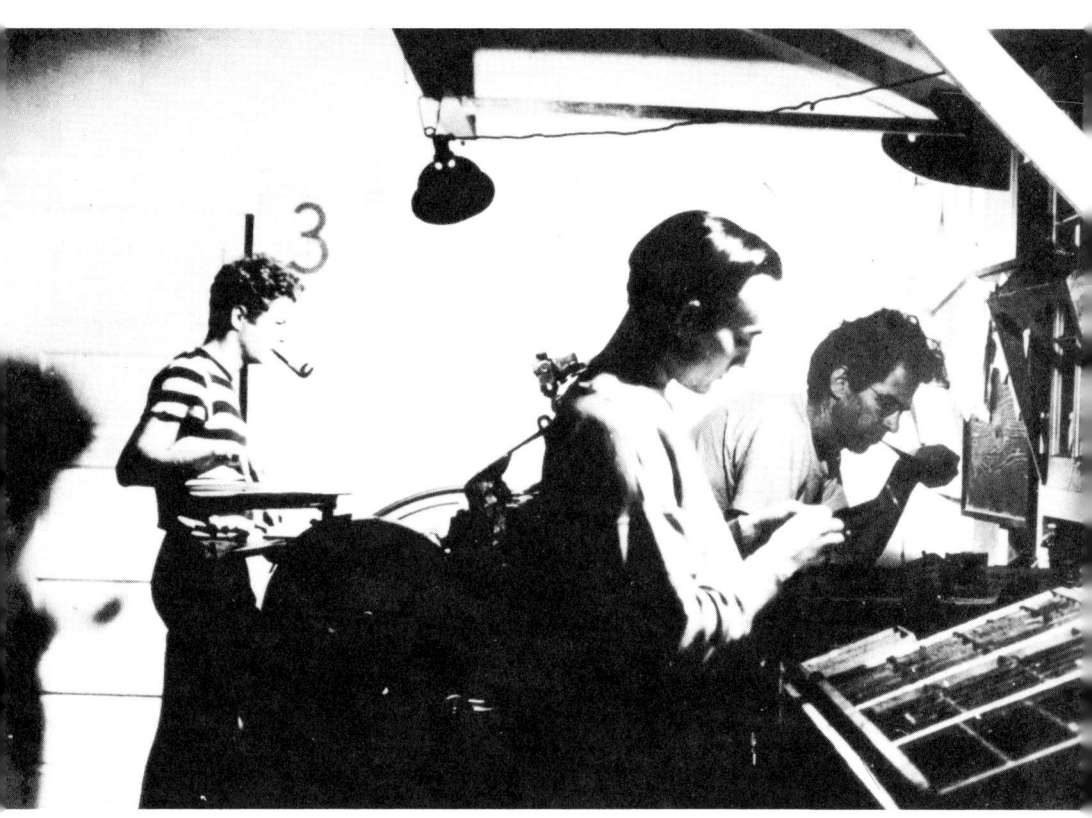

Vladimir Dupre, William Eschelman, William Everson in print shop at CPS Camp 56, Waldor

William Everson

From *THE WALDPORT POEMS*

NOTE

This series of poems is an attempt to render whole the emotional implications of a kind of life that has become almost universal: the life of the camp, the life of enforced confinement, individual repression, sexual segregation. Everywhere in the world these centers exist, huge impermanent cities housing millions of men—conscription camps, concentration camps, prison camps, internment camps, labor camps. Their effect upon the human spirit is not to be measured within the framework of a generation; the scars will remain for decades.

I wrote these poems during my first six months in a labor camp for conscientious objectors, at the period when emotional reaction to the disruption of my life was at its most intense. I had left behind me a marriage of five years' standing, a new farm, a region wherein I was completely adjusted and had no wish to leave. I was thirty years old, and after an unstable coming-up, I had tasted enough of the good life to be quite reluctant to forgo it.

I point these things out because as a pacifist I perceive clearly that whatever I say should be a testament to the integrity of which the history of pacifism is full: an ability to overlook the irritation of detail for the historical perspective. But as a poet I wanted to grasp the overtones of my immediate experience, to weigh the particular against the general, and try to find between them what would be common to all men. I did not wish to once again concern myself against the war. I had said my say in a previous series, and I knew that the uses of poetry are best directed toward other ends. When I came to write I found that what manifested itself, below my participatory acts, my intentions, my concern for a cause to which I had committed myself, remained the basic mood of separation, of loss, a primal injustice, a huge dissatisfaction that stands as basic a protest to the coercive life as any summary of detail I could muster. It is the kind of attitude which is impossible to hide, and my one concern was to let it speak for itself. It is my hope that it speaks also for The Conscripted Man, wherever he might be.

William Everson
10 July 1944
Camp Angel
Waldport, Oregon

ONE

That morning we rose,
And broke the fast as had been our custom,
Having fashioned between us too long a time
The pattern of living to scant it at last.
There was haste to be made,
And to that end we strove,
But neither the schedule in its compulsion,
Nor the host of pressures that verge on departure,
Could loosen the brittle clamp of abstraction
That fastened our minds.

For this, we had nothing,
As the patient, prone on the table,
Cannot encompass the massing years
Divorced of his limb.
We moved in our trance,
In utter unrealness,
Till the clock,
That had pulled itself toward its ultimate hour,
Tocked once in its orbit,
And toppled the heavy hanging wave
That taught us the knowledge of loss.

THREE

This, then, is our world.
Having entered the gate
Who is there to measure the length of our stay?
The factors that manage that endurance have yet to be formed.
This much we know:
Blood will be poured,
The world in constriction must loosen, unlock,
And the tides withdraw,
And all the wide chaos,
That dwarfs our meager participation,
Must have its great way.
Yet the impassive calendar governs our minds;
And the gate remains,
Broad for departure,
To pass if we choose.
Some of us do,
Openly asking the consequent hurt,
Or by stealth and deceit in the moon's blindness.
Only rumor returns.
We others remain,
Holding within us the vast temptation and the obscure threat,
And nurse the wide cleavage of will.

SEVEN

No man is alone.
Side by side in the long room
We mingle and touch,
Nudge at the table,
Shout on the walks,
Lie head to heel in the close beds.
Even at stool we squat in our row—
The private act revealed and made known to the corporate eye.

Yet after a time the mind erects its own defenses.
The tongue chatters,
The mobile mouth smiles and flouts,
In the steaming baths the nudists dance
And wrestle with joy,
But behind the bone wall
The spirit whistles and sings to itself,
Keeping its inward motion and its transitory grace
While the bodies touch.

But the body itself,
Though it turns and cavorts,
And schools forever to the avid throng,
Does it not tire?

Will it not also,
Some subsequent day,
Aware of stillness and a strange peace,
Be glad to be wholly alone?

EIGHT

    The man struck from the woman—
    That is the crime.
    As the armies grow so gathers the guilt,
    So bloom the perversions,
    So flower the fears,
    So breed the deep cruelties
    And the secretive hurts.
    And each, the man and the woman,
    Too much alone,
    Age and grow cold.

    Let the man touch the woman.

    Now the husband dreams of the wife,
    Recalling her clear singing and her solitary grace.

    We are not whole.

And she?
Sadly apart she stirs in sleep and makes moan,
Turns and makes moan,
Needing the all-encompassing arm
That now is not there.

ELEVEN

But at length we learn,
Finding the chastening pattern to school desire:
Not tamper with time,
Neither rowel the future nor finger the past.
The world wars on,
Our subsequent fate involved in its toil,
But the abstract voice that spills from the box
Cannot bring it clear.
Even the purpose by which we have come
Loses distinction,
With the lover's face and the wife's affection,
Here in the wilderness,
The waste of the world,
Bounded between the continent's back
And the absolute West.
We rise in the dawns,
Enter the day;
We eye the weather and watch the sea,
In its manifest purpose,
Marshall itself for another assault.
Whether or not we are heroes or fools
Is hardly the point,
Who have learned in this
That all achievement is only attained
By the thick sequence of forced beginnings
Composing an act
As the soldier,
Crouching and killing,
Must also know,

Bent by his gun.
Having fastened on this we can only endure,
Immersed in the corework of the will,
And wade up time,
Where the glacial future,
Frozen and formed in the stone ranges beyond our sight,
Yields only the irridescent trickle
That bleeds from its throat.

THE WALDPORT POEMS

was published in an edition of 975 copies,
and completed in the month of July, 1944.
It was printed on Linweave paper,
in Goudy Light and Lydian types,
and executed upon a clam-action monster
of incalculable vintage.
It is the second printed publication of
The Untide Press,
the venture of a group of pacifists
at Camp Angel, Waldport, Oregon,
who, from under the mantle of conscription,
submit it as one of the manifestations
of those who seek to affirm the creative man.

William Stafford

From *THE ILLITERATI*, Summer 1943
Wyeth, Oregon

SEARCH

I went in every house and every room.
I climbed the stairs, descended the basement steps,
    and followed the narrow halls;
And my feet picked up more dust.
And I often stopped, rich with thought.
And when I came to the doors again,
I knew each house.
But it was not home.

CO'S WORK ON MOUNTAIN ROAD

Like bay trees on the edge of La Cumbro Peak,
liking with wistful scent and the swooping world below,
we few dreamers
on the edge of the now savage years, jagged beyond sight,
audaciously lean, suspiring a few old messages from
    the old earth still under our trustful foot.
The pines have left us and are marching;
the sycamores fly angry tints;
the oaks present overworked postures, extreme.
Who cares in a big country for a few egret trees,
    on one cliff, on an edge, leaning far out,
    on a scent like a memory?

Glen Coffield

From *THE ILLITERATI*, Summer, 1945

CONSIDER THE UNSPEAKABLE PARDONS

    Consider the unspeakable pardons
    The mind owes the body;
    For earth in its wielding breaks bone,
    Shatters nerve for unreasonable asking;
    And the sad dilapidated onion,
    That leaves its taste in the mouth,
    Is the principle ally of late hours;
    In rooms of private study,
    Or in the desperate fling under stars,
    When the mind bows out,
    And begs to apologize.

    It is in resolute desire
    The mind breaks open its blossom and fails.
    But not in confusion's roar,
    Which knows no clear turning,
    No lathework, or a crystal promise;
    For here speaks the long view,
    The unshaped vista,
    The day a man were foolish to die for,
    Till he knows.

    Only in simple comprehension
    Is the word made fact,
    And yet what language
    Never known at all
    Except by craving of a singer's frown,

And what mistaken meaning,
First construed the depth of ruin
That was born as real
To a gibbering idiot child
With a broken doll?
These shapes, these vessels halved,
Are not the goal, nor plan,
Nor children of kings,
But only the toys
That prophets shape for gold.

Glen Coffield 1944.

Sophus Keith Winther

From *BEYOND THE GARDEN GATE* (1946)

Nobody Tells The Truth (chapter 4)

While Tom was preparing the second breakfast, his mind kept turning to Forrest. It seemed to Tom that something from his own past was catching up with him, and with Forrest; perhaps with the whole world. "That might be it," he said aloud as he slipped the coffee pot on the stove and began to cut the bacon. He let himself go. He liked following a thought like this one. It had the fascination of the unpractical. It was his own, and it was not subject to contradiction. Something, he thought, was catching up with everything in the world. Old, deep, long buried forces were beginning to assert themselves. The world was being pursued by something it had for the moment outstripped in its mad onward plunge toward a doubtful goal. If he looked back along the road leading into the past there wasn't a thing in sight; but as soon as he started forward again he could feel it coming. It was creeping over the plains, along the dark mountain passes, it was in hot pursuit and one day it would overtake him and the whole world.

The coffee pot burst into violent agitation, spilling water out on the hot burner. "All right, all right," said Tom, turning to the coffee pot. "Go ahead. Raise hell." It's just as well, he thought, I would get nowhere on that road anyway. "At least not yet," he said aloud as if promising himself that he would return to that idea later. Probably at night, in bed, that would be the time to go on such a journey. He smiled. "I'll get Emily Brontë to go with me. She could tell me or any man how to go places in a world like that. It must have been wonderful in Gondal land. Strange, beautiful, weird, and full of all the wild terrors that pursue the imagination of man."

But he could not escape the mood that had come over him. His mind turned to the past and all at once he began to think about his grandfather. He remembered his red beard, and his hard calloused hands. He remembered as a boy how those hands hurt him even when grandfather meant to be gentle. Tom remembered things his father had told him about the old man. How Breckridge Bailey had come to Eugene in a covered wagon with the early pioneers. His outfit had been snowbound in the mountains on the Upper Willamette, and saved on Christmas Day by a rescue party from Goshen. "Your grandfather was a devout man." Tom had heard that often enough. Lord, he thought, I wonder if my sons ever think of me the way I thought of my father? We never had a serious talk without warning and moralizing platitudes. He must have learned them from his father. It must have been the fear of the wilderness that made them talk that way. Or just the fear of life. Why did grandfather ever leave Iowa? He had a good farm there. Then he sold it and came this long journey to end up in debt to the bankers. Why did he do it? Maybe Bertrand Russell is right. People want to go to war, to fight, to leave their homes, burn up their security for a hazard at adventure because life is monotonous. Its economic routine is dull. So is their sex life, or what little most people have. Suddenly Tom laughed so loudly that Elizabeth came to the door in wonder. She was forty-six, she admitted that, but as he saw her in the doorway—in a pair of gray slacks, her hair caught back from her ears with two silver pins and hanging loose down her back, and her naked breasts, not small like ripe apples as they once were, but still well shaped with sharp nipples pointing right out at him—to him she was beautiful. "Elizabeth, I think you're lovely. Damn it, I think you're beautiful."

She rushed over to him, threw her arms around his neck, and pressed her naked body against him. "I could cry," she whispered.

"Well, don't," he said as he kissed her.

"What were you laughing at?" she asked.

"Laughing? Oh, I happened to think of Reverend Davis. Didn't I tell you? Mr. Barker who lives in the apartment below the Reverend at Berkeley Court told me that last Saturday night he was having a little party. They must have been noisy, for the preacher complained."

"What's funny about that?"

"The reason he gave for objecting to the noise. He said that Saturday night was his love-night, and the noise interfered."

Westside Eugene.

Ferry Street Bridge on the Willamette. The Chambers Rowboat.

"Shame on you," Elizabeth said. "You shouldn't laugh at such things."

"No, perhaps not. But think of having a love-night, just one every week, like prayer meeting night. What if one should have the belly-ache on Saturday night? Then I suppose you would just skip that week.

"Go on with the breakfast," said Elizabeth, and left him to his work.

Real pancakes. None of this prepared stuff. How can people eat pancakes thick as a thumb and dry as a toadstool? He mixed his with sour buttermilk in which there were hundreds of little globules of yellow butter. Then just the right amount of soda, a pinch of salt, and two eggs. That would make nine pancakes about the thickness of a plate. While he was frying the cakes he had another pan filled with strips of bacon, not the dried-up package stuff, but real bacon, home-smoked by a farmer, and cut fresh from the slab. In the meantime the coffee had begun to perk; nothing like well perked coffee, with fine rich cream.

Maybe it did all begin long ago on that farm in Iowa. Wonder what happened? Did grandpa start out to the horse pasture one day to repair a section of the fence, and then when he reached the little hill beyond the creek did he look to the west? Did it flash over him all at once that this security was deadly? Did he dream of great adventure on the plains, and did he hurry home to order his wife to begin packing? Did he say, "We're going to Oregon— great country out there—all the land you want for the taking— great timber land, rivers so clear you can see the trout at a depth of twenty feet"? Was that it? Was that the way grandpa began his move west? Or was it something else? Had there been a shady deal of some kind? Many emigrants came west, just as their ancestors before them came from across tre Atlantic, because of trouble with the law. Maybe they had cheated some one. Maybe they had signed a false mortgage. That might be the answer. Still grandfather had money when he came to Eugene. The old Applegates admitted that, and no one doubted an Applegate on matters concerning the early settlers. Somebody should study the Applegate family. That winter on the new trail. That was a saga as good as the story of the Donners. The Applegates were great people. No doubt about it. Why did grandpa leave? Women. Maybe it was women. The Mormons were not the only people who moved from comfort into the wilderness because of woman trouble. That's something that began a long time ago. Not a once-a-week affair either. Joseph had woman trouble in Egypt. Menelaus had plenty of it. So did the Puritans. No wonder they had to burn witches and write secret diaries. But grandfather! Tom smiled to himself at the thought. Could be, though. It was an amusing idea. He resolved to give it some further thought. Maybe something started back there in Iowa that would not end until the family moved again.

The breakfast was done. Elizabeth came out, fully dressed this time. "It looks wonderful," she said as she took her place at the table and poured the coffee. "Did you make enough for the thermos?"

"Sure. I already filled it."

"You know what I was thinking in there?" She gestured with a shake of her head in the direction of her dressing room.

"No. But I know what I was thinking. There is something about this day that recalls the past. As I grow older I begin to realize that one of these days I'm going to read Proust and know what he meant. Do you remember when we started *Swann's Way*, reading it aloud? We didn't like it, did we? I think it will be different now. I was thinking about my grandfather. There was something eating on him. Somewhere back in Iowa he walked along the corn rows one day, and then it happened. It struck him that what he wanted was beyond the law, beyond anything man had made, and then he thought of Oregon. He didn't know anything about Oregon. None of the pioneers knew anything, really, about the land they set out for. Pioneers never have. They run toward a dream; but far more impelling is the fact that they run away from something."

"That is just what I was thinking," said Elizabeth. "Or, at least, nearly the same. I was thinking that if man were happy there would be neither poetry nor art of any kind. Did you ever read a happy story that wasn't insipid, or just plain gruesome nonsense, like Tennyson's 'Happy, Happy, Happy'? It makes your good pancakes taste as though they were fried in gall even to think about it."

"Most anything of Tennyson tastes like that to me. He was trying to run away from something, like most of the Victorians."

"Or like us?" said Elizabeth.

"Well, yes. I guess so. We do it differently. Still I think we try to tell the truth even when we fail, but Tennyson ran like a scared hound whenever he saw the face of truth."

"All right, let's forget it. We're going on a picnic. Remember? We're going to have fun recovering our lost youth. Didn't you know that?"

Tom smiled. "What do people talk about when they are having fun? I have fun talking about Tennyson because I hate him so much. Engaged for seventeen years. What do you suppose Emily was doing, besides drying up?"

Tom paused for an answer.

"Do you know we are almost out of pepper?" said Elizabeth.

"No! Really?"

"Yes. Really. And I don't like that fine-ground pepper. It tastes like something swept off the floor late at night. I want the nice coarse-ground pepper. Do you think you could remember that?"

"All right. I'll remember," said Tom, willing for Elizabeth to lead for the moment. "If you'll pack the lunch, I'll get dressed, and then we'll head for the mountains. There is the place to talk, where the mighty crags speak as if a voice were in them."

"Goodbye, Mr. Wordsworth. I'll see you when you're dressed."

William O. Douglas

from *OF MEN AND MOUNTAINS* (1950)

It was a cold July day in 1948. The snow had been particularly heavy the preceding winter. There were seven feet of it on the level around our cabin in the Wallowas on April 15, and two feet of it were still there on May 15. When I arrived from Washington, D.C., in mid-June, the snow was gone from the Lostine canyon but big drifts hung on the ridges and blocked all trails. Aerial reports showed the high lakes wholly or partially frozen. It would be a brief season for fishermen, and almost as brief for the trout. There would be only a few weeks for the bug hatches on which trout fatten. July would be almost gone before the water was rid of its icy chill, and September frosts would be on the heels of the dog days of August.

Green Lake is one of the first of the high lakes to open in the spring. It lies 7100 feet up, nestled under granite crags of the ridge that bounds the North Minam Meadows on the south. The mountains rim it in horseshoe fashion, the north side being open. That side of the lake laps the edge of a great saucer. Almost 2000 feet below the rim is the North Minam. The mountain drops off from that edge in a great tangle of lava rock and conifers, as wild and broken terrain as one can find in the mountains. This pocket in the Wallowas is a high shelf. One sits high in the heavens on the edge of this lake. At the south side of the lake is a rich meadow with a small stream that in late August is only inches wide but ice cold. This is an ideal place to camp. There is feed for the horses; and if they tire of that, there is the sweet mountain fescue or bunchgrass (*Festuca viridula*) on the ridges above.

There are conies (carrying Stanley Jewett's name) in the rock slides to scold and chatter. There are does and bucks on the rim; and there are cougar and coyote to hunt them—hunters that know no law against taking does and fawns, hunters that have no legal limit on the kill. If one watches carefully he may see the gray-crowned rosy finch, the red crossbill. He might even see the Rocky

Mountain pine grosbeak, a ruffed grouse or possibly a fool hen (Franklin's grouse).

The water of the lake is deep green from the rich algae that cover its bottom and give it its name. The fish are especially sweet. They are eastern brook, fat and lively. Isaak Walton said, "If I catch a trout in one Meadow, he shall be white and faint, and very like to be lousy; and as certainly if I catch a Trout in the next Meadow, he shall be strong, and read, and lusty and much better meat." I think I could take a taste test and find the one Green Lake trout in the frying pan. They have the sweetest taste of any eastern brook I have eaten. One of them is worth a half-dozen of any others I have known.

These fish were a part of the magnet that drew me over the mountains. I left our cabin around 5 a.m.—an early start because the snow promised slow travel. Normally it takes three hours to go the seven miles to the North Minam Meadows on horseback. My daughter Millie set the record for that trip when she was sixteen— the time when Dick McDaniel was thrown from a horse and had a concussion. Then Millie rode Lightning out to Lapover for a doctor in an hour and a half, without putting the horse beyond a walk. I would be lucky to make the trip in four hours this July day. Brownie Basin lies about 2000 feet above the Lostine. This morning it was filled with drifts of snow. Towering over it are jagged granite cliffs. There was a stark grandeur about them. Huge avalanches of snow perched on their shoulders, with ten-foot drifts all the way to the top. The saddle, half as wide as a city street, was filled with broken blocks of snow more than a dozen feet thick. Below the saddle to the west are Wilson Basin and John Henry Lake. The sun was high and John Henry was sparkling as if a million mirrors were casting light on it.

The hillside snow was too soft for horses, so I walked, leading Dan. We both floundered in it for a half-mile or more and did not leave it until we reached the basin, a rich meadow dotted with pine and fir and lying about 7000 feet high.

Here I saw young whitebark pines, bent even as the bunch grass from the pressure of heavy snow that had burdened them that winter. Hundreds of them had been crushed under the terrific weight, some never to straighten again. I remembered one in particular, a whitebark pine 15 or 20 feet high. It bowed at a crazy angle; and so it would be shaped throughout its life. But already it had turned its tip straight as an arrow to the sky. It reminded me of England, crushed under the burden of war but raising her proud head to the sky where freedom lives.

I went down the pitch of trail that leads to the North Minam Meadows—the old Bowman, which dropped off the mountain like a spiral staircase. It often lay thick in powdered dust in August. Today it was wet with snow water and had been heavily washed and gouged by spring floods.

In the Meadows I found elk grazing, and I heard coyotes yapping at them from the mountainside. From Wilson Basin the trail had been lined with flowers and shrubs in bloom. The Meadows were ablaze with colors, wild flowers rioting in the late spring that had suddenly arrived in the Wallowas. The North Minam River was so far over its banks as to transform the Meadows into a lake. Dan had to swim the middle stretch. I held my feet on his shoulders, and the water lapped at my saddle seat.

We went into the woods on the other side and found the Culbertson Trail to Green Lake—most of it a treacherous series of cutbacks that climb for a mile at 45 degrees or more. I leaned forward against Dan's neck and rested him frequently, since it was his first strenuous exercise of the season.

There was much down timber that had to be cut away, for we were the first travelers of the year. There was a lot of snow at the lake. But the water itself was clear of ice and snow; and so was the half of the meadow nearest the lake. There was not a sign of life on the surface. I took a yellow and black woolly worm from my box, tied it onto a nine-foot gut leader, and at the head of the leader put a small split shot. Usually I trim off the fuzz, leaving only a shank wound tight with wool yarn, but this time I left it on. On the retrieve from the first cast I had a strike. On the fourth I had an 11-inch eastern brook. In short order I caught six trout, ranging from 11 to 13 inches.

I kneeled by the icy brook to clean them. Then I appreciated for the first time the full glory of the meadow. The grass was beginning to appear, only a quarter-or half-inch above the group, not yet high enough for a horse to take in his lips. Ahead of the grass were the buttercups. The meadow was golden with them in the late sun. There were spots of star moss on some of the rotten tree trunks. Hellebore, its leaves all furled in conical shape, was beginning to poke its head out of the ground, but no other plants were in evidence.

Serviceberry, chokecherry, red willow or dogwood, elderberry, currant and snowbrush were the shrubs in bloom. Yellow columbine, stickweed, pussytoes, western valerian, skunk cabbage, tall groundsel, sweetroot, western wallflower, wild rose, windflower, miner's lettuce, alumroot, twinberry, heartleaf arnica, wild carrot, buttercup, yellow violet, sheep bluebells (liked more by sheep and cattle than by horses), Solomon's-seal, several penstemon, strawberry, Richardson's geranium, Oregon grape, yarrow, forget-me-nots, larkspur, honeysuckle (gilia), and lupine—these were the wild flowers I picked in the dusk.

The most fragrant of all was the snowbrush (*Ceanothus velutinus*), sometimes known as tobacco brush, mountain balm, and sticky laurel. It is popularly called chaparral, a term applied loosely to describe various types of shrubby vegetation. Chamise is its prototype on the desert. As Walt Dutton of the Forest Service once told me, "It's chaparral if you can't ride a horse through it; chamise, if you can."

Snowbrush comes into a region on the heels of a forest fire and often takes over. Many of the snowbrush areas of the Northwest are almost impenetrable. They are a nightmare to fire fighters. The shrub can't be pulled because it is too deeply rooted. It can't be chopped readily because it is too loose and springy at the base. But it can be snapped off easily—if one knows how—because it is extremely brittle at the ground level. Digging a fire trench through it is a fine art, as the men of the Forest Service know.

Deer like to bed down in snowbrush and they browse somewhat on it. Cattle and horses leave it alone; and it is far down on the menu of an elk. The resinous varnish of its leaves adds to the inflammability of the shrub. The leaves contain volatile aromatic oils which on a warm sunny day give off a pleasant odor. When crushed they have the fragrance of cinnamon.

This July day the snowbrush had been in bloom for most of the way along the trail from Lapover to the North Minam Meadows. Acres of it had surrounded me. Its odor in bloom is more fragrant than the locust or the lilac or any other blossom I recall—sweet and penetrating, subtle and suggestive. Its fragrance seemed to fill the whole canyon of the North Minam. I last saw it when I was on the lip of the Lostine canyon on my way home. It was dusk; 1000 feet or more below me was a vast yawning pit lined with fir and pine and filled with a haze that made it seem miles deep. I stopped Dan for a moment. An evening breeze swept off the mountain from the west. It carried the perfume of the snowbrush with it. That fragrance made this darkening canyon a place of enchantment, a land where only imagination can carry a man.

Coming through Brownie Basin I had heard the wheezy notes of the white-crowned sparrow. Now from some undisclosed thicket came the sweet song of Audubon's hermit thrush—the delicate singer who, as Gabrielson and Jewett once put it, produces "the music of the stars."

These were my memories as I unsaddled Dan at the barn and entered our cabin. Friends had arrived during my absence. They were seated before a roaring fireplace. They gathered around me at the sink as I separated flowers from fish under the glare of a gasoline lantern. In that light they could not see the glory of my botanical collection. I was too tired to describe the beauty of the scenes I had witnessed on my trip. But the memories of this journey were so poignant that I laughed out loud when a friend who prefers a soft chair by the fire said, "So you rode twenty miles of rough trail for six trout?"

Chief Joseph with General O. O. Howard, below.

Stewart Holbrook

from *THE COLUMBIA* (1956)

From Kettle Falls to the sea the Indian economy was based on salmon. The mysterious migrations of these great fish were held to be the work of gods whose moods were uncertain and had best be propitiated by prayers and often by elaborate ceremonial appeals. If you lived along the lower seven hundred miles of the Columbia or its tributaries, you depended chiefly on salmon. There were elk, of course, and deer, and other animals fit to eat, and roots and berries, but red fish was the diet just as it was the principal medium of exchange among the tribes.

Lewis and Clark encountered their first sign of salmon economy on the Lemhi, a tributary of the Salmon River which is a tributary of the Snake, which is a tributary of the Columbia. Pacific salmon were surpassing rangers. These fish which the two explorers found so far inland may well have grown mature in the high latitudes and distant waters of Alaska, but they had been born there in Idaho waters and to Idaho waters they had returned to spawn another generation, then to die. No matter the rapids, the falls, or other obstructions, including the nets and spears of the red men, these fish by a compulsion of awesome power and a memory undimmed after two or four years in foreign salt waters, simply *had* to return to an obscure stream that rose in the mountains of Idaho. It was the same elsewhere. At the Columbia's headwaters, David Thompson saw battered chinooks that had come more than a thousand weary and often tempestuous miles from the sea and God alone knew how much farther. Had some of these fish spent the best part of their lives around the island where Vitus Bering died? Had they plowed the Aleutian Trough? What an odyssey it was to have returned from a voyage measured in the thousands of miles, and what an abiding urge had prompted it.

In their Journals, Lewis and Clark noted the increasing intensity of the salmon belt. By the time they reached the mouth of the

Snake, they had passed several large villages devoted to fishing; and here, on the main river, Clark made a map showing more than one hundred "fishing establishments" on the lower portion of the Snake, the Yakima River system, the Wenatchee, and another stream which probably represented the Spokane River. On their way down the Columbia they came upon whole villages engaged in making pemmican of dried fish which had been pulverized, then packed into basketlike sacks lined with fishskins. This food went everywhere, even over the Rockies, and remained in good condition for years. The sacks weighed at least ninety pounds each. The Indians told the explorers they traded what pemmican they did not need with tribes of the lower river in exchange for materials which they wanted from the Coast region. From the Cascades to the sea, the explorers remark again and again on the prevalence of salmon as native food.

Far up the Columbia, at Kettle Falls, as noted in a previous chapter, David Thompson was struck by the large village there which appeared to be devoted almost wholly to fishing and smoking fish. Thirty years later, Captain Wilkes saw the Kettle Falls fishermen take nine hundred salmon in a twenty-four-hour period; while at Spokane Falls he estimated the number of men engaged at one thousand. The natives used dip nets, spears, and traps to take the fish. Their nets were made of inner bark of white cedar, or from the long surface roots of spruce. Willows formed their weirs. Between Celilo and the sea, the natives fished and got about with dugout canoes, a few of them fifty feet long.

When the white men began coming in numbers, they found the salmon hordes tempting. Nathaniel Wyeth, John Couch, the Hudson's Bay Company and others established fisheries along the lower river, to catch and salt salmon for export, but the business amounted to little until 1867 when Andrew Hapgood, and the Humes—William, George, and Robert—came to begin the first canning of fish in the Pacific Northwest. These men were from Maine where Tinsmith Hapgood had been canning lobster by a "secret process" he had devised. They had come first to California in 1864 and opened a salmon cannery on the Sacramento River. The run of fish there proved disappointing. There was also trouble with the canned fish exploding. After investigating the Columbia, they moved to Eagle Cliff on the north bank of that stream in Wahkiakum County, Washington. In their first year of operation they packed four thousand cases of forty-eight cans each. Next year the pack rose to eighteen thousand cases. Within twenty years they were operating twenty of the thirty-five canneries along the river. In the legendry of the river, the Humes stand out as efficient and ruthless men. William Hume built a large house described as a mansion overlooking the Columbia near Eagle Cliff, and was long known as King of the Canneries.

Canning salmon was something new. For a time Hapgood and one trusted assistant did all the cooking in a room separated from the rest of the plant by a tight partition. No one else was allowed there. Into this secret place the filled cans came through a small opening. The process was at first very crude. The bodies of the cans were cut with a pair of big shears. Each fish was butchered separately, packed into cans, and each can was a single soldering job. But the technology quickly caught up with the needs of this brand-new industry, and, long before the end of the century, a can concern in Astoria was turning out fifteen million cans annually; and the process of canning was also much improved.

Within a year of the Hume-Hapgood's first pack, Captain John West opened a cannery at Westport on the Oregon side of the river. Others soon followed, the Cook Brothers at Clifton; Sam Elmore, M. J. Kinney, and Badollet & Company in Astoria; McGowan at Ilwaco; while away up the river near the Cascades and Celilo, the Warrens and the Seuferts opened canneries. By the early eighties, thirty-nine outfits were packing salmon. This was the peak, and '83 was the top of the peak, the pack that season running to 630,000 cases, a figure that was also reached in 1895, but when a part of the catch was made offshore and not in the Columbia proper.

By the time the Columbia River Packers Association was organized in the middle nineties, Astoria had long been recognized as the center of the river's fishing industry. When young Mont Hawthorne first saw it, in 1883, "there wasn't no railroad to Astoria." Whether you got there from the north, south, east or west, you came by boat. It was quite a place. Most of it was built on piling, including the saloons which were believed to be more numerous per capita of population than in any other town in Oregon. There were several dance halls, and honky-tonk theaters, one of which had a sort of salt-water pen near the door. If you didn't have the price of admission, you tossed a big fresh salmon into the tank and were admitted to the show. A similar arrangement was to be found also at a couple of the red-light establishments, of which there were many. The major industries after dark appeared to be harlotry and shanghaiing.

The Astoria canneries were going full stride when Mont Hawthorne arrived. He recalled that the waste of fish was sickening. In the place where he worked they might heave as many as five hundred dead salmon into the river at night. And the refuse of those that were canned was dumped too. When the tide changed, the dead fish and the offal drifted onto the beach and stayed there. After much complaint, the city felt obliged to hire men with skiffs to haul the remains out into the channel. That is, most of the remains. Enough stayed on the beach to attract bears who came to eat their fill and to cause more complaints against the canneries. The canners did not mind. It was a period when complaints of the sort mattered little. The canners provided the main payrolls of the town and could ignore ill-tempered people who considered the water-front aroma too strong.

But there was another menace which the fishermen's union and the canners rose as one to defeat: When herds of sea lions got the habit of tearing nets to pieces in their efforts to get at salmon, a dead shot, Clark Lowry, was hired to hunt and shoot the marauders.

Along the evil-smelling water front were long bunkhouses to accommodate the two thousand Chinese who were the chief help in canneries all along the Columbia. Their settlement was complete with a theater, firecrackers on occasion, and opium that was sold openly in flat round cans. Abused and bedeviled on every hand, these old men and young boys from Canton had built railroad grades, washed gold in all the diggings, and were now providing the main labor force of a new industry.

That part of Astoria called Uniontown was gradually filling up with a few Italians, a few Portuguese, and many, many more Scandinavians and Finns. The latter came in time to do the major portion of the fishing. The Chinese were not allowed to fish, ever. They filled all the inside cannery jobs, such as making the cans and cutting up the fish. A sketch artist's picture of an Astoria cannery of the time shows two score Orientals, pigtails wrapped neatly up on the backs of their necks, their faces classically impassive, going about their work in a huge room that is steaming from the cooking apparatus. Another sketch shows a few Chinese in rubber boots contemplating a room strewn with "15 tons of Royal Chinook Salmon." The Chinese were so closely allied with canning that when, some twenty years later an automatic machine was devised to open and clean fish, it became known at once as the Iron Chink. Despite its efficiency elsewhere, this machine was not used on the Columbia because of the wide variation in the size of Columbia chinooks—from five to sixty pounds. The Iron Chink worked better on fish more evenly sized. Incidentally, the technology of canning was being continuously improved, and the elapsed time between the moment a salmon was lifted from the river and the moment his meat was filling several cans grew shorter by the year, until it was said that a fish was hardly done flopping when he was inside a can.

Catching fish in early years was done largely by vagrant fishermen, many of whom came from California; and by people who lived along the lower river and worked part time at logging. Somehow or other these crews got the reputation of being wild men, undependable in all things save hell-raising, at which they had few peers. The quality of the fishing crews began to improve in the eighties as a few Scandinavians and Finns settled in Astoria. They went to catching fish, an occupation they knew from childhood. They worked hard. They quickly learned some of the subtleties of Pacific salmon, an education that could be had almost only from empirical methods. And in the pattern of American emigration from the old world, these few pioneers from Scandinavia and Finland attracted their countrymen. In a few more years almost half of Astoria's population was made up of Finnish, Swedish, Norwegian and Danish nationals and their American-born sons and daughters.

These were mostly literate people. It wasn't long before they could support newspapers printed in their own languages. The Finns even had a daily and a tri-weekly. Social and "benefit" lodges were formed. With them, too, the Finns brought their *sauna*, or steam-bath house, and when conventional bathrooms came in, they installed them also, but no true Finn, it was said, would let a Saturday night pass without visit to a *sauna*, of which downtown Astoria still has many.

The many Finns, together with the numerous Scandinavians,

were not tardy in sensing the group action of the salmon packing houses which made agreements as to how much they would pay for a salmon; and almost from the first they had a fishermen's protective union. In time, too, these realistic people organized their own packing concerns, the first one known as the Scandinavian Cannery. The most successful, which flourishes today, was founded in 1896 as the Union Fishermen's Co-operative Packing Company.

Catching and canning salmon on the Columbia was marked for decades by periodic violence when strikes disrupted fishing or canning, or both. There were even more violent times when contending groups of fishermen fought each other over sand bars favored for operating haul seines. Fists, clubs, knives, even guns were used; and though the industry has never known the ferocity that went with the Wobbly (IWW) troubles in the logging woods and sawmills, fishing the river has not been an occupation for weaklings.

Over the years, a goodly part of the catch has been canned by outfits affiliated as the Columbia River Packers Association, organized in the nineties. This group still operates the biggest cannery on the river. For more than half a century it has also operated in Alaska.

The salmon of the Columbia are worthy of the big blond men who go out in boats to get them, and of the smaller red men who used to stand precariously at the roaring fishways of Celilo and Kettle Falls to net, spear and gaff them. All Pacific salmon are anadromous, a useful word meaning that these fish are hatched in fresh water, descend to the ocean where they attain most of their growth, then return to their home or native streams to spawn. They are distinguished from Atlantic salmon chiefly by the fact that the latter may spawn more than once, while the Pacific species always die after spawning.

Once upon a time, in Indian days, any salmon in the river was considered of value, though the red men had their preferences. But since canning by white men began, only four species have been of commercial importance in the Columbia. These are the chinook, the silver, the blueback, and the chum. The chinook is the king of salmon—of all salmon—and is often called Royal Chinook, and tyee, an Indian term for chief. It will average twenty-two pounds, and reaches ninety pounds. The spring chinook run enters the Columbia in late winter or early spring and continues through the lower river until August. The fall chinooks are more numerous but of less value commercially. There is another difference between the two runs: The spring chinooks mostly head well upriver, only four divisions of that run entering tributaries below the Cascades; but the fall chinooks are common to all the tributaries of the lower river.

Silver salmon are fall-run fish and appear in small numbers before August. There used to be large migrations of silvers to rivers entering the middle Columbia, like the Methow, Wenatchee, Yakima, and Grand Ronde, but of late years the majority spawn in tributaries below the Cascades. Silvers average ten pounds. The bluebacks come in June and July and continue upriver. They average four pounds. The lowest grade of salmon, the chum, migrate up the river's lower tributaries in the fall, and will average around twelve pounds.

For a time it seemed as if the catching of sturgeon might grow into a large industry. These huge fish, often running well over one thousand pounds each, were occasionally taken for food by the Indians, and early settlers ate them. They were not, however, highly esteemed, and as late as 1874 the *Weekly Astorian* said that a sturgeon weighing 1,250 pounds had been taken there and was sold for twenty-five cents. That is, for the entire fish. More than a decade later, some ninety-odd tons of sturgeon were salted at Astoria. But frozen sturgeon awaited the advent of railroads and ice.

By 1888, when a railroad had come down the Columbia as far as Portland, a New York firm established what was called a sturgeon camp at Oneonta, Oregon, below the Cascades. Eighty-five tons were shipped in iced cars during the first season. Three other companies later went into the business. The sturgeon catch suddenly dwindled, and one by one the camps were closed. It was generally believed that the use of gear called Chinese lines was responsible for overfishing the river, even as far inland as Wieser, Idaho, on the Snake. A Chinese line was a real killer. It carried from two hundred to four hundred hooks. Once entangled, few sturgeon escaped. Long after the sturgeon camps closed, a few ingenious and patient fishermen made a small industry of sturgeon farms. A small bay would be staked off like a marine pasture, and into it the farmer put as many of the big fish as possible, feeding them like so many barned cattle until the market was good. Then they were hauled out, killed, dressed, and shipped. One of these pasture fish was a true whale of one thousand eight-hundred pounds. In recent years legislation has virtually prohibited the taking of Columbia River sturgeon except by Indians in reservation waters.

At the other pole from the armored monsters are Columbia River smelt. Mature smelt seldom run more than eight inches long and are so rich in fat they used to be called candlefish because a dried smelt wrapped around a wick and lighted would supply a sort of illumination. In December to February they arrive in the Columbia in such numbers as to call for editorial notice. The editorialists, and almost nobody else, refer to smelt as eulachon; and the papers send reporters and cameramen to cover the thousands of smelt-dippers who line the Cowlitz, Lewis and Sandy rivers which are the home waters of these fish. Because they do not freeze suitably, the smelt industry is mostly local. In Portland smelt become so numerous as the season wears on that one of the best stories concerns the newcomer to the region who is deluged with free smelt to the point of embarrassment, sometimes to the point of desperation, and clogs his plumbing in frenzied efforts to rid himself of enough fish to feed a multitude. But fried in corn meal, the Columbia smelt is a dish that many compare favorably with brook trout.

In regard to trout, the Columbia is the principal Pacific Coast stream of the steelhead. In the 1920s the Columbia pack of this fish occasionally totaled more than two million pounds, with another million pounds sold frozen. These figures have declined by approximately half, due in part to reclassification of the steelhead as a game fish. On the Oregon side, a part of the steelhead catch is still packed, but by far the greater portion is frozen.

Of fishing gear used in the Columbia, the gill net has always been of first importance in taking salmon. It is of record that the first gill net here came from Maine's Kennebec River and was used, in 1853, on the Columbia near Oak Point, Washington. It is basically a rectangular piece of webbing weighted on the lower side with leads, buoyed on the upper by corks, and is fished by laying it out across a section of the stream. It is then allowed to drift with the current. When fish encounter it, they penetrate as far as the region just behind the gills, and are thus caught. The gill net's efficiency varies with the skill used in laying it out and taking it in, and also in the manner it is hung. Fishermen will hang and rehang a net again and again until they believe it is just right.

There are two ways of fishing gill nets. One is constructed so that its top edge floats at or near the surface; the other, called a diver, drifts with its bottom edge on or near the bottom of the river. When the stream is muddy, a gill net is used day or night, but when the water is clear, it is fished mostly at night. Nearly all gill nets today are used with an additional net called a trammel of large-mesh webbing. This serves to catch the salmon too big to gill in the small-mesh web.

Because the efficiency of the diver-type gill nets depends on a bottom free of snags, sunken logs and other debris, the gill-net fishermen organize themselves into "snag unions" to clear the location they fish. It is said to be an unwritten and well-enforced law that the men composing a snag union have exclusive rights to that territory. The wars between fishermen have seldom been caused over gill-net locations, but have had to do with sand bars and other places where haul seines were used. Outlawed now for several years, horse-seining was a common sight for half a century. On some sand bar or other, often a mile or so from either shore, one could see six to eight teams pulling a vast net one thousand five-hundred feet long, or longer, plodding steadily through the water up to their bellies, hauling the net's offshore end, to beach a few tons of fish that flopped twenty feet on the sands. In those days, the animals were often played-out relics of the Portland streetcar system, later veterans of the fire department, and it is told that their sore feet never failed to respond to healing qualities of the water, and aged horses were much rejuvenated, living years beyond their natural time. One seldom saw them above the first seventy miles of the river where, in season, they lived in stables built on piling at the sand bars.

In the early era of commercial fishing, Chinook Beach was often in the news because of the efforts of rival packers to monopolize this fine spot for seining. The McGowans were said to have inspired Indians to claim their legal seining rights here, while competing firms got other Indians to attack the seining claims. The matter was settled only after many years' resort to the United

States courts. Another center for seining was Sand Island, and here, too, the courts had to intervene after men had been beaten and shot in the seine wars.

Then, there were the fish wheels. This device was first used on the Columbia in 1879 by the Williams Brothers, one of whom patented the idea, though the principle of a wheel had been used elsewhere previously. It was a framework with scoop nets made of wire netting. These were the buckets of the wheel, so arranged that the wheel was kept in constant motion by the current, picking up all fish that tried to swim the channel. The wheels ran from nine to thirty-two feet diameter. They were used mostly from a point above Portland to as far as Celilo Falls.

It is recorded that one wheel built near present Bonneville Dam took an average of three-thousand salmon a day during the season of 1881. By the turn of the century seventy-six wheels were turning, day and night. But they were of little use except when the surface water was at the proper height. Their use began to decline in 1900, long before both Oregon and Washington outlawed them, at which time less than forty wheels were in operation. Statistics indicate that even at the height of their popularity wheels were never a large factor in the total catch. It was the net, in one form or another, that had taken the main catch of Columbia river salmon, and gill nets topped all other types. The nets were once knitted by the Chinese, and are now made of nylon by machines.

Laying out gill nets was first done from small open rowboats. Then came sail, with the boats longer and of wider beam. This period presented something of a sight during the season. The wide estuary was alive with small craft each carrying sail and looking, as more than one observer has said, like an armada of tiny junks. In 1889, there were 2,596 of these boats operating between Portland and the mouth of the river, most of them within sight of Astoria. The first power boats came in about 1905, and later an Astoria fisherman, Matt Tolonen, started a trend by fitting a flat stern to his gill-net boat.

One of the spectacular shows of fishing the Columbia was that of the Indians swarming the rocky canyon at Celilo Falls. The first explorers saw them dipping and spearing salmon there, and they continued to dip without hindrance for nigh one hundred and fifty years more, "protected," as the terminology had it, "by a treaty guaranteeing them exclusive and perpetual fishing rights" and stipulating they might use any method they saw fit.

And it must have seemed to the Indians that here at the falls of Celilo was something the white men simply could not take away from them. This was their chief fishing ground, their source of food, since time began. They still gather there, as this is written, and many of them stay there the year around, to net and spear and gaff at will. Standing on jerry-built platforms jutting out over the boiling water, or in a basket lowered by rope down the sheer side of a cliff, they will be motionless for long periods, then lunge suddenly to bring up a whopper that calls for stout arms.

The several tribes which fish here keep what they need and sell the surplus to cannery buyers, or people driving along the highway. Fishing laws have never applied to them. Celilo, as the legend goes on millions of picture postcards, is "the Indians' happy hunting grounds where they may catch the big Chinook salmon in any way they choose."

That was all well enough when it was written, but it was written in sand. A dam is rising not far below Celilo at The Dalles, and it will soon bury the falls so deep in a lake that not a ripple of their fury will trouble the surface. The redskins have been defeated once more, this time not by the United States Cavalry, but by the genial dam builders of the United States Army, Corps of Engineers. Custer is revenged again. And if the Indians at Celilo should persist in their age-old liking for salmon as food, then they may buy it in cans, by the case if need be.

Construction of Celilo Canal 1915.